Environmental Policy Integration

Environmental Policy Integration

Greening Sectoral Policies in Europe

Edited by
Andrea Lenschow

Earthscan Publications Ltd
London and Sterling, VA

First published in the UK and USA in 2002
by Earthscan Publications Ltd

ISBN: 1 85383 709 1 paperback
       1 85383 708 3 hardback

Typesetting by PCS Mapping & DTP, Newcastle upon Tyne
Printed and bound in the UK by Creative Print and Design Wales, Ebbw Vale
Cover design by Danny Gillespie

For a full list of publications please contact:

Earthscan Publications Ltd
120 Pentonville Road, London, N1 9JN, UK
Tel: +44 (0)20 7278 0433
Fax: +44 (0)20 7278 1142
Email: earthinfo@earthscan.co.uk
Web: **www.earthscan.co.uk**

22883 Quicksilver Drive, Sterling, VA 20166-2012, USA

Earthscan is an editorially independent subsidiary of Kogan Page Ltd and publishes in
association with WWF-UK and the International Institute for Environment and
Development

A catalogue record for this book is available from the British Library

Library of Congress Cataloging-in-Publication Data

Lenschow, Andrea
    Environmental policy integration : greening sectoral policies in Europe / Andrea
    Lenschow.
        p. cm.
    Includes bibliographical references (p.).
    ISBN 1-85383-708-3 (cloth) — ISBN 1-85383-709-1 (pbk.)
      1. Environmental policy—European Union countries. I. Title.

  GE190.E85 L46 2001
  363.7'056'094—dc21

                                                              2001023290

Contents

PART IV   CONCLUSION

List of Tables and Figures

TABLES

FIGURES

About the Contributors

Henry Buller is Professor of Rural Studies at the Countryside and Community Research Unit of Cheltenham and Gloucester College, UK, and researcher at the French CNRS Research laboratory LADYSS at the University of Paris X. He is also Maitre de Conférences en géographie at the University of Paris VII and author and editor of numerous books, chapters, research reports and articles on rural development, agricultural and environmental policy and European rural policy.

Ute Collier has been the Head of WWF-UK's Climate Change Programme since April 1998. Her work focuses on energy efficiency and renewable energy, as well as the impacts of climate change on biodiversity. Prior to this, Ute was Senior Research Officer on Climate Change with Friends of the Earth (FoE) in London. Before moving to the NGO sector in 1997, she researched at a number of academic institutions, including the European University Institute in Florence, Sussex and Cambridge Universities. She also worked as a lecturer in environmental studies and European studies at the University of Hertfordshire, UK.

Christian Hey is Secretary General of the German Environmental Council and former EU Policy Director within the European Environmental Bureau. He received a Diploma in the Science of Public Administation at the University of Konstanz and a PhD at the Free University of Berlin. He was project coordinator at the Institute for Regional Studies in Europe between 1990 and 1997.

Andrew Jordan lectures in environmental politics in the School of Environmental Sciences at the University of East Anglia, UK. He has published extensively on the long-term impact of the European Union (EU) on the traditional style, structures and procedures of British environmental policy.

Volkmar Lauber is Professor of Political Science at the University of Salzburg, Austria. Together with Artur Mol and Duncan Liefferink, he co-edited *The Voluntary Approach to Environmental Policy* (Oxford University Press, 2000). His chief current interest is in the politics of regulating renewable energy sources.

Andrea Lenschow is lecturer of political science at the University of Salzburg. She received her PhD at New York University in 1996 and has been Research

Fellow at the Erasmus University in Rotterdam and Jean Monnet Fellow at the European University Institute. Together with Christoph Knill, she co-edited *Implementing EU Environmental Policy. New direction and Old Problems* (Manchester University Press, 2000).

Rodolfo Lewanski is associate professor at the Faculty of Political Science, University of Bologna, Italy. His main research interests are in the fields of public policies, environmental policy and public administration, with specific emphasis on the Italian case.

Edda Müller is Executive Director of the Federation of German Consumer Organizations, former Deputy Executive Director of the European Environment Agency, former Minister for Nature and the Environment of the German state Schleswig-Holstein and former senior civil servant of the Federal Ministry for the Environment.

André Nollkaemper is Professor of Public International Law and Director of the Amsterdam Center for International Law at the Universiteit van Amsterdam, the Netherlands and Of-counsel, Van den Biesen Prakken Böhler, Attorneys, Amsterdam. He published widely in the field of international and European environmental law.

Acknowledgements

This book has its roots in the Third Environmental Summer School of the Robert Schuman Centre of the European University Institute in Florence in July 1998. I was fortunate to be able to organize this event and to coordinate the publication of its results. The success of the summer school and the publication of this book owe much to the generous and continuous support of the Robert Schuman Centre as well to the financial assistance of the European Commission.

My particular thanks are due to Professor Yves Mény, director of the Robert Schuman Centre. Professor Mény initiated many of the activities on environmental policy-making at the centre; he always actively supported the Institute's Working Group on Environmental Studies and helped to organize regular workshops and the summer schools on specific environmental issues. Without his support, I would not have been able to bring many of the authors who contributed to this book together to discuss the topic of environmental policy integration (EPI) in such an intensive but at the same time pleasant working climate. I am especially grateful to Yves that he arranged for me to return to the Robert Schuman Centre for several months in the first half of 2000 to complete the editing of this book. Furthermore, I am indebted to Monique Cavallari for her administrative and logical support during the organization of the summer school, as well as to Kathinka Espana for being such great help in the follow-up of the project.

But a summer school does not consist only of organizers and speakers; it depends on the active input of the participants. More than 20 young scholars of environmental policy-making from across the world came together for a week-long discussion in which we jointly made some progress in tracing the compliance with the EPI principle across policy sectors and across countries and in understanding the nature of the integration problem. I am grateful to all participants for their inspired contributions.

This book is not a carbon copy of the summer school presentations. All authors who prepared papers for the summer school put much effort into revising their contributions in light of the summer school discussions and of recent developments, as well as with the aim of responding to the general framework of the book. Thank you for being such good and responsive colleagues! I would like especially to thank Ute Collier and Andrew Jordan who were willing to join the book project after the summer school and to contribute important chapters on energy policy and on the UK.

Finally, thank you to my friends and colleagues in Florence, Salzburg and Bonn for open doors and telephone lines and for providing the feedback that I much needed during the final editing phase of the book.

Andrea Lenschow
Salzburg, April 2001

Acronyms and Abbreviations

ALTENER	EU renewable energy programme
ANPA	Agenzia Nazionale per la Protezione dell'Ambiente (Italian National Environmental Protection Agency)
BAT	best available technology
CAP	Common Agricultural Policy (EU)
CO_2	carbon dioxide
CEC	Commission of the European Communities
CFC	chlorofluorocarbon
CH_4	methane
CHP	combined heat and power
CIPRA	Commissione Internazionale per la Protezione delle Alpi (Italy)
CITES	Convention on International Trade in Endangered Species of Wild Fauna and Flora
CLM	Centre for Agriculture and Environment (The Netherlands)
CRE	Centre for Rural Economy (UK)
DEFRA	Department for Environment, Food and Rural Affairs (UK)
DETR	Department of the Environment, Transport and the Regions (*now* DTLR) (UK)
DG	Directorate-General
DG II	Economic and Financial Affairs Directorate-General
DG VI	Agriculture Directorate-General
DG VII	Energy and Transport Directorate-General
DG XI	Environment Directorate-General
DG XVI	Regional Policy Directorate-General
DG XIX	Budget Directorate-General
DM	Deutschmark
DoE	Department of the Environment (*now* DEFRA) (UK)
DoT	Department of Transport (*now* DTLR) (UK)
DTI	Department of Trade and Industry
DTLR	Department for Transport, Local Government and the Regions (UK)
EAGGF	European Agricultural Guarantee and Guidance Fund
EAP	Environmental Action Programme
EC	European Community
ECA	European Court of Auditors
ECCP	European Climate Change Programme
ECIS	European Centre for Infrastructure Studies
ECMT	European Conference of Ministers of Transport

ECOFIN	Council for Economic and Financial Affairs (EU)
ECR	*European Court Reports*
ECU	European Currency Unit
EEA	European Economic Area
EEA	European Environmental Agency
EEB	European Environment Bureau
EEC	European Economic Community
EIA	environmental impact assessment
ENDS	Environmental Data Services
ENEA	Ente per le Nuove Technologie, l'Energia e l'Ambiente (Italian Agency for Energy and the Environment)
ENEL	Ente Nazionale per l'Energia Elettrica (Italian National Electricity Board)
ENV	UK Cabinet Committee on the Environment
EP	European Parliament
EPI	environmental policy integration
ERDF	European Regional Development Fund
ESA	environmentally sensitive area
ESF	European Social Fund
EU	European Union
Euro	currency of the European Monetary Union
EWE	*Environment Watch Europe*
EWWE	*Environment Watch Western Europe* (*now* EWE)
FARRE	Forum de l'Agriculture Raisonnée Respectueuse de l'Environnement
FIFG	Financial Instrument for Fisheries Guidance
FS	Ferrovie dello stato (Italian National Railway Company)
GAEPS	General Agri-Environmental Protection Scheme
GATT	General Agreement on Tariffs and Trade
GDP	gross domestic product
GDR	German Democratic Republic
GNP	gross national product
GWh	gigawatt hours
HC	House of Commons
HFC	hydrofluorocarbon
HL	House of Lords
IEEP	Institute for European Environmental Policy
IEM	internal energy market
IGC	intergovernmental conference
ILM	*International Legal Materials*
IPPC	Integrated Pollution Prevention and Control
IRU	International Road Union
IUCN	World Conservation Union (*formerly* International Union for Conservation of Nature and Natural Resources)
kWh	kilowatt hour
LFA	less favoured area
LSVA	Leistungsabhängige Schwerverkehrsabgabe (road pricing for trucks)

MAFF	Ministry of Agriculture, Fisheries and Food (*now* DEFRA) (UK)
MEKA	*Marktentlastungs- und Kulturlandschaftsausgleich*
MEP	member of the European Parliament
MP	member of parliament
MW	megawatt
NATO	North Atlantic Treaty Organization
NEAT	Neue Eisenbahn–Alpentransversale railroad project
NFFO	non-fossil fuel obligation
NGO	non-governmental organization
N_2O	nitrous oxide
NO_x	nitrogen oxide
OECD	Organisation for Economic Co-operation and Development
OFFER	Office of Electricity Regulation (UK)
OJ	*Official Journal of the European Communities*
OPUL	*Ökologische Evaluierung des Umweltprogrammes*
PET	petroleum equivalent tonnes
PFC	perfluorocarbon
PV	photovoltaic
RCEP	Royal Commission on Environmental Pollution
SAVE	EU energy efficiency programme
SEA	Single European Act
SEA	strategic environmental assessment
SEIA	strategic environmental impact assessment
SF_6	sulphur hexafluoride
SO_2	sulphur dioxide
SoSE	secretary of state for the environment
SVP	Südtiroler Volkspartei, South Tyrol
T&E	Transport & Environment
TENS	Trans-European Networks
TEU	Treaty on European Union
TGAP	*taxe générale sur les activités polluantes*
toe	tonnes of oil equivalent
UAA	utilized agricultural area
UK	United Kingdom
UNCCC	United Nations Convention on Climate Change
UNCED	United Nations Conference on the Environment and Development
UNCHE	United Nations Conference on the Human Environment
UNEP	United Nations Environment Programme
UNFCCC	United Nations Framework Convention on Climate Change
US	United States
VW	Volkswagen
WCED	World Commission on Environment and Development
WTO	World Trade Organization
WWF	*formerly known as* World Wide Fund For Nature

Part I

INTRODUCTION

1

Greening the European Union: An Introduction

Andrea Lenschow

INTRODUCTION

Effective environmental protection requires the consideration of environmental consequences in all 'technical planning and decision-making processes' at national and Community level (OJ, 1973, p6). So stated the first Environmental Action Programme (EAP) of the European Community in 1973. In 1999, Environment Commissioner Margot Wallström described current integration strategies (adopted in the fifth EAP) as 'the start of an important process... the *beginning of a learning process* in our thinking and attitudes' (EWWE, 1999a, p12, emphasis added). For more than a quarter of a century, the issue of environmental policy integration (EPI) had been neglected in the European Union (EU), despite its widely recognized importance for environmental protection. This book traces the bottlenecks hampering effective EPI in Community and national policy-making and identifies possible opportunities and solutions for dealing with this problem.

By the late 1990s, the process and the problem of achieving EPI had become very topical. Since the European Council meeting in Luxembourg in December 1997, the issue of EPI has been a regular concern for the European heads of state or government. Arguably, achieving EPI has become 'the critical challenge confronting European environmental policy-makers at the dawn of the new millennium' (Jordan and Lenschow, 1999, p31). In view of barely satisfactory results of environmental regulatory policy to improve the state of the environment in Europe, and also in response to an increasingly deregulatory policy-making climate, attention has shifted towards changing the nature and outlook of sectoral policies. 'Sustainable development' is the new paradigm that is supposed to guide all policy-makers. However, despite these recent political commitments, progress towards achieving the integration of environmental concerns in all sectoral policy-making on the EU and the national level remains slow. The appearance of a wide consensus on the EPI principle among political leaders contrasts with considerable resistance among the stakeholders to apply an integrative approach in practice. The Commission notes that the 'commitment by other sectors and by Member States ... is partial' (CEC, 1999a, p3). Analytically even more interesting, the degree of policy integration varies from policy area to policy area and from country to country. It is the objective of this book to investigate the nature of the challenge and the reasons for such variation.

In short, what are the bottlenecks obstructing EPI in spite of the emerging 'conventional wisdom ... that the environment must be an integral factor of other policy areas' (Jordan, 1998a, p12)? What are the opportunities for advancing the goal of EPI? What are the factors that explain different performance levels between states and what factors are responsible for sectoral variation? The structure of this book permits some insights into these questions. The three country studies on the UK, Germany and Italy in Part II allow us to investigate the role of political leadership, constitutional and administrative structure and the role of societal actors. Subsequent policy studies in Part III, focusing on sectoral changes in the context of the EU multilevel system, alert us to sector-specific interest constellations, reform options, costs and benefits.

This introductory chapter presents the background to the subsequent analysis. It introduces the concept of EPI and provides an overview of the evolution and present significance of the principle in Europe. Considering that EPI is widely perceived as a vital prerequisite for improving the state of the environment, the varied but generally deficient application of the principle is worrisome. This chapter illustrates this policy challenge and previews some of the performance assessments aired in the policy discourse. It offers a 'flavour' of the issues that are discussed in depth in the subsequent chapters. The chapter closes with several possible explanations for the currently unhappy state of affairs. These options are reviewed in the concluding chapter, in light of the case and country studies in Parts II and III.

THE EPI PRINCIPLE: THE IDEA AND ITS HISTORY IN THE EU

The principle of environmental policy integration emerged in the context of a paradigm shift on the international level and as a response to an internal performance crisis. On the one hand, it is closely related to the concept of sustainable development, which – though not new – began to shape the general thinking on environmental protection since the publication in 1987 of the report of the United Nations' World Commission on Environment and Development, entitled *Our Common Future* and commonly referred to as the Brundtland Report (WCED, 1987). The EU's fifth EAP followed the language of the Brundtland Report in calling for cross-sectoral policy integration as a means to 'green' all economic activities already at the planning stage. The linking of EPI to the rhetorically powerful paradigm of sustainable development contributed to its political acceptance, but it has done less to facilitate adaptation on the operational level (see later in this chapter).

The acceptance of the need for a more integrative approach was equally triggered by a gloomy internal assessment of past policy practices. Traditionally, the EU has treated the protection of the environment as the sole responsibility of environmental policy-makers in the Commission's Environment Directorate-General (DG XI) and the national environment ministries rather than a common responsibility. In this framework, the EU made use of regulatory, mostly 'command-and-control', policy instruments. Neither the general state of the environment (cf EEA, 1999) nor the implementation of concrete EU regulations gave much evidence that the EU was on the right path with this strategy (CEC, 1996; Collins and Earnshaw, 1992). Present efforts to establish the environment as a horizontal policy matter and to build a cross-sectoral 'Partnership for Integration' (CEC, 1998) reflect the lessons drawn from policy failure, while borrowing recipes from the new international discourse on environmental protection. However, the ones who were made responsible for policy failure in the environmental field and therefore contemplated new solutions and those to carry the main burden of the proposed changes were not the same. Neither policy failure nor a paradigm shift led by the environmental community necessarily made much of an impression on sectoral policy-makers. On the following pages, I will provide an overview of the ideational process as well as the legal and institutional changes that followed from internal and external pressures, as well as of the obstacles that remained.

EPI and sustainable development: Consequences of a conceptual linkage

The principle of environmental policy integration may be considered a core application of the concept of sustainable development, which has gained much influence in the international environmental discourse since the 1970s. I suggest that this conceptual linkage has contributed to the political legitimation of EPI in the EU. EPI has become a firmly embedded normative principle in the EU *acquis*. At the same time, however, the EPI principle suffers from some ambiguities and weaknesses of its 'mother principle', with the risk of undermining its legitimacy in sectoral policy-making.

The core idea of 'sustainable development' is that *environmental protection, economic growth and social development are mutually compatible*, rather than conflicting, objectives. Environmental protection ensures that the very foundation for economic activity and the human existence are not destroyed. Economic and social development, in turn, are considered possible without further depleting non-renewable resources and reducing biodiversity. This idea entered the international political agenda in 1972 when the United Nations Conference on the Human Environment (UNCHE) was convened in Stockholm. During preparatory meetings, the notion of 'eco-development', emphasizing the interdependence between ecological and developmental goals, was developed and subsequently formed the basis for the sustainable development debate (Alker and Haas, 1993, pp5–6, citing UNEP (1981) as a main reference). In

1980, the International Union for the Conservation of Nature and Natural Resources presented the *World Conservation Strategy* (IUCN, 1980) which focused on the ecological dimension of sustainable development – that is, the conservation of living and non-renewable resources.

The publication of the Brundtland Report broadened this perspective to the social and political sphere and firmly established the concept on the European political agenda. The report defined sustainable development as 'a process of change in which the exploitation of resources, the direction of investment, the orientation of technological development, and institutional change are made consistent with future as well as present needs' (WCED, 1987, pp8–9). It presumes that 'technology and social organization can be both managed and improved to make way for a new era of economic growth' (p8) and that policies 'that sustain and expand the environmental resource base' can be devised (p1). The introductory note that '[o]ur message is, above all, directed towards people, whose well-being is the ultimate goal of all environment and development policies' (pxiv) and the compatibility assumptions behind the concept resonate well with the economic mainstream, while equally responding to the emerging environmental concerns in Western Europe. 'Sustainable development' represents an idea able to facilitate political consensus; it offers a story that is attractive to many actors because it provides a conceptual foundation for the pursuit of widely accepted ethical values (intergenerational equity, alleviation of poverty, environmental protection) at seemingly low financial and political costs.[1]

It gained particular currency in EU circles where the problem of squaring the objective of economic competitiveness with the goal of environmental protection had resulted in increasingly controversial debates, which even resulted in several court cases dealing with the priority or compatibility of economic and environmental objectives (Koppen, 1993). The old regulatory-based approach began to face a serious legitimacy crisis, as it seemed to impose high costs on economic actors without producing the desired environmental improvements. It is therefore hardly surprising that the new 'no trade-off' conceptualization of the economy–environment relationship and the related 'softening' of the top-down regulatory approach found increasing acceptance.

Clearly implicit in the notion that environmental, economic and social objectives may be achieved in a mutually compatible way is the integration principle. In Angela Liberatore's words (1997, p107):

> *The relevance of integration for moving towards sustainable development is straightforward: if environmental factors are not taken into consideration in the formulation and implementation of the policies that regulate economic activities and other forms of social organization, a new model of development that can be environmentally and socially sustainable in the long term cannot be achieved.*

Put differently, EPI represents a first-order operational principle to implement and institutionalize the idea of sustainable development. However, its legitimacy was based not only on this conceptual linkage, but equally on the evolution of the EU treaties. By the early 1980s, the concept of sustainable development had entered the policy programmes of most European governments and the EU; the legal obligation to policy integration was established with the Single European Act in 1987; and a commitment to 'sustainable development' was made in the Amsterdam Treaty (1999).

Nevertheless, the fact that EPI is widely perceived as tied to sustainable development is not unproblematic. The concrete interpretations of the concept and the political consequences of having made a commitment to sustainable development vary widely. For instance, the Dutch government adopted in its National Environmental Policy Plan a holistic notion of the relationship between environment and the economy, and inferred from it the need for deep attitudinal changes in society, which are to be developed 'bottom up'. The German government and industry tend to perceive sustainable development as a chance to market environmental technologies, focusing otherwise on the correction of market failures through top-down regulatory environmental policies. In Britain, by contrast, the emphasis has been on rationalizing government and the elimination of policy contradictions between regulatory environmental policy and sectoral policies, which could quite possibly result in the dilution of existing policies to protect the environment (Lenschow, 1999a; Jordan and Lenschow, 1999).[2] The EU itself has not yet adopted a very strong version of the concept of 'sustainable development' as a policy-guiding idea.[3]

Ambiguity may have served the quick and continuing acceptance of the concept and made it a reference point in defining policy problems. However, it may also undermine a clear and effective operationalization. EPI means something else in a context where sustainable development aims at the rationalization of government compared to where sustainable development implies holistic planning. As we will see below, EPI has been understood in the EU first as a political aspiration and a mainly *procedural* principle (cf Nollkaemper in Chapter 2 on the normative and legal ambiguities of EPI). It implies that policy-makers in non-environmental sectors recognize the environmental repercussions of their decisions and adjust them when they undermine sustainable development. The European Environment Agency (EEA) defines EPI as a process of shifting the focus of environmental policy away 'from the environmental problems themselves to their causes ... [and] [f]rom "end of pipe" environment ministries to "driving force" sector ministries' (EEA, 1998, p283). In the absence of clearly defined policy goals, indicators and timetables, however, there remains ample room for sectoral policy-makers to evade such substantive environmental responsibilities. The integration process currently faces the challenge of ensuring that substance follows from procedure.

The impact of EPI may be reduced not only due to conceptual and hence operational ambiguities, its impact may suffer even more due to conceptual inconsistencies in connection with its 'mother concept'. The compatibility assumptions inherent in sustainable development apply to a highly aggregated (possibly global) level, while EPI applies to sector or even sub-sector policies where there may be real winners and losers as a consequence of policy integration. EPI is likely to encounter conflict which sustainable development causes us to forget. Therefore, the legitimating power of sustainable development may collapse on the operational level of EPI. Subsequent chapters in this book investigate this dilemma further on the basis of concrete case material.

From the conception to the operation of EPI

This chapter will continue to focus on EU developments. While their role was mostly declaratory in the beginning, EU institutions – since the early 1990s – have attempted to move from the policy idea to a policy in operation. During the past few years, in particular, efforts were increased to make EPI procedures effective rather than mere bureaucratic exercises. The analysis of this process may provide first hints on how to deal with conflict and resistance.

The EPI principle in the Environmental Action Programmes (EAPs) of the EU

During the 25 years in which an identifiable EU environmental policy has existed, the legal basis for the pursuit of environmental protection has evolved and the idea of EPI has increasingly been accepted. The growth of a general concern for environmental protection is reflected in the series of EAPs of the EU. As indicated above, the first EAP hinted at the need for an integrated approach. This was made more explicit in the third EAP in 1983, which stated (OJ, 1983, Section I, 8):

> *[T]he Community should seek to integrate concern for the environment into the policy and development of certain economic activities as much as possible and thus promote the creation of an overall strategy making environmental policy part of economic and social development. This should result in a greater awareness of the environmental dimension, notably in the fields of agriculture (including forestry and fisheries), energy, industry, transport and tourism.*

The fourth EAP of 1986 (OJ, 1986) devoted a whole subsection to discussing 'Integration with other Community Policies' (Section 2.3) and announced that the 'Commission will develop internal procedures and practices to ensure that this integration of environmental factors takes place routinely in relation to all other policy areas' (paragraph 2.3.28). The fifth – and most recent – EAP, which came into force in 1993 (CEC, 1992), placed great emphasis on the integration principle. It identified five key areas – industry, energy, agriculture, transport and tourism – where policy integration seemed most urgent and developed an approach of dialogue and joint responsibilities to pursue the sustainable development agenda. Rather than attempting to regulate integration, the fifth EAP hoped to involve policy-makers and stakeholders in a cooperative *process* that would result in the penetration of the idea of sustainable development and EPI into all sectors of society and public policy. The fifth EAP was also most explicit in pointing to the limits of top-down regulation and the promise of 'soft law' to achieve the desired attitude change. In the words of the Commission (CEC, 1992, p49):

> *[T]he basic strategy therefore is to achieve full integration of environmental and other relevant policies through the active participation of all the main actors in society (administrations, enterprises, general public) through a broadening and deepening of the instruments for control and behavioural change including, in particular, greater use of market forces.*

Evolution of the treaty base for sustainable development and EPI

The EAPs are reflections of the policy-planning process within the formal agenda setter of the EU: the European Commission. Legally, however, the EAPs are non-binding and they may amount to little more than a wish list for ambitious policy-makers. In the case of the EPI principle, the publication of new EAPs, however, was paralleled – responding to Commission initiatives, in particular – in the treaty evolution of the EU. The Single European Act, which entered into force in June 1987, first established a legal basis for environmental policy in general and formulated the objective of integrating environmental considerations into other policies at all levels in the new Environment Title (Title VI, Article 130r). The Treaty on European Union (Maastricht Treaty), which was ratified by late 1993, strengthened Article 130r by requiring that 'Environmental protection *must* be integrated into the definition and implementation of other Community policies' (Article 130r(2), emphasis added). It also approached the 'sustainable development' language by inserting a new Article 2 into the treaty that read: 'The Community shall have as its task ... to promote throughout the Community a harmonious and balanced development of economic activities, sustainable and non-inflationary growth respecting the environment'. Despite the much-criticized phrasing, calling for 'sustainable ... growth', this article moved the environmental objective to the front of the treaty and hence added weight to it. This process was continued in the Treaty of Amsterdam that elevated in Article 6 the integration principle to a guiding objective of the EU. Furthermore, the achievement of sustainable *development* becomes a fundamental objective of the EU, mentioned in the preamble and Article 2 of the treaty. The process of institutionalizing the legal principles involved plenty of conflict (cf Jordan, 1998b; Verhoeve, Bennett and Wilkinson, 1992). The problem of sustainable development and EPI now is to put a legal principle[4] into practice.

Achieving EPI: The path to and from 'Cardiff'

As hinted above, neither the concept of sustainable development nor the principle of environmental policy integration implies a clearly developed plan of action. Despite the longer history of these concepts in the EU, rhetoric efforts to elaborate the operational side began only in the early 1990s with the drafting of the fifth EAP. Today, we observe a critical stocktaking of the results of the action programme and renewed attempts to give substance to the EPI principle. This section reviews the operational development of the integration process. It suggests that the EU has been undergoing a learning process towards implementing the EPI principle, which involves a gradual extension of the scope of actors directly targeted as well as an increasingly active and strong leadership approach to facilitate and enforce EPI.

The EU's initial attempts to apply the EPI principle were cautious and followed a bottom-up approach, meaning that influence rather than formal power were applied to change the attitude and behaviour of the stakeholders in non-environment sectors (cf Wilkinson, 1997). The fifth EAP provided the general framework for these first activities. But, even though the action programme addressed all levels of government (from the local to the EU level), and private as well as public actors, even proposing actions, targets and timetables, only the European Commission made deliberate efforts to put the EPI principle into operational practice. The Commission's integration arrangements were set out in an internal communication (CEC, 1993), drafted under the leadership of the Environment DG and adopted by all commissioners in May 1993. It included the following measures:

- A new *integration unit* was placed in DG XI, reporting directly to the director-general.
- Each Directorate-General (DG) was to designate an *integration correspondent*, who would liaise with the Environment DG and ensure that environmental concern would be given proper account.
- Policy proposals with significant environmental effects would be signified with a *green star* in the annual legislative programmes of the Commission and be subject to an environmental appraisal.
- Each DG was called to conduct an *annual evaluation* of its environmental performance.
- A *code of environmental conduct* was to be drawn up for the Commission itself.

Even though these internal procedures were incorporated into the Commission's internal manual of operational procedures, their impact on the practices in the non-environment DGs was disappointing. In 1997, in the context of the publication of the Commission's work programme for 1998, Environment Commissioner Bjerregaard admitted that the internal measures to improve integration 'have not been particularly effective' even though progress had been achieved in areas such as regional spending, development policy, transport and energy (EWWE, 1997, p14). The Commission was supported in its critique by assessments conducted by the EEA, such as the *Dobris Assessment*. As a result of these critical reviews, the Commission renewed its commitment to adapt its internal procedures to the task of policy integration by reinforcing old measures and adding new ones. It proposed an analysis of the environmental impact of funding from the EU budget. It also attempted to strengthen the overall process by introducing an independent evaluation of the EPI process conducted by the Environment DG and the development of training programmes for Commission staff on environmental appraisal and integration (EWWE, 1997, p14–15; ENV Press, 1997). It therefore added components of capacity-building and more central (environmental) control. The Commission realized, however, that *substantive guidelines* needed to be developed for the sectoral integration process and that the effectiveness of policy reforms crucially depended upon the political commitment in the Member State governments. Only if the leadership of the process shifted from the Commission's

Environment DG to the European Council, the Councils of Ministers and the Member States would it be possible to legitimately impose some real pressure to change old practices.

Pressure for a more active EPI agenda developed after the so-called northern enlargement of the EU that brought Austria, Finland and Sweden – three 'pioneers' in the area of environmental policy (Skou Andersen and Liefferink, 1997) – into the EU. With the help of those countries the integration clause was strengthened in the Amsterdam Treaty and new pressure developed on the heads of state and government level to put this clause into practice. At the 1997 Luxembourg Summit, work on the current process of EU environmental policy integration was launched on the basis of a Swedish initiative. Surprisingly, the UK presidency followed up and placed the environmental integration project at the top of its agenda. Besides organizing the first ever joint council of environment and transport ministers and raising environmental concerns in other councils such as energy and fisheries, the UK supported and gave weight to a new Commission strategy on integrating the environment (Jordan, 1998a).

The Commission's communication 'Partnership for Integration' (CEC, 1998) implies a change from the previous cautious perspective in explicitly calling on the Council of Ministers and the European Parliament to take responsibility in the integration process. This process goes hand in hand with pressures emanating from the United Nations Conference on the Environment and Development (UNCED) process, begun in Rio in 1992, that requires all participating states to develop strategies for sustainable development. While the Commission still hopes to improve its implementation of the internal rules that had been agreed in 1997, the councils are now asked to:

- collect experiences and evidence of best practices of EPI in the Member States and develop a basis for improved Community procedures;
- identify a set of priority actions in order to incorporate environmental requirements and to foresee effective mechanisms for monitoring their implementation;
- ensure that environmental requirements are explicitly reflected in their decisions on new proposals;
- commit themselves to review their current organizational arrangements to ensure effective implementation of this integration strategy.

The European Council will periodically review environmental integration within key sectoral policies. The European Parliament is called to join the partnership by identifying its priorities in the integration process and by reviewing its current organizational arrangements to facilitate integrated decision-making (CEC, 1998).

The four summit meetings that followed the publication of this latest EPI strategy seem indeed to indicate a strengthened commitment from the European Council and, consequently, some real progress in the stocktaking of past activities and a targeting of procedure at substantive advancement. Most relevant sectoral councils were assigned to review their integration performance of the past and develop an EPI strategy for the future. The first reports were critically reviewed – also in the light of a rather negative assessment of the EEA of the state of the environment in Europe. First results on the development of EPI indicators were presented, which might provide guidance for sectoral policy-makers, but will also function as a standard for future monitoring and assessment. Table 1.1 summarizes the history of the EPI process, so far.

Evidence of sectoral change

The history of the EPI principle until the year 2000 reveals a real success in widespread agenda-setting. The concept has travelled from international fora to the Environment DG in the European Commission and via the European Council to leading sectoral policy-makers in the EU and the Member States. The combination of the legal commitment to EPI and such top-level monitoring is likely to make a difference in the future. Pressure from EU leaders as well as international commitments are today contributing to a shift of the EPI as a general principle to an operational framework (cf EPI indicators). Nevertheless, we must not ignore that the actual progress towards achieving EPI has been disappointing so far. Most recent and also most devastating is the Commission's 1999 *Global Assessment* of the Community's fifth EAP. 'Despite some improvements', it says, 'the state of the environment overall remains a cause for concern and pressures on the environment are predicted to grow even further in some areas.'[5] The Commission laments (CEC, 1999a, pp2–3):

> ... *the commitment by other sectors and by Member States to the Programme is partial, and the patterns of production and consumption in our countries prevent us from achieving a clean and safe environment and protecting the world's natural resources... [W]ithout a reinforced integration of environmental concerns into economic sectors to address the origins of environmental problems and without a stronger involvement and commitment by citizens and stakeholders, our development will remain environmentally unsustainable overall.*

It is not the function of this chapter to investigate the reasons for continuing resistance in great detail. Rather, it previews some of the evidence analysed in subsequent chapters and highlights the different reactions to the EPI agenda.

Agricultural policy has been identified as particularly problematic (cf Buller, Chapter 6). In the context of preparing the EU for eastern enlargement, as well as facing the pressure of external trading partners, the EU policy-makers have decided some major reforms of the Common Agricultural Policy (CAP), which from an environmental perspective are considered rather timid (EWWE, 1998, p12). Lone Johnsen, president of the European Environmental Bureau (EEB), for instance, said in March 1999 during a meeting with European Commission President Santer: 'The rhetoric about the environmental integration and sustainable development becomes better day by day. But practice is stubborn. The latest negotiations on the CAP reform show that environmental policy by and large is not improving' (EEB, 1999). UK Environment Minister Meacher considered the draft agriculture document submitted to the Cardiff process as

Table 1.1 *Development of the Integration Process*

1972	Stockholm Conference	Develops notion of 'eco-development', emphasising the interdependence between ecological and developmental goals. This subsequently forms the basis of the sustainable development debate.
1973	First EAP (OJ, 1973)	Establishes that effective environmental protection requires the consideration of environmental consequences in all 'technical planning and decision-making processes' at national and Community level.
1983	Third EAP (OJ, 1983)	'[T]he Community should seek to integrate concern for the environment into the policy and development of certain economic activities as much as possible and thus promote the creation of an overall strategy making environmental policy part of economic and social development. This should result in a greater awareness of the environmental dimension, notably in the fields of agriculture (including forestry and fisheries), energy, industry, transport and tourism.'
1986	Brundtland Report (WCED, 1987)	Introduces the notion that environmental protection and economic and social development are compatible goals and establishes the EPI principle. 'The major central economic and sectoral agencies of governments should now be made directly responsible and fully accountable for ensuring that their policies, programmes, and budget support development that is ecologically as well as economically sustainable' (p314). The report serves as a reference point for subsequent EU environmental policy, particularly the fifth EAP.
1986	Single European Act	New Environment Title (Article 130r) introduces the objective of integrating environment into other policies at all levels.
1987	Fourth EAP (OJ, 1986)	Devotes a subsection to the 'Integration with other Community Policies' and announces that 'the Commission will develop internal procedures and practices to ensure that this integration of environmental factors takes place routinely in relation to all other policy areas'.
March 1992	Fifth EAP (CEC 1992a)	Promotion of integration in five economic sectors: agriculture, energy, industry, transport and tourism. EPI is to be achieved in a spirit of shared responsibility among all key actors and by making use of a range of policy instruments (including economic and communicative instrument and voluntary agreements).
June 1992	UNCED (Rio Earth Summit)	Gave rise to Agenda 21, the UNCED process and led to the integration focus of the fifth EAP.
1992	Signing of the Treaty on European Union (came into force	The new Article 2 of the EEC treaty states: 'The Community shall have as its task … to promote throughout the Community a harmonious and balanced development of economic activities, sustainable and non-inflationary growth

	in November 1993)	respecting the environment'. Article 130r(2) includes the requirement that: 'Environmental protection requirements must be integrated into the definition and implementation of other Community policies.'
1997	Signing of the Amsterdam Treaty (came into force in May 1999)	Establishes sustainable development as one of the objectives of the EU and an overarching task of the Community. Article 6 requires that: 'environmental considerations should be integrated into other policies in order to deliver sustainable development'.
December 1997	Luxembourg Summit	Work on the current process of EU environmental policy integration launched.
June 1998	Cardiff Summit	'The European Council welcomes the Commission's submission of a draft strategy [for integration of the environment into other EU policies] and commits itself to consider it rapidly in view of the implementation of the new Treaty provisions. It invites the Commission to report to future European Councils on the Community's progress' (Cardiff European Council,1998, paragraph 32). European Council invites all relevant sectoral councils to establish their own strategies for integrating the environment and sustainable development. Transport, energy and agriculture are asked to start this progress and provided reports to the Vienna Summit.
December 1998	Vienna Summit	Transport, agriculture and energy councils produce initial reports. Further integration plans are invited from development cooperation, internal market and industry councils for Helsinki.
June 1999	Cologne Summit	European Council called upon the fisheries, general affairs and ecofin (finance) councils to report on the EPI process and sustainable development in 2000. Commission submitted its report (of 26 May 1999) on mainstreaming of environmental policy (CEC, 1999b).
December 1999	Helsinki Summit	European Council calls on nine Councils of Ministers (energy, transport, agriculture, development cooperation, internal market, industry, general affairs, ecofin (finance) and fisheries) to complete work on environmental policy integration and to submit comprehensive strategies by June 2001. The Commission submits a report on 'environment and integration indicators' (CEC, 1999c), a report reviewing the integration process 'from Cardiff to Helsinki and beyond' (CEC, 1999d), and a 'global assessment' of the results of the fifth EAP (CEC, 1999a). The European Commission is invited to prepare a long-term policy proposal on sustainable development by June 2001.

Source: adapted from HOC (1999, ppxi–xii)

the 'weakest' and 'least satisfactory' (HOC, 1999, pxxiv). The CAP's resistance is explained by the strong institutional acceptance of environmentally harmful practices and by a strong clientele in favour of the status quo.

The transport sector produces 'remarkable' trends of increasing pollution levels with regard to specific pollutants such as carbon dioxide (CO_2). While significant progress has been made in recent years to improve the environmental quality of cars and fuels, the traffic volume has increased to such an extent that it more than neutralizes technological advances. A persistent belief that economic development and competitiveness depend upon infrastructure expansion and that interference in the mobility of people will represent an unacceptable restriction of personal freedom have obstructed EPI with regard to the non-technical dimension of transport policy. However, the EU seems closest in developing substantive EPI guidelines and performance indicators for the transport sector (EWWE, 1999b, p8; CEC, 1999c, Annex 2). Furthermore, according to the assessment of Meacher at a hearing in front of the Environmental Audit Committee of the House of Commons, the transport document 'is probably the best' among the first reports submitted in the context of the Cardiff process (HOC, 1999, p51). Hence, there might be a change of attitude on the EU level, though Hey (Chapter 7) introduces us to the ups and downs that tend to occur between policy formulation and actual decision-making. Lauber (Chapter 8) confirms that the economic interests of national and regional actors have been quite capable of suppressing EPI policies in the past.

With the growing evidence that the EU will have problems in achieving the Kyoto Protocol targets on the reduction of emissions responsible for climate change, the energy sector is receiving increasingly critical attention. Only a few years ago the energy sector seemed to be the leading sector in terms of complying with the EPI principle. The win–win situation proclaimed in the Brundtland Report appeared most evident here as energy saving and efficiency as well as the development of new and renewable energy sources presented solutions to environmental problems and the energy dependency trap. In the meantime, however, little has happened. In its recent *Global Assessment*, the Commission states bluntly that the EU will not meet its Kyoto commitments and observes that the EU schemes supporting renewable energy and energy efficiency have had little impact, not least because several Community measures have received less funding than originally proposed (CEC, 1999a, pp6–7). Collier (Chapter 9) takes a closer look at the negative turn this sector has taken, and points to interesting innovations in several Member States that might diffuse 'from below'.

The EU regional development and cohesion policy has been identified as an area where considerable improvements were made on the EU level (Lenschow, 1997 and 1999b). In a recent assessment, the Commission itself argues 'the new regulations offer a host of tools for a better integration of the environmental dimension into regional and cohesion policy. It is now up to the Member States to draw on them in the actual implementation of the funds' (CEC, 1999b, p5). With respect to this implementation performance in the Member States, some serious doubts remain as to the degree of sharing the idea of EPI. The small number of designated Natura 2000 sites (as required under the 1992 Habitat

Directive), which compromise the 'green dimension' in future regional development plans, serves as evidence for this national resistance (Lenschow, Chapter 10).

The country studies on the UK, Germany and Italy included in this book (Jordan, Müller and Lewanski, Chapters 3–5) reveal that traditional notions of 'pioneers' and 'laggards' (Skou Andersen and Liefferink, 1997; Sbragia, 1996) are of little help in understanding national differences in EPI. Leadership commitment to the principle seems a necessary condition, though institutional structures, regulatory style and political culture are crucial intervening factors. The three country studies looking at federal Germany, unitary Britain and Italy, with its notoriously weak centre, will further advance our understanding of the interaction between these factors.

Overall, the spell of activity during the so-called Cardiff process indicates that the implementation of the EPI principle finally got into motion outside the narrow scope of the European Commission. The 'stick' of a now legally binding treaty obligation (as opposed to previously non-binding action programmes), as well as an emerging political commitment at the top political level to the integration agenda, have contributed to an increasing activity on the sectoral level. Nevertheless, the first integration reports that were submitted by sectoral councils also suggest that attitudes have not yet changed and a certain resistance persists. The question remains whether the amount of paper that has been produced in the last two years will translate into actual progress towards EPI.

In order to tackle this question we must gain a better understanding of the conditions that will contribute to EPI. What explains the general rise of attention to EPI, on the one hand, and the remaining differences between policy sectors and between countries, on the other? What is the impact of the European multilevel governance structure on implementing the integration principle; what has been the impact of international commitments? Is the process towards EPI characterized by learning from policy failures, by a diffusion of new ideas or by external political pressure? The following concluding section briefly suggests some explanatory avenues. These will be explored further in the case and country studies, and in the concluding chapter of this book.

EXPLANATORY FRAMEWORK

Three dimensions are worth investigating in order to explain patterns of EPI in policy sectors and in Member States: actors, ideas and institutions.

The role of actors

In searching for the bottlenecks holding back integration, we might focus on the policy preferences of relevant policy actors and their relative power or influence in the decision-making process. Considering the often marginal position of environmental policy-makers in the overall political structure, progress towards EPI depends upon the political commitment of sectoral policy-makers. This commitment may differ between sectors, explaining variation in the EPI process. The commitment may equally vary between political levels – for example, between Commission officials and local implementers or between elected politicians and bureaucrats explaining the episodic 'greening' of the entire policy cycle and influencing the nature of the outcome of the EPI process. Assuming a tendency towards inertia on the routine levels of policy-making and implementation, change may need to be pursued either through political leadership from above or societal movements pressuring from below. The extent to which top-level political commitment and pressure or the mobilization of societal actors (as voters or as non-governmental organization (NGO) activists, for instance) are necessary requisites for the EPI process is an empirical question; the subsequent case studies provide more concrete evidence.

The role of ideas

Policy preferences or interests, which are central to an actor-centred perspective, are not necessarily predetermined. As a result, an alternative explanation searches for the sources of interests. It is helpful to consider policy interests as embedded in a frame of reference, which prestructures the thinking within a policy sector, a segment of society or any given echelon in an organization. As indicated earlier in this chapter the idea of sustainable development constitutes a new frame of reference for analysing the link between the economy and environmental protection. The acceptance of the idea implies a modification of interests among the stakeholders in the policy process and indeed a smoothening of the conflict of interests that was referred to above.

As hinted earlier, the promise of win–win solutions and the relative ambiguity of the sustainable development concept have helped its general acceptance in the EU, as well as that of its associated concept of EPI. Poor progress towards EPI may result if this acceptance begins to falter. For instance, moving from the aggregate sector level to the level of individual industries, farmers or car drivers, the 'causal story' (Stone, 1989) establishing the win–win scenario may collapse. The relative persuasiveness of the causal story on the sectoral level may also explain variation across areas. The spread and stability of a policy idea, however, is not only linked to daily evidence of its 'truth', but also in a general inclination to believe that it is 'true'. In this sense, it will be of importance that sustainable development and the EPI principle have been given treaty status and therefore cannot easily be dismissed and ignored in the political debates.

The role of policy traditions and institutions

The previous two explanatory approaches have focused on the attitudinal level of relevant actors. However, even if the general attitude toward EPI is positive, progress may be slow due to the magnitude of the task. The literature on adaptive processes in a multilevel polity such as the EU has introduced the notion of 'level of fit' (Caporaso et al, 2001; Knill and Lenschow, 2000), suggesting that the EU *acquis* will have a greater impact on national policies and institutions if it is compatible with the given structures and practices. This notion can be applied to the problem of policy integration as well. Simply stated, it suggests that change will be more difficult the more it departs from traditional practices. Along these lines, this chapter has argued that the 'greening' of the European agricultural policy, for instance, is moving slowly and the impact remains moderate because the very task of dismantling the CAP and changing the patterns of production in Europe is indeed enormous (Favoino et al, 2000).

Besides this impact of the structure of the policy, administrative structure also matters and can produce obstacles to integration. The EU and most Member States organize policy-making in a sectorally divided and often fragmented way (Armstrong and Bulmer, 1998). The horizontal coordination that is the key to EPI requires that the DGs in the Commission, the Councils of Ministers and the parliamentary committees work with their respective colleagues in other areas. On the Member State level, ministerial bureaucracies will need to collaborate. It is easy to see why this poses a large administrative challenge.

In this context, the structure of the political system may make a difference. If policy-making is relatively centralized, a large reform may be more feasible than if a variety of policy centres are involved in the decision of comprehensive reforms. Along these lines, Scharpf (1988) argues that the reform capacity of federal systems is relatively low, suffering from 'joint decision traps'. Focusing only on the EU level, the multilevel structure of the EU seems to be prone to suffering from decision traps. But, there is also variation across sectors.

The institutional dimension is closely linked to the other dimensions mentioned above. Institutional structures intervene in the dissemination of new policy ideas and hence the learning process or the adaptation of policy interests of the actors involved. Equally, of course, institutional arrangements impact on the distribution as well as the exercise of political power. The following chapters examine the influence of these factors on the EPI process, as well as on the interaction of explanatory factors. It is not intended for this book to propose a common explanatory framework from the start but, rather, to explore the impact of a range of factors. The authors of the case and country studies approach the issue of EPI from various analytical and empirical viewpoints. The Conclusion attempts to connect the individual studies from the perspective of the overarching question: what are the reasons for an overall tardy – though slowly accelerating – yet sectorally varied process towards EPI in the EU?

REFERENCES

Alker, H R and Haas, P M (1993) 'The Rise of Global Ecopolitics' in N Choucri (ed) *Global Accord. Environmental Challenges and International Responses,* MIT Press, Cambridge, MA, and London, pp133–171

Armstrong, K and Bulmer, S (1998) *The Governance of the Single European Market,* St Martin's Press, New York

Baker, S, Kousis, M, Richardson, D and Young, S (eds) (1997a) *The Politics of Sustainable Development. Theory, Policy and Practice Within the European Union,* Routledge, London, New York

Baker, S, Kousis, M, Richardson, D and Young, S (1997b) 'Introduction: The Theory and Practice of Sustainable Development in EU Perspective' in S Baker et al (eds) (1997a), pp1–40

Caporaso, J, Cowles, M and Risse, T (2001) (eds) *Transforming Europe*, Cornell University Press, Ithaca NY

Cardiff European Council (1998) 'Cardiff European Council, 15 and 16 June 1998, Presidency Conclusions',
http://europa.eu.int/council/off/conclu/jun98.htm#C31

Commission of the European Communities (CEC) (1992) *Towards Sustainability. A European Community Programme of Policy and Action in Relation to the Environment and Sustainable Development*, COM (92) 23/fin, CEC, Brussels

CEC (1993) *Integrating the Environment into Other Policy Areas Within the Commission*, Communication to the Commission from Mr Paleocrassas and Mr van Miert, CEC, Brussels

CEC (1996) *Thirteenth Annual Report on Monitoring the Application of Community Law (1995)* Office for Official Publications of the EC, Luxembourg

CEC (1998) *Partnership for Integration. A strategy for Integrating Environment into EU Policies. Cardiff – June 1998*, Communication from the Commission to the European Council, COM(98) 333, CEC, Brussels

CEC (1999a) *Europe's Environment: What Directions for the Future? The Global Assessment of the European Community Programme of Policy and Action in Relation to the Environment and Sustainable Development, 'Towards Sustainability'*, Communication from the Commission, COM(1999) 543 final, CEC, Brussels

CEC (1999b) *The Cologne Report on Environmental Integration. Mainstreaming of Environmental Policy*, Commission Working Paper addressed to the European Council, SEC(1999) 777 final, CEC, Brussels

CEC (1999c) *Report on Environment and Integration Indicators to Helsinki Summit*, Commission Working Document, SEC(1999) 1942 final, CEC, Brussels

CEC (1999d) *From Cardiff to Helsinki and Beyond. Report to the European Council on Integrating Environmental Concerns and Sustainable Development into Community Policies*, Commission Working Document, SEC(1999) 1941 final, CEC, Brussels

Collins, K and Earnshaw, D (1992) 'The Implementation and Enforcement of European Community Environment Legislation', *Environmental Politics*, vol 1, no 4, pp213–249

ENDS Environment Daily (1999) 'EU Chiefs Promote Sustainable Development', *ENDS Environment Daily*, 13 December

ENV Press (1997), *The Commission Renews Its Commitment to Integrate the Environment in Its Policy-Making*, IP/97/636,
http://europa.eu.int/comm/environment/press/ip97636.htm

European Environment Agency (EEA) (1998) *Europe's Environment. A Second Assessment*, EEA, Copenhagen

EEA (1999) *Environment in the European Union at the Turn of the Century*, Environmental Assessment Report No 2, Copenhagen

Environment Watch Western Europe (EWWE) (1997) *EU Executive Renews Bid to Integrate Environment into Other Policies, Own Operations*, 1 August, Cutter Information Corp

European Environment Bureau (EEB) (1999) 'Santer urged to lead integration process and promote public participation',
http://www.eeb.org/press/santer_urged_to_lead_integration.htm, 1 March, Brussels

EWWE (1998) *Environment Measures Disappoint in EU Policy Reform Plans,* 20 March, Cutter Information Corp

EWWE (1999a) *EU Should Have Sustainable Development Strategy by 2001,* 12 November, Agra Europe, London

EWWE (1999b) *Finish Presidency Makes Environmental Integration A Priority,* 1 October, Agra Europe, London

Favoino, M, Knill, C and Lenschow, A (2000) 'New Structures for Environmental Governance in the European Commission: The Institutional Limits of Governance Change' in C Knill and A Lenschow (eds), *Implementing EU Environmental Policy: New Directions and Old Problems,* Manchester University Press, Manchester, pp39-61

International Union for Conservation of Nature and Natural Resources (IUCN) (1980) *World Conservation Strategy: Living Resource Conservation for Sustainable Development,* IUNC, UNEP and WWF, Gland, Switzerland

Jordan, A (1998a) 'European Union: Greener Policies', *Oxford Analytica Daily Brief,* vol 4, 14 July, pp12–14

Jordan, A (1998b) 'Step change or stasis? EC environmental policy after the Amsterdam Treaty', *Environmental Politics,* vol 7, pp227–236

Jordan, A and Lenschow, A (1999) 'Memorandum' in House of Commons, Environmental Audit Committee, First Report and Proceedings (Session 1999–2000) *EU Policy and the Environment: An Agenda for the Helsinki Summit,* HOC, London

Knill, C and Lenschow, A (eds) (2000) *Implementing EU Environmental Policies: New Directions and Old Problems,* Manchester University Press, Manchester

Koppen, I J (1993) 'The Role of the European Court of Justice' in J D Liefferink, P D Lowe and A P J Mol (eds) *European Integration and Environmental Policy,* Belhaven Press, London and New York, pp126–149

Lenschow, A, (1997) 'Variation in EC environmental policy integration: agency push within complex institutional structures', *Journal of European Public Policy,* vol 4, no 1, pp109–127

Lenschow, A (1999) 'Transformation in European Environmental Governance' in B Kohler-Koch and R Eising (eds) *The Transformation of European Governance,* Routledge, London, pp39–60

Lenschow, A (1999b) 'The greening of the EU: the Common Agricultural Policy and the Structural Funds', *Environment and Planning C: Government and Policy,* vol 17, pp91–108

Liberatore, A (1997) 'The integration of sustainable development objective into EU policy-making. Barriers and prospects' in S Baker et al (eds) (1997a), pp107–126

Official Journal of the European Communities (OJ) (1973) 'Declaration of the Council of the European Communities and the Representatives of the Governments of the Member States Meeting in the Council of 22 November 1973 on the Programme of Action of the European Communities on the Environment', C112 (20 December)

OJ (1983) 'Resolution of the Council of the European Communities and of the Representatives of the Governments of the Member States Meeting Within the Council of 7 February 1983 on the Continuation and Implementation of a European Community Policy and Action Programme on the Environment (1983–1986)', C46 (17 February)

OJ (1987) 'Resolution of the Council of the European Communities and of the Representatives of the Governments of the Member States Meeting Within the Council of 19 October 1987 on the Continuation and Implementation of a

European Community Policy and Action Programme on the Environment (1987–1992)', C328 (7 December)

O'Riordan, T and Voisey, H (eds) (1997) *Sustainable Development in Western Europe: Coming to Terms with Agenda 21,* Frank Cass, London and Portland, OR

Richardson, D (1997) 'The Politics of Sustainable Development' in S Baker et al (eds) (1997a), pp43–60

Sbragia, A (1996) 'Environmental Policy' in H Wallace and W Wallace (eds) *Policy Making in the European Union,* Oxford University Press, Oxford, pp235–255

Scharpf, F W (1988) 'The Joint-Decision Trap: Lessons from German Federalism and European Integration', *Public Administration,* vol 66, no 3, pp239–278

Skou Andersen, M and Liefferink, D (1997) *European Environmental Policy: The Pioneers,* Manchester University Press, Manchester and New York

Stone, D (1989) 'Causal Stories and the Formation of Policy Agendas', *Political Studies Quarterly,* vol 104, pp281–300

United Nations Environment Programme (UNEP) (1981) 'Development and Environment: The Founex Report: In Defense of the Earth', *The Basic Texts on Environment,* UNEP Executive Series 1, Nairobi

Verhoeve, B, Bennett, G and Wilkinson, D (1992) *Maastricht and the Environment,* IEEP, Arnhem and London

Wilkinson, D (1997) 'Towards Sustainability in the European Union? Steps within the European Commission Towards Integrating the Environment into other Policy Sectors' in T O'Riordan and H Voisey (eds), pp153–173

World Commission on Environment and Development (WCED) (1987) *Our Common Future,* Oxford University Press, Oxford and New York

NOTES

1   The concept's ambiguity with respect to the true costs and demand for change implied by achieving sustainable development has been criticized as allowing actors to share in the political correctness of the term without changing behaviour (Richardson, 1997).

2   See also Baker et al (1997a) and O'Riordan and Voisey (1997) for good collections.

3   Compare Baker et al for a 'ladder of sustainable development' distinguishing between the treadmill, weak, strong and ideal approaches. The weak approach engages in market-reliant environmental policy and targets for changes in patterns, rather than levels, of consumption and production (1997b, pp8–18).

4   Nollkaemper argues in Chapter 2 that ambiguities regarding the nature of the legal principle may already cause problems for developing the operational side of the story.

5   The Commission refers to the European Environment Agency's state of the environment report (EEA, 1999).

2

Three Conceptions of the Integration Principle in International Environmental Law

André Nollkaemper

PRELIMINARY REMARKS

In April 2000, almost 28 years after the first formulation of the integration principle in the 1972 Stockholm Declaration and 13 years after its entry into European Community (EC) law through the Single European Act, the legal meaning and significance of the environmental integration principle remains yet to be defined. Is integration only an objective to be achieved? Or is it also a principle of law? And if so, what does that mean? Furthermore, how would such a principle be related to more specific legal obligations set forth in treaties, regulations and directives?

This chapter explores the legal dimensions of the integration principle and distinguishes between three different conceptions of the principle. It argues that in dominant thought, the principle is intended to develop into the third conception: an autonomous normative principle that seeks to provide closure to the otherwise incomplete normative system of European and international environmental law. It further argues that, in practice, this conception is not easily achieved. While normative space beyond existing law can be found, there is as yet little practice that suggests that the integration principle will fill that space.

The prime objective of the chapter is to provide doctrinal clarity on the meaning and significance of the integration principle in the already dense normative field of European and international environmental law. But the chapter also has a pragmatic relevance. It often has been said that one of the major stumbling blocks encountered in implementing the integration principle is its uncertain legal status. There is some circularity in the critique, as the lack of efforts to implement the principle certainly have contributed to the alleged uncertain legal status and meaning of the principle. Yet, it may also be true that the incidence and effect of such efforts may be enhanced by *prior* clarity on meaning and status of the principle. That, indeed, is an additional reason for exploring the legal meaning of the integration principle.

Two descriptions of the scope of the chapter are in order. Firstly, the observations in this chapter generally are relevant to both the integration principle in EC law and in public international law. While most of the illustrative examples are taken from EC law, the conceptual aspects of the chapter apply equally to public international law. Therefore, no strict separation between the two fields will be observed. Secondly, to the extent that the chapter refers to EC law, the principle will be used as one that applies to individual states rather than one that applies (only) to Community institutions. In its most limited meaning, the principle addresses only the Community institutions. This is the meaning adhered to in Article 6 of the Treaty on the European Community. There is also a broader construction, however. In this broader construction, the principle goes beyond the Community institutions and addresses *Member States*. There is sufficient authority for this broader meaning to make this the starting point of our inquiry. The Commission stated in its fourth Environmental Action Programme (EAP) that it aspires to apply the integration principle to Member States. The action programme formulated the ultimate goal that '*all* economic and social developments throughout the Community [obviously including activities of Member States] ... would have environmental requirements built fully into their planning and execution'.[1] The Commission's ambitions have been buttressed by legal developments outside of the Community. Principle 4 of the 1992 Rio Declaration on Environment and Development,[2] accepted by *all* Member States of the Community, proclaims, 'in order to achieve sustainable development, environmental protection shall constitute an integral part of the development process and cannot be considered in isolation from it'. Clear authority for the proposition that the integration principle applies to Member States can be found in treaties that bind the Community and its Member States. For instance, Article 3(4) of the Climate Change Convention stipulates that: 'Policies and measures to protect the climate system against human-induced change ... should be integrated with national development programmes'.[3] Finally, the ongoing so-called Cardiff process on environmental policy integration (see Chapter 1) clearly addresses both Community institutions and the Member States.

THE INTEGRATION PRINCIPLE AS A PART OF INTERNATIONAL ENVIRONMENTAL LAW

As a first step in analysing the principle, some observations need to be made on the focus of this chapter on the *legal* dimensions of the integration principle. The problem of environmental integration may not strike the interested observer as a quintessentially normative problem. The divide between environmental policy, on the one hand, and policies that pursue economic progress by bolstering transport, tourism, energy and industrial policy, on the other, indicates primarily problems of public management, coordination and political will. Indeed, it is no mishap that most contributions to this book will deal with these matters, rather than with the legal dimensions of the integration principle.

Yet, the fact of the matter is that the drafters of the 1987 Single European Act, the 1992 Maastricht Treaty and the 1997 Amsterdam Treaty *did* perceive the lack of environmental integration as a normative problem. They attempted to solve it in the archetypal 'integration-through-law' manner that has characterized the Community throughout its history. The law-making powers proclaimed that environmental requirements 'must be integrated in sectoral policies'. Integration through law, once again. Likewise, numerous treaties now have incorporated, either expressly or implicitly, the integration principle.

This does not necessarily mean that the integration principle is a general principle of international law. It is noticeable that the International Court of Justice in its judgement in the Gabcíkovo-Nagymaros (Hungary/Slovakia) case referred to the principle of sustainable development as a 'concept' rather than as a principle.[4] This appraisal invoked a critical dissent by Judge Weerymantry, who considered the word 'concept' to be something of an understatement. Judge Weerymantry argued that authority and precedent do allow us to speak of sustainable development as a principle.[5] The court apparently disagreed. It may well be that the court would take a similarly reluctant position when asked to apply the integration principle. After all, authority for the integration principle is hardly stronger than that for the more general principle of sustainable development.

Nevertheless, in this chapter I will not draw hard and fast lines around the legal status of the integration principle. Modern international legal scholarship has substantially qualified the significance of the positivist characterization of law that seems to underlie the statement of the court. It portrays a much more diffuse model of normativity. Writers such as Reisman (1988), Baxter (1980) and Fastenrath (1993) have deformalized the distinction between law and non-law in favour of informal sources of law. They argue, rightly so, that for most practical purposes the positivistic divide between law and non-law is simplistic. It is a matter of fact that principles that do not pass the sources test play an important role in determining the decision-making of states and other actors. It also is a matter of fact that principles that *do* pass the sources test, and that properly can be called 'legal principles', can be meaningless.

In view of the variety of sources in which the integration principle has been included, partly legal and partly non-legal, Phillipe Sands in his textbook on international environmental law characterizes the integration principle as a principle of international environmental law (1995, pp205–206). This chapter argues later that the integration principle fulfils a variety of legally relevant functions, which do not seem to hinge on a formal legal status of the principle. The assumption is made that the principle is part of international and European law and the most difficult problem is enforcing the principle.

While it may be easy to gloss over the uncertain *legal* status of the integration principle, this is less easily done with the substance of the principle. There is not *one* integration principle. The integration principle acquires different meanings depending upon the context in which it is invoked. Three possible constructions of the integration principle are presented.

THREE CONSTRUCTIONS OF THE
INTEGRATION PRINCIPLE

The integration principle can be construed as an objective, a rule of reference or an autonomous principle.

The Integration Principle as an Objective

It is unobjectionable to consider the integration principle as an objective or, as Dworkin would call it, a 'policy' (1978, p22ff). Most, if not all, everyday policies pursue the integration of something into something else. We talk about integration of safety in transport policy; integration of minorities in housing policy; integration of disabled persons in the private sector; integration of Russia in the North Atlantic Treaty Organization's (NATO) structures; and so on. Similarly, we can talk about integration of environmental protection in developmental policy as an objective.

As a policy or objective, the integration principle fulfils an important function. Arguments of policy provide reasons for legislative bodies to develop the law in order to further the objective. As such, we can assume that the integration principle as a policy has coinspired more particular legal rules. Indeed, the entire body of European Community environmental law can be perceived as a means to achieve the policy of environmental integration and, beyond that, of sustainable development. Similarly, one could consider many provisions of international environmental law as a form of application or implementation of the integration policy.

Yet, from the perspective of a legal analysis this is not a helpful way of construing the integration principle. For one thing, lawyers generally are not very interested in policies, unless they are involved in determining the competence of legislative bodies that have to fulfil certain policies. Courts or other bodies empowered to review activities with harmful effects generally do not review activities in the light of 'policies'. It may be a valid question whether various parts of Community law, such as the policy on structural funds, properly worked towards the objective of the integration principle. It is arguable that they do not. However, as long as integration is only an objective, courts are unlikely to invalidate any decisions that have not brought that objective any closer.

There is also a more conceptual problem with this first construction of the integration principle. Constructing the integration principle as a policy is little else than saying that the environment should be protected. If we want to protect the environment, we should impose constraints on those activities that are harmful. This is simply another way of saying that environment should be integrated into the formulation and implementation of these activities. The integration principle then does not have any distinct conceptual meaning. Furthermore, it adds little to our understanding to say that environmental protection should be integrated in development policy when what we really mean is that the environment should be protected from the harmful effects of development – except for the fact that due to the foggy word 'integration', the first statement is far less clear and less likely to mobilize the forces that are necessary to realize the aspired degree of protection.

The Integration Principle as a Rule of Reference

The integration principle can be construed in a second way. This second construction portrays the integration principle as a rule of reference. The principle does not have any autonomous normative meaning, but refers to other applicable rules. For a proper understanding of this construction, it is necessary to distinguish between situations where the principle addresses the Community and where it addresses states.

This construction has its prime application to the Community and finds its source in what essentially was a problem of interpretation raised by the original text that was to be inserted in the EC treaty by the Single European Act. The question was: would the objectives and principles of environmental policy, which were to be formulated in Article 130r (old), *only* be applicable to those policies that could be qualified as 'environmental policy' in terms of Article 130r-t (old)? Or would they also apply to the so-called sectoral policies, such as policies on transport and agriculture? It was fairly plausible that the better interpretation was that the objectives and principles *did* apply to other policies. However, there was room for legitimate legal dispute on this point. The Single European Act introduced the integration principle as a solution to this potential interpretation problem. After the Single European Act, and in any case after the Maastricht and Amsterdam treaties, it now is clear that the requirements of Article 174 (ex-Article 130(1–3)) do not only apply to measures adopted as environmental policies proper. They also apply to sectoral developmental policies with potential environmental effects. This has been implicit recognized by the court, among other cases in Case 300/89 (Titanium-Dioxide).[6]

In this construction, the integration principle does not have any autonomous normative meaning. Rather, it essentially is a rule of reference. That is, it refers to 'environmental protection requirements' that are defined by *other* norms – not by the integration principle itself.

This construction of the integration principle is also found in secondary legislation, such as the Regulations on Trans-European Networks and Structural Funds. Article 7 of Regulation 2052/88 provides: 'Measures financed by the Funds ... shall be in keeping with *Community policies*, including those concerning ... environmental protection'.[7] Likewise, Regulation 2236/95, laying down general rules for the granting of Community aid in the field of trans-European networks, states that projects financed under the regulation will comply with Community law and Community policies in relation to environmental protection.[8] Furthermore, in these legal instruments, the integration principle itself does not have an autonomous normative meaning. It refers to norms defined elsewhere.

What are these norms? There are various answers to this question. Probably the best answer is that the clause 'environmental protection requirements' in Article 6 of the treaty refers to the objectives, principles and criteria of Article

174 (ex-Article 130r). The integration principle makes these objectives, principles and criteria applicable to development policies.

Another interpretation is that the integration principle means that secondary legislation must be complied with. But this interpretation should be rejected since it would be wholly tautological: what is obligatory is obligatory. This interpretation of the integration principle as a rule of reference would not add anything to the existing legal situation.

Yet another interpretation of the integration principle as a rule of reference holds that 'environmental protection requirements' do not only refer to Community *legal rules* but also to Community *policies* – a category that apparently is meant to be broader than existing legal requirements. This interpretation is supported by Article 7 of Regulation 2052/88 that provides: 'Measures financed by the Funds ... shall be in keeping with *Community policies*, including those concerning ... environmental protection'. This interpretation would open the door to a legal obligation to apply norms that in themselves are not legally binding – such as policies contained in action programmes or resolutions. This raises important normative problems. It would undermine in the field of environmental policy any distinction between legal and non-legal norms. This would have substantial consequences. An interpretation that would make non-binding norms become directly binding by virtue of a rule of reference would undermine the already limited powers of democratic control vested in national parliaments and the European Parliament. This chapter does not explore these issues. What is important here is that in this meaning the rule referred to would be a written and prior agreed norm, so that the integration principle itself would not add any normative requirements.

The integration principle possesses in none of these interpretations of the integration principle as a rule of reference applicable to the Community any autonomous normativity, since it derived the norm from other rules and principles, not from the integration principle itself. It does not require anything *more*, nor does it solve problems relating to the interpretation and enforceability of the objectives and principles of Article 174, secondary law and possibly non-legal instruments. The integration principle in itself does not force any other change in the balance between environmental protection and economic development than the requirements of Article 174 and secondary legislation do. If we approach this from the perspective of enforcement, the question is not whether the integration principle can be administered before a court of law – it is whether the objectives, principles and criteria of Article 174 can be enforced.

This section deals with the construction of the integration principle as a rule of reference as it applies to the Community. The construction can also be applied to individual states. The same analysis then applies. The integration principle would mean that states have to incorporate requirements presented by other environmental rules in their development policies. Such an interpretation would likewise be meaningless. It would add nothing to the existing normative situation. States would be obliged to comply with the norms of international law that apply to them. The integration principle cannot change this and surely does not render applicable norms that otherwise would not apply.

The Integration Principle as an Autonomous Principle

There is also a third and broader meaning of the integration principle. In this construction the integration principle is not only an objective but also a *principle*, and is not only a rule of reference, but also a principle that carries autonomous normativity.

The construction differs from the first construction since it is not only an objective but also a principle. What does it mean to argue that the integration principle is a legal principle? The *Longman Dictionary of Contemporary English* tells us that a principle is 'a belief that is accepted as a reason for action' (1995, p1122). Dworkin defines a principle as 'a standard that is to be observed' (1978, p22). When we say that a particular principle is a principle of our law, we mean that 'the principle is one which officials must take into account, if it is relevant, as a consideration inclining in one direction or the other' (Dworkin, 1978, p26). This clearly is different from a policy; a policy may justify regulatory action, but in itself does not constitute a norm that the regulatory action should be taken and does not provide a basis for review of that action.

The third construction differs from the second construction since it does not only constitute a rule of reference, but has an autonomous normative meaning. It does not ask the Community or the Member States to apply prior agreed norms to their development policies, but to integrate 'the environment', or 'environmental interests' into development policies. This is the form in which the integration principle was incorporated in Principle 4 of the Rio Declaration. This states, '*environmental protection* shall constitute an integral part of the development process'. In contrast to the first meaning, this construction has an autonomous normative identity. It requires integration of environmental interests that in themselves are not contained in legal principles or norms. In this respect, the integration principle goes beyond the normative structure of existing international law.

Interesting in this context are the proceedings in Case 321/95 (Greenpeace versus Commission) concerning the legality of decisions taken by the Commission pursuant to Council Regulation 1787/84 on the European Regional Development Fund.[9] In these decisions, the Commission granted Spain financial assistance for the construction of two electricity power stations in the Canary Islands. A number of plaintiffs, including Greenpeace, argued that the decisions of the Commission were not in keeping with Community law, in particular the requirements for environmental impact assessment. The court declined to hear the case for lack of *locus standi* – incidentally, an interesting and somewhat disconcerting illustration of the barriers encountered in enforcing the integration principle. Of current interest is the approach of Advocate-General Comas. Comas stated that the treaty provisions concerning the environment – including the integration principle – 'are not mere proclamations of principle'.[10] He stated that the integration principle 'appears to impose on the Community institutions a specific and clear obligation which could be deemed to produce direct effect in the Community legal order'.[11] Comas continued to state that this obligation has not remained a 'dead letter' but has been imported into secondary Community law, and indeed in the context of legislation on the financing by the Community of certain actions having an impact on the environment. Significantly, he pointed to the importance of: 'observance, in the present case, of the Commission's *specific and clear obligation to take into account the safeguarding environmental interests* at the same time as adhering to the relevant Community legislation during the financing of the relevant works in the Canary Island'.[12]

The advocate-general thus distinguishes Community legislation from 'environmental interests' and argued that the Commission was obliged to take into account both categories. It is only in this third meaning that the integration principle adds something to the normative framework of international and European environmental law.

ENVIRONMENTAL INTEGRATION AND THE ASPIRATION OF NORMATIVE CLOSURE

In this third and most ambitious construction, the integration principle seeks to close the normative spaces that are left open by the otherwise fragmented norms of European and international environmental law.

In international law, the basic authority of states is governed by what commonly is called the Lotus principle. In the 'Lotus' decision, the Permanent Court of International Justice addressed its inquiry to the question: 'whether or not under international law there is a principle which would have prohibited Turkey, in the circumstances of the case before the Court, from prosecuting Lieutenant Demons'.[13] The court held that in the absence of such a principle or of a specific rule to which it had expressly consented, the authority of a state could not be limited.

This holding is often implicitly extrapolated to other areas of law, including environmental law. The argument is then that the discretionary authority of states is only limited when there is a *specific* rule of law that curtails their authority. If there were no such rule, freedom would reign.

While the Lotus holding has often been critiqued, it appears that it correctly depicts the normative structure of European and international environmental law. States have accepted many more or less specific environmental norms. Yet, these have not fully occupied the normative space. Directives, regulations and treaties govern certain activities and do not govern others. For instance, the Habitat Directive protects certain species and habitats but not other species and habitats. Even if its general provisions apply to *all* species and habitats, it does not apply to the *trade* in all species. And while the Convention on International Trade in Endangered Species of Wild Fauna and Flora (CITES) and the EC's CITES regulation cover many species, they do not cover all species. The Environmental Impact Assessment Directive requires impact assessments for a variety of activities, but not for others. And so on. In short, European and international environmental law leaves gaps that are not, or not expressly, governed by special norms. In such gaps, the Community and Member States can make their policy decisions unhindered.

The emergence of and support for the integration principle can be seen as an attempt to close the normative space that is left open by special norms. Together with the precautionary principle, the principle of sustainable development and other principles, the integration principle constitutes an attempt to fill pre-existing gaps and to function as a 'closing norm' in the normative system of international and European environmental law.

Implications of Reaching Normative Closure

In the third meaning, the integration has a procedural and a more substantive component. With regard to the procedural function, the principle requires, at a very minimum, that interests of environmental protection are considered in decision-making procedures. Of course, this requirement overlaps with the already applicable requirement of environmental impact assessment. It can, however, have a procedural significance in those cases where these requirements do not apply. Whereas the question to what extent such interests should be given protection generally lies beyond judicial scrutiny (that is, if only the integration principle would apply), the requirement that such interest should be considered in a procedural sense is a requirement that can be applied by courts and other supervisory mechanisms.

The European Court of Justice has showed itself prepared to review policies in the light of general principles of autonomous normativity, such as the principle of prevention at source. There does not seem to be a reason why this would be different for the integration principle – it is vague and undefined, but vagueness has never been a sufficient reason for courts or other reviewing bodies not to apply a principle.

There is also a more substantive dimension to the integration principle in this third conception. Even where specific substantive or procedural norms do exist (and, as such, there is no gap), these often may collide or conflict and leave a normatively ambiguous situation. The integration principle provides a means of balancing two competing norms. Consideration of conflicting norms that protect development, on the one hand, and the environment, on the other, can be aided and given focus by introducing the integration principle in that consideration. In this respect, the principle can fulfil a similar function as the principle of sustainable development. As Lowe observes: principles such as the principle of sustainable development 'are free agents, which may in principle be combined with any other rule, modifying that rule... Modifying norms establish the relationship between other, primary norms' (1999, p33).

It is in this sense that the International Court of Justice used the term of sustainable development in the Gabcíkovo case. The court argued that 'the need to reconcile economic development with protection of the environment is aptly expressed in the concept of sustainable development',[14] and subsequently formulated a way to achieve that reconciliation. The court used the reference to sustainable development as a means and a perspective to reconcile development and environment. Some have criticized the reference to the concept as being vague and meaningless, but this critique would appear to miss the function of the principle as a principle that has a normative direction and is linked and attached to other norms. The principle of integration can likewise fulfil a role in finding solutions in cases where the applicable norms point in different directions.

CONCLUSIONS

It appears that the integration principle may play three distinct roles in international and European environmental law. Firstly, it will serve as an objective that underlies and inspires more specific environmental law. As such, the principle is unobjectionable, though not distinguishable from environmental policy proper.

Secondly, the integration principle can, as a rule of reference, be used as a vehicle to encourage the Community and other international institutions to comply with relevant norms of international law in their various activities.

Thirdly, the integration principle may come to play as an autonomous normative principle. Whether it will play that role depends upon the identification of normative space and the development of criteria to evaluate integration. This will be an area where much will depend upon the energies and activities of interested actors to make the principle effective and practicable.

REFERENCES

Baxter, R R (1980) 'International Law in the "Infinite Variety"', *International and Comparative Law Quarterly*, vol 29, pp549–566

Dworkin, R (1978) *Taking Rights Seriously*, Harvard University Press, Cambridge MA

Fastenrath, U (1993) 'Relative Normativity in International Law', *European Journal of International Law*, vol 4, pp305–340

Longman Dictionary of Contemporary English (1995), third edition, Longman House, Burnt Mill, Harlow

Lowe, V (1999) 'Sustainable Development and Unsustainable Arguments' in A Boyle and D Freestone (eds), *International Law and Sustainable Development: Past Achievements and Future Challenges*, Oxford University Press, Oxford, pp19–37

Reisman, M (1988) 'Remarks in Panel "A Hard Look at Soft Law"', *Proceedings of the American Society of International Law*, vol 82, pp373–377

Sands, P (1995) *Principles of International Environmental Law*, I, Manchester University Press, Manchester

NOTES

1   *Official Journal of the European Communities* (OJ) (1987), C 139/1
2   31 *International Legal Materials* (ILM) 874 (1992)
3   31 ILM 849 (1992)
4   32 ILM 1247 (1993)
5   *Id*, par A.c.
6   1 *European Court Reports* (ECR) 6103, 559
7   OJ (1988), L 165/9

8   OJ (1995), L 228/1
9   1998 ECR I-1651
10 *Id* par 62
11 *Id*
12 *Id*, par 63–65
13 P C I J, Series A, no 10, p21
14 32 ILM 1247 (1993), par 140

Part II

COUNTRY STUDIES

Efficient Hardware and Light Green Software: Environmental Policy Integration in the UK

Andrew Jordan

[P]olicies and programmes, local and national, [must] tackle the issues facing society ... in a joined up way, regardless of the organisational structure of government. (Cabinet Office, 1999, 'Modernising Government', paragraph 7)

THE PARADOXES OF UK ENVIRONMENTAL GOVERNANCE

UK policy-makers fully appreciate the fundamental mismatch between 'the integrated, holistic functioning of environmental systems and the disjointed nature of the policy-making machine' (Weale et al, 1991, p25). However, the UK's experience in trying to bring the two more closely together by implementing environmental policy integration (EPI) presents a number of interesting paradoxes. On the one hand, the UK has often been the back-marker in the 'regulatory competition' (Héritier et al, 1996) to set higher environmental standards in Europe. More often than not, it has been in the group of Member States trying to delay or weaken environmental protection measures. Haigh describes the UK as a 'median' state 'between the Danes, Dutch and Germans ... and Ireland and the Mediterranean countries' (Haigh and Lanigan, 1995, p35). But when it comes to implementing EPI at home and promoting it abroad, Britain has been in the vanguard of European states, providing both political and intellectual leadership for the rest of the European Union (EU).

The second paradox is that although the UK is widely recognized as having one of the strongest and most effective systems for coordinating departmental policies of any Member State in the EU, it struggles to implement EPI in core areas of domestic policy-making. To borrow one of Albert Weale's analogies (Weale, 1993, p214), the UK possesses the necessary 'hardware' (that is, the organizations and procedures of governance) needed to coordinate policy across the various strands of government activity, and the intellectual 'software' (that is, the knowledge needed to implement EPI)[1] to make the government machine run in a more environmental direction. But even with these two vital prerequisites in place, until relatively recently implementation of EPI has been extremely patchy and fitful. Even under the present Labour government, which is politically committed to 'greening government' by joining up policy-making across different policy domains, EPI is manifestly failing to permeate the 'core' areas of government activity, such as financial budgeting, taxation and energy supply.

What explains these two paradoxes? Part of the explanation has to do with the emphasis that the UK places on achieving good European governance. The British like to see themselves as a positive force for efficiency and effectiveness in the EU. In the UK, EPI, poor implementation and the other 'meta' policy problems afflicting EU environmental policy are regarded as equally, if not more, important than the political race to set higher standards for so-called 'end-of-pipe' activities (the waste products of industrial production). However, there is more than a hint of political opportunism in the UK Department of the Environment, Transport and the Regions' (DETR's) espousal of EPI, because integration is an issue where it can safely take the initiative in Europe without incurring a bill for new environmental spending (and with it the ire of other national departments).

Secondly, the continuing failure to 'plug' the software of EPI into the efficient hardware of government is due in large part to the historically low political position of environmental issues in UK policy-making. Significantly, EPI has tended to enter mainstream political discourse when environment is at or near the top of Anthony Downs's political attention cycle. British experience suggests that EPI is only ever implemented when it secures the political backing not only of environment agencies and departments, but the very heart of government – the 'core executive' (that is, the prime minister, his/her personal office and the cabinet (Rhodes and Dunleavy, 1995, p12)). The core executive is important because it is the only organization capable of brigading the various sectoral departments of state. *Political will*, therefore, is the vital catalyst – the electricity, so to speak – which energizes the hardware and the software of government to work in pursuit of sustainable development. Without it, EPI in the UK has foundered on the rocks of interdepartmental wrangling. Simply put, EPI has failed to advance as far as one might have expected it to in the UK because a succession of governments has seen no political reason to promote it. Consequently, the stock of 'software' techniques for achieving EPI has been greatly underutilized, leaving the hyper-efficient hardware with little to chew on.

This chapter explores these paradoxes in a little more detail by investigating the history of EPI in the UK from the late 1960s, through the 1990s to 'new' Labour's recent efforts to achieve 'joined-up policy-making' to address so-called 'wicked' issues such as environmental damage that spill over departmental divisions – Blairspeak for horizontal coordination. It argues that EPI needs to overcome endemic features of government, which have served to frustrate just about every previous attempt to improve the 'horizontality' of action (Peters, 1998a, p295; Marsh et al, 2000). The chapter examines the progress made both in implementing EPI at home and selling it abroad as a policy idea. New Labour regards EPI as a central plank of its sustainability strategy. It has also signalled its determination to make Whitehall more receptive 'to new ideas that take the long-term view and cut across organizational boundaries to get to the root of the problem' (Cabinet Office, 1999, p49). Therefore, the chapter concludes with a brief assessment of how well EPI is being applied in two key policy sectors of the UK, namely transport and energy, which are especially vital to the sustainability transition.

THE INSTITUTIONAL 'HARDWARE' OF UK GOVERNMENT

Coordinated action is notoriously difficult for *all* large bureaucracies to achieve, none more so than governments, which are typically divided into different departments of state. In one important sense, the UK already has a very coordinated system of government. While many countries struggle to present a united front in international negotiations, Britain boasts an extremely 'tight' set of internal coordination mechanisms, which ensure that departments speak with one voice on foreign matters. Overseen by the Cabinet Office, these mechanisms are the envy of other Member States (Metcalfe, 1994; Spence, 1995). The mechanisms (a combination of information sharing and consensus-forming discussion) are underpinned by the informal cabinet principle of collective responsibility. The UK, which is a relatively cohesive unitary state, also has a relatively homogenous and highly trained civil service; so the sort of internal coordination problems found in more politicized and federal systems of government are much less pronounced. Together, these features provide UK policy-makers with one of the most effective policy machines to formulate, coordinate and implement EU policy (Wallace, 1997, p687). At least in principle, it is difficult to conceive of a bureaucratic context that is more conducive to achieving that 'great Holy Grail' of all governments (Peters, 1998b, p1): horizontal coordination.

These centralized mechanisms have been designed to operate centripetally by coordinating policy development from the top down. But pulling in the opposite direction are powerful centrifugal forces operating at a much lower level in the departmental structure of government. By far the most powerful force springs from the basic bureaucratic structure of Her Majesty's government, which remains deeply fragmented into competing departments of state. Richardson and Jordan (1979, pp26, 28) first coined the phrase 'departmental pluralism' to describe the marked tendency for the various parts to compete with one another to realize their sectoral interests. Those interests often reflect a well-entrenched ideology or philosophy of working which pre-exists any 'rational' assessment of a new policy problem. This aspect of policy-making is captured by the popular aphorism 'the departmental view', but it is also closely connected to the concept of policy paradigms. The best example in Britain is to be found in the agricultural sector, which under the UK Ministry for Agriculture (MAFF) has concentrated on intensifying production and protecting farmers' incomes regardless of the environmental cost. Similarly, before it was integrated into the DETR, the Department of Transport (DoT) believed in building more roads to meet a predicted level of demand instead of taking active steps to manage (reduce) that demand. Hence, EPI is a central plank of sustainability, which is the DETR's main policy paradigm.

These vertical divisions serve to frustrate cross-cutting initiatives such as sustainability and EPI. According to one Labour minister, the 'danger' is that ministers find themselves 'locked into silos... one department does one thing, another does another, and they actually undermine each other and never talk to each other' (HC 517-II, Session 1997–1998, p145). Potentially 'overriding issues' such as the environment tend to fall into the cracks between departments or are simply dissipated unless the core executive exercises strong leadership and pulls departments into line (Peters, 1998a, p306), or the department in question manages to win cognate departments around to its way of thinking.

The problem faced by environmental departments the world over is that the driving forces of pollution, habitat loss and development reside in virtually every sectoral ministry of state. Indeed, with the exception, perhaps, of economic policy, environment is probably *the* most cross-cutting of all policy issues confronting governments. Former Environment Commissioner Ritt Bjerregaard (Bjerregaard, 1995) admitted that she was:

> ... *a bit like someone in charge of a car park where none of the issues which are parked there under the name of the environment are really ones I could call my own. In reality, they are in fact issues which really need to be resolved elsewhere by some of my other ... colleagues with responsibility for agriculture, for industry, for energy.*

Expressed in these simple bureaucratic terms, EPI will only occur if and when the DETR colonizes the key centres of power in the UK political system, by winning over older and more influential departments of state to its paradigm or way of thinking. The difficulty of achieving such an outcome through the deeply institutionalized game of interdepartmental bargaining in Whitehall should not be underestimated.

COORDINATING GOVERNANCE

The overall level of coordination achieved by the government on any particular issue will be determined by the interaction between these centripetal and centrifugal tendencies. The resulting level of policy coordination can be measured using a typology developed by the Organisation for Economic Co-operation and Development (OECD, 1996). This identifies various levels or 'styles' of coordination ranging from the most minimal (simply making others aware of what you are doing by sharing information) through to highly centralized, top-down management systems for remedying interdepartmental conflict.

Box 3.1 Levels of Policy Coordination

Level 1

Independence: each department retains autonomy within its own policy area irrespective of spillover impacts on cognate departments/areas.

Level 2

Communication: departments inform one another of activities in their areas via accepted channels of communication.

Level 3

Consultation: departments consult one another in the process of formulating their own policies to avoid overlaps and inconsistencies.

Level 4

Avoiding divergence in policy: departments actively seek to ensure their policies converge.

Level 5

Seeking consensus: departments move beyond simply hiding differences and avoiding overlaps/spillovers to work together constructively through joint committees and teams.

Level 6

External arbitration: central bodies are called in by, or are imposed upon, departments to settle irresolvable interdepartmental disputes.

Level 7

Limiting autonomy: Parameters are predefined which demarcate what departments can and cannot do in their own policy areas.

Level 8

Establishing and achieving common priorities: the core executive sets down and secures, through coordinated action, the main lines of policy.

Source: adapted from OECD (1996)

On some issues such as the coordination of UK foreign policy, the level of coordination routinely achieves levels 6 and 8 in Box 3.1 (Metcalfe, 1994). This is because departments themselves recognize the value of having a single policy position in Europe and not operating behind one another's backs. The UK government's economic policy routinely achieves a similar level of coordination because it is backed by strong Treasury controls on spending which all departments are forced to comply with. However, when it comes to domestic policy concerns with a much lower political profile (such as EPI), the level of coordination achieved is much lower because 'non-environmental' departments tend to fight fiercely to protect their own turf. A recent parliamentary committee, which investigated how well EPI initiatives were performing, concluded that (HC 517-I, Session 1997–1998, paragraph 4):

> *Successive governments have always had strong machinery for ensuring that the economic aspects of policies and programmes are kept under regular and close review. The environmental and social aspects have not always been similarly treated… [A]ll the recent indicators and monitoring efforts … show that there is still much to be done to protect the environment and to reverse damaging trends.*

The failure to attain higher levels of coordination on environmental issues (ie, stronger EPI) is partly the result of weak leadership shown by the core executive, and partly disinterest bordering on outright hostility shown by other departments. The DETR's relatively weak position in the cabinet hierarchy[2] means that it cannot force them to acquiesce, so EPI struggles to make any serious headway. It is important to remember that the Cabinet coordinating mechanisms described above are designed to resolve conflicts between departments; they do not substantially disturb the existing balance of departmental power in the cabinet. In any case, the DETR is not and never has been a purely 'environmental' department. Its responsibilities cover such a vast array of different policy issues (for example, local government finance, housing and transport, through to regional development) that units dealing with concerns such as pollution control and land-use planning have always struggled to secure ministerial time and hence political backing in intra-departmental wrangles (McQuail, 1994a,b).

Because of these political and institutional characteristics of UK policy-making, EPI has tended to operate at a very 'weak' level (where 'non-environmental' departments simply take environmental considerations 'into account', corresponding to levels 1–3 in Box 3.1) (Hill and Jordan, 1993, p5). Conversely, for 'strong' integration (where policies are produced in non-environmental spheres that *consistently* benefit the environment) fully to take root, EPI would need to function at much higher levels in Box 3.1. At the moment, this seems unlikely, although in the last decade the prospects have improved. This is because key economic departments such as trade and industry are now beginning to see environment policies on climate change, for example, as a positive enabler of wealth generation rather than a crude brake on innovation and enterprise.

THE HISTORY OF EPI IN THE UK

In the UK, EPI is conventionally defined as 'the creation of procedures and mechanisms, political and administrative, which … ensure that environmental priorities … are built into the planning and execution of policies in other non-environmental spheres' (HL 27, Session 1992–1993, p5). This section explains why recent UK governments have taken active steps to improve EPI, describes the means selected for doing so and examines their overall performance to date.

The Key Drivers of EPI in the UK

Three developments have encouraged UK governments to examine ways of improving EPI:

1   new modes of thinking;
2   international policy commitments;
3   domestic political pressure.

Sustainability: a new paradigm of environmental policy?
The 1980s witnessed the emergence of sustainable development as the main organizing principle of modern environmental policy the world over. The 1987 Brundtland Report defined sustainable development as 'development that meets the needs of the present without compromising the ability of future generations to meet their own needs' (WCED, 1987, p43). Sustainable policies are polices which minimize pollution, reduce non-renewable resource use (such as oil and gas), close product loops, use renewable resources carefully, and care for the environment so that it can continue to supply these services now and forever. However, sustainability is proving much harder to implement than environmental policy because it involves moving beyond environmental regulation to address the driving forces of environmental change at their roots. Brundtland's diagnosis was simple (WCED, 1987, p9):

> *Those responsible for managing natural resources and protecting the environment are institutionally separated from those responsible for managing the economy. The real world of interlocked economic and ecological systems will not change; the policies and institutions concerned must.*

At first, the UK (DoE, 1989, p13) denied the need for greater EPI, claiming that the existing coordination mechanisms were up to the task of implementing sustainability. But like most other countries, it was eventually forced to confront the mismatch identified by Weale described at the beginning of this chapter.

International and European commitments
Although sustainability has emerged as the dominant paradigm of modern environmental policy, international obligations continue to provide the main impetus to UK environmental policy. Currently, over 80 per cent of UK environmental policy originates in the EU. Unlike some other aspects of domestic environmental policy, the EU has not been a consistent force promoting higher levels of EPI in Britain. To the contrary, the UK has done much to sell the need for EPI to other EU states. However, the steady internationalization of environmental policy in the 1980s did increase the need for cross-departmental coordination, both in terms of developing national negotiating positions prior to the development of policy and implementing whatever commitments are eventually entered into. When policy-making is purely domestic, governments have the 'luxury' of leaving the resolution of coordination problems to the implementation phase (Peters, 1998a, p306).

During the 1980s, the arrival onto the international agenda of issues such as acid rain, nitrate pollution from agriculture, ozone depletion and water pollution forced other 'non-environmental' departments in the UK such as agriculture and industry to routinely pay much more attention to the detailed aspects of environmental policy. The privatization of the water and energy utilities was especially important in this respect, as they powerfully revealed the extent to which the government's hands had been tied through the UK's membership of the EU (Jordan, 1999a).

Over time, the DETR and its predecessor, the Department of the Environment (DoE), have learned to use international commitments to gain leverage over other departments. Strictly speaking, the big political battles that the DETR won in the Cabinet during the 1980s on issues such as acid rain (1984–1988), sewage treatment (1990), climate change (1988–1992) and chlorofluorocarbon (CFC) production (1987) were not EPI because they were discrete events, rather than a structured, long-term process of policy integration. But one of the recurring themes of the British experience with EPI is that environmental departments have to continue winning strategic interdepartmental battles; EPI does not occur automatically. Insofar as they raised the level of environmental awareness in Whitehall, these interdepartmental victories provided a vitally important foundation for the EPI initiatives that followed.

Domestic political pressure

Until relatively recently, the environment was regarded by most UK politicians as an unimportant and largely self-contained area of political activity. In the past, 'non-environmental' departments interpreted any escape of environmental issues from the 'environmental ghetto' (HC 517-I, Session 1997–1998, pxvii) as unwarranted interference to be resisted wherever possible. However, the growing scale and scope of environmental legislation, and the steady politicization of the environment throughout the 1980s, made it progressively harder for them to stand aloof. Pressure from groups such as Greenpeace and Friends of the Earth has forced all departments to learn, often painfully, to justify their policies in environmental terms to a more environmentally astute public. The Brent Spar crisis brilliantly revealed how poorly prepared the Department of Trade and Industry (DTI) was to meet the new political demands that the sustainability agenda is bringing.

British non-governmental organizations (NGOs) have also provided a rich pool of political support and ideas about how to implement EPI. At home, a tiny environmental NGO in London called the Green Alliance, whose motto is 'to put the environment at the heart of decision-making', ran a 'greening government' campaign throughout the early 1990s which tried to audit each department's performance against its EPI commitments. In spite of its small size, the Green Alliance was the only NGO that tried to track routinely the implementation of EPI. For well over two decades, British groups such as the Institute for European Environmental Policy (IEEP) have used various channels, including parliamentary committees, to promote the cause of EPI in Europe.[3]

EPI by Organizational Means: the 1970s

Guy Peters (1998b, pp27–46) outlines the various kinds of 'procedures and mechanisms' (see above section) for achieving horizontally coordinated EPI. These range from creating new organizations (such as super-ministries) through to strengthening the core executive (for example, the cabinet or prime minister's private office), forming coordinating committees (for example, at the interdepartmental or cabinet level) and introducing processes (such as budgeting, evaluation and regulatory reviews). At one time or another, the UK has employed all four – organizational, central control, coordination by committee and process based – in its bid to 'green government'.

Alterations to the organizational hardware of government to achieve EPI have tended to occur only very infrequently in the UK. The first came in 1970 with the creation of the DoE. The DoE was one of Prime Minister Heath's sprawling super-ministries, which, at its founding, employed over 74,000 staff (Draper, 1977, p9). It has never, as reported above, been a purely 'environmental department' (Jordan, 2002). In 1980, just 3.2 per cent of its staff was allocated to environmental functions (McQuail, 1994a, p3). The rationale for brigading all the government's 'environmental' functions into one department was to facilitate holistic policy problem-solving. But in reality, 'building big' failed to tame the centrifugal tendencies in government (Painter, 1980; Radcliffe, 1985), and the DoE lasted just six years as a super-ministry before the last Labour government (1974–1979) hived transport off into a separate department. At the time, politicians claimed that the creation of the DoE, a Royal Commission on Environmental Pollution (RCEP) and a Central Unit on Environmental Pollution in the Cabinet Office reflected the government's determination to implement EPI by organizational means. In truth, neither the creation of the DoE nor the modifications subsequently made to it were primarily motivated by political (for example, the wish to increase/decrease the number of places in cabinet) rather than environmental considerations (Radcliffe, 1985, p123; McQuail, 1994b, p17).

Meanwhile in Europe, the Commission's Environment Directorate-General (DG) was weak and in any case too preoccupied with laying the foundations of EU environmental policy to colonize other 'non-environmental' policy areas (Jordan, 1999b). The UK flatly rejected the advice of the House of Lords to promote the greening of the EU. If the Commission wanted new resources to advance EPI in Europe, it should divert them from existing areas of regulatory activity such as water pollution, which UK authorities believed were greatly overregulated by the EU (ENDS, 1981, p14):

> *Controlling pollution will continue to be a major concern and the [UK] Government [does] not want to see … commitments neglected in order to extend [environmental policy] into other areas. They would rather see a change of approach towards forms of action which would be more manageable than hitherto, thus allowing resources to be used for other areas of concern.*

EPI under the Conservatives: The 1990 White Paper Process

Efforts to achieve EPI in the UK continued at a fairly low level until the late 1980s when, in the frantic aftermath of Mrs Thatcher's famous environmental speech to the Royal Society in September 1988, the environment suddenly entered the political mainstream. Chris Patten was appointed to be a 'credible' environment secretary. With his more media-friendly image and strategic vision, he persuaded Thatcher of the need for a coordinated White Paper on environmental policy, setting out the government's environmental agenda. Crucially, this statement would need to have the backing of every government department. Patten (Her Majesty's Government, 1990, p230) was particularly anxious to ensure that: 'all the environmental implications of policy decisions are considered before conclusions are reached... [We must] integrate environmental concerns more effectively in to all policy areas'.

The result was an annually updated White Paper series entitled 'This Common Inheritance' in which policies were summarized, new initiatives announced, some targets set and departmental performance reviewed. The paper announced the creation of four mechanisms to improve EPI:

1   The retention of the Cabinet Committee that had prepared the White Paper.
2   A network of 'green ministers', one from every department, to follow up the implementation of White Paper commitments and to systematically consider the environmental implications of all departmental policies.
3   A system through which departments would report on how well they had implemented EPI.
4   The publication of guidance on how departments should undertake environmental appraisals of their own policies.

These were the objectives. In fact, as has been widely reported (Hill and Jordan, 1993), the exercise proved rather disappointing. Ambitious targets were not set, parliamentary departmental committees did not take up the challenge of assessing performance, and very few policy initiatives were created that would not have occurred anyway. Aside from the Green Alliance (eg Hill and Jordan, 1995, pp539–541), the large environmental pressure groups never showed much interest and what could have been a promising development began to atrophy. For instance, the cabinet coordinating committee met very infrequently and always in secret. The so-called green ministers hardly ever met together as a group and consequently their political profile in Whitehall remained very low. When they did meet, they considered routine 'housekeeping' issues such as departmental purchasing policy and never really got to grips with the more strategic aspects of EPI. The policy appraisal guide was issued by the DoE (*not* the Cabinet Office as part of a cross-departmental initiative) in 1991 (DoE, 1991). Three years later the DoE was forced to admit that it 'would be wrong to pretend that [it was] being applied in every case as systematically and consistently as ideally we should like' (DoE, 1994, piii), and issued a supplementary guide to best practice to raise awareness. An independent review subsequently commissioned by the DETR revealed that the reality was a lot bleaker than the DoE's worst fears: most departments chose to politely ignore it (DETR, 1997).

The clear impression given by a parliamentary committee which investigated the White Paper process in 1995 (HL 72, Session 1994–1995) was that there was no systematic interpolicy coordination on environmental matters outside that dictated by EU directives and political expediency generated by controversial political events and electoral considerations. The task of the green Cabinet committee was only to resolve contentious interdepartmental conflicts, not to systematically integrate environmental concerns into all areas of policy formulation and implementation. In an attempt to breathe life into the initiative, their Lordships (HL 72, Session 1994–1995, p56) requested a 'clear and prompt re-statement of the functions and purpose of the Government's own internal integration mechanisms'. Some hope. In a parliamentary reply shortly afterwards, former Chancellor of the Exchequer Kenneth Clarke said he believed the government's strategy on sustainable development was primarily the DoE's responsibility, not the Treasury's (HC, 1995)!

By the mid 1980s, EU environmental policy was beginning to address some of its meta-policy failing such as poor integration and implementation. The DoE sought to exploit these new opportunities, though not always to enthusiastic audiences. For instance, former Environment Minister William Waldegrave, remembers having been 'goaded' by British environmental NGOs into:

> *... putting down statements and boring our colleagues silly in the Environment Council by making long speeches at 6 o'clock in the morning about the importance of integration of agricultural and environmental policy. When we started doing that, people did rather rush for their aeroplanes home, with one or two exceptions... [But] I do believe that ... we [gave] ... [Environment] DG people clout in their discussions with their agricultural colleagues within the Commission... [I now] think the agricultural discussions have been very successfully infected with the sort of environmental concerns we all want to see.*
> (HL 135, Session 1986–1987, p92)

Building on this success, the DoE succeeded in getting EPI on the UK's list of demands during the 1991 Maastricht Treaty (political union) intergovernmental conference (IGC). The UK's main environmental proposal was to ensure that all new Commission proposals received an environmental appraisal. The UK also suggested that the Environment DG should immediately establish an environmental appraisal unit to audit the environmental performance of the other DGs (ENDS, 1991, p3). These proposals, which were quite clearly modelled on the White Paper mechanisms, were potentially far reaching and went well beyond current practice in Britain – an example, perhaps, of former Secretary of State for the Environment (SoSE) Michael Heseltine playing national departmental politics by international means? More importantly, they chimed with the UK's wider agenda of promoting subsidiarity, good governance and deregulation, and found a receptive audience in the Environment DG. But the other DGs flatly opposed the UK's initiatives and they failed to make the final text of the Maastricht Treaty.[4]

During its presidency of the EU in 1992 (when the treaty was still undergoing ratification), the UK again sought to revive interest in integration. EPI was discussed at length during the informal Environment Council at Gleneagles in the autumn of 1992. However, the discussion, which was informed by a document specially prepared for the DoE by the IEEP (IEEP, 1992), failed to give the initiative sufficient political impetus and momentum drained away. This may in part have been due to the perception that the British were behaving somewhat duplicitously, in seeking to impose EPI on the Commission while blocking the Commission's proposed Directive on Strategic Environmental Assessment (Hanley, 1998, p63).

New Labour: 'Greening Government' and the 'Cardiff Process'

New Labour entered office promising to breathe fresh life into the White Paper process. In opposition, it had promised to make a number of minor changes to the hardware of government to reflect this (Labour Party, 1994). However, its first act, the reintegration of the departments of transport and environment, came out of the blue. The move was, of course, warmly received by environmentalists, who also drew encouragement from the appointment of Deputy Prime Minister John Prescott as its first head. However, as previous prime ministers discovered, EPI requires more than a slight rearrangement of departmental portfolios; it must incorporate mechanisms that green other departments from the inside out. EPI has undoubtedly fired the imagination of the Blair administration as it fits neatly with Labour's long-term political project of promoting 'joined-up' thinking as a means of 'modernizing government' (Cabinet Office, 1999).

Once in power, Labour quickly set about implementing a new EPI initiative, which it termed 'greening government' (HC 517-I, Session 1997–1998) after the Green Alliance campaign of the early 1990s. The main elements are as follows:

- a Parliamentary Audit Committee on Sustainable Development to ensure EPI is implemented across all government departments;
- a special cross-departmental Sustainable Development Unit located in the DETR to issue guidance, promote best practice and report on progress made by all departments (it was coordinated by Stephen Tindale, a former director of the Green Alliance);
- a Green Globe Task Force to inform and review the Foreign Office's new greener and more 'ethical' foreign policy.

New Labour also:

- increased the status of the Green Ministers Network and opened it up to greater external scrutiny;

- announced comprehensive policy reviews of energy and transport policy – two critical drivers of environmental change;
- produced a new strategy on sustainable development which placed much greater emphasis on EPI, on increasing social equity and on managing demand for environmentally damaging services;
- raised the political profile of the Cabinet Committee on the Environment (ENV) by placing it under the chairmanship of the deputy prime minister;
- introduced a set of key sustainability indicators to sit along side the headline inflation and gross domestic product (GDP) figures (these are meant to show whether or not the UK is on a sustainable growth path and to flag the need for appropriate policy interventions);
- reviewed the use of existing environmental appraisal guidance and introduced new supplementary guidance on best practice.

On paper, these go considerably further than anything introduced by the Conservatives. But, how well have they fared in practice? In its first progress report the Audit Committee (HC 517-I, Session 1997–1998), detected 'some failure to grasp the overarching nature of sustainable development' – diplomatic code for 'thwarted by departmental resistance and weak central leadership'. Apparently, ENV hardly ever meets and its activities remain secret. In evidence, the DETR sought to reassure members of parliament (MPs) that the committee's failure to meet was in fact a good sign, in that it reflected consensus in Whitehall on the need for EPI. However, the committee strongly disagreed and suggested that if there is no disagreement then the whole initiative is not proceeding nearly as fast as the government claims. In effect, it rated the performance of the greening government initiative as being somewhere closer to levels 1–4 in Box 3.1 than level 6. Significantly, ENV is supposed to resolve contentious interdepartmental conflicts, not systematically integrate environmental concerns within all areas of policy formulation and implementation. But it meets too infrequently to attain even this very modest goal. The committee was told, for example, that ENV did not consider the environmental implications of the 1997 Budget before it was announced (HC 517-II, Session 1997–1998, p272) – surely, an important acid test of how well greening government is really performing. It also discovered that the 1998 Comprehensive Spending Review, which determined the shape of public spending well into the new century and whose environmental implications are obviously enormous, was undertaken separately from the DETR's sustainability initiative. In fact, the DETR was the only department to include sustainability in its terms of reference for the review. Under close questioning from MPs, Michael Meacher conceded that there was simply too much at stake for the whole budgetary process to be held up by the greening government process:

> *It would not have been reasonable to have postponed the [UK£300 billion review] given the sheer weight of impact of public expenditure, until DETR has completed its sustainable development strategy and got agreement around Whitehall for it.* (HC 517-II, Session 1997–1998, p275)

The green ministers, who met just seven times in five years under the Tories and twice in the first year of the Blair government, are still not very visible and seem to spend most of their time on 'housekeeping' issues. The fact that the Sustainable Development Unit was placed in the DETR rather than in the Cabinet Office, where Labour had promised to put it when in opposition (Labour Party, 1994, p43), underlines the relatively lowly status of EPI relative to other cross-cutting initiatives, such as social exclusion, which have their own designated unit in the Cabinet Office.

The Audit Committee returned to the topic of EPI in 1998–1999 to see whether the government had remedied any of these failings. It discovered that major government strategies on tourism and, most surprisingly, sustainable development, had not come before ENV, and instructed it to take a 'more interventionist' approach in future (HC 426-I, Session 1998–1999, paragraph 2). The committee probably had in mind the sort of interventionist body found on level 7 of the OECD's guidelines (see Box 3.1). Currently, though, ENV is 'not driving the Government's pursuit of sustainable development nor acting in a positive way to unearth and deal with related policy conflicts' (HC 426-I, Session 1998–1999, paragraph 12). Too much is left to ad hoc interdepartmental wrangling – hardly a recipe for coordinated EPI.

The committee reserved its harshest criticism for the environmental policy appraisal process. It discovered to its dismay that only eight departments, covering 14–25 separate policy issues, could actually list the environmental appraisals they had undertaken in the preceding year. The majority reported that they had not undertaken any at all. This state of affairs persists because there is still no formal requirement on departments to produce or publish assessments. The committee (HC 426-I, Session 1998–1999, paragraph 49) courteously remarked that:

> ... *the limited list of environmental appraisals cannot reflect the full extent of departments' relevant policy work and must reflect either a very different, more limited, interpretation of whether they have undertaken environmental appraisal or indicate that environmental impacts have not been addressed where they might have been expected.*

Worse still, the committee discovered clear evidence that appraisals were being used as 'after the event justification and mitigation of environmental impacts – the "green proofing" of policy decisions already taken'. Green proofing is a very good example of what the OECD terms 'negative coordination', which is a feature of levels 1–4 in Box 3.1. The committee also examined how far EPI had actually penetrated into that most hallowed of all governmental activities: the setting of a national budget (HC 326, Session 1998–1999, p3). It discovered to its alarm that parts of the March 1999 Budget had been subject to an environmental appraisal, but not the whole. Tellingly, the government had overlooked 'the fundamental point that economic growth of itself conflicts with two core aspects of sustainable development, the use of natural resources and the protection of the environment'. In 2000, the government conceded that only 5.5 per cent of the government-sponsored bills for new legislation in that parliamentary year contained an environmental appraisal (HC, 2000). Clearly, EPI still has a long way to go.

In 1998, Labour sought to revitalize EPI in the EU by making environment one of three political priorities during its six-month presidency (ENDS, 1998a, p47). This time the context was more propitious than it had been in 1992: the recently signed (1997) Amsterdam Treaty had just granted EPI much stronger legal backing; with 'greening government', the UK had something genuinely ambitious to export to the rest of the EU; and the new (post-1995) Scandinavian Member States were keen to raise the profile of environmental issues such as EPI in the Commission and the Environment Council. The UK succeeded in organizing an unprecedented joint meeting of environment and energy ministers, and joint policy initiatives on environment and transport. The Cardiff European Council, which addressed EPI, was the first time that heads of state really debated any environmental issue at great length. The council set in train the so-called 'Cardiff process' whereby sectoral councils report on the environmental impact of their activities (Jordan and Lenschow, 2000; see also Chapter 1 in this book). The UK presidency therefore succeeded in extending the discussion about the scope of EPI to encompass the Council of Ministers, where policies are actually adopted, as well as the Commission, which simply proposes legislation. However, the UK's continuing refusal to back the Commission's strategic environmental assessment (SEA) proposal again raised fresh doubts about its long-term commitment to EPI.

TESTING THE EFFICACY OF 'GREENING GOVERNMENT'

If EPI is to have a long-term impact on policy-making, it has to suffuse the daily processes of policy-making in government. Therefore, this final section looks at two policy areas – transport and energy supply – which are currently on an unsustainable track, and asks whether the greening government initiative has had much, if any, impact.

Transport: A Policy Mess?

There is no better example of the need for improved interdepartmental coordination than transport policy. The rising costs of congestion, coupled to health fears about smog in urban areas (childhood asthma rates have doubled in the last 20 years), and a rising wave of protest about plans to run new roads through greenfield sites in the affluent parts of the south and south-east of the UK (Doherty, 1998) have greatly politicized the issue of transport in the last five years. Transport is an example par excellence of a 'policy mess' which typically arises 'when policy problems do not correspond to the structure of government' (Rhodes, 1986, p28).

Conflicting policy paradigms
For the past 40 years, transport policy has worked on the 'predict and provide' principle that forecasted levels of growth should be catered for by a continuous

road-building programme. This policy paradigm suited the interests of a tightly integrated policy community of engineers, haulage firms, car producers and road builders that surrounded the DoT, insulating it from external political pressure. Realizing that the situation was both socially and environmentally unsustainable, the DoE fought hard to impose a ceiling on future traffic growth but found itself blocked by the DoT (ENDS, 1994, p19). During the 1990s, the DoE announced new planning guidelines to curb the sort of new out-of-town developments that stimulate and sustain car use, but this did not deflect the main thrust of the road-building programme. Worse still for the DoE, its attempts to reduce car dependency were challenged by the privatization–deregulation agenda pursued by the DoT under the Conservatives, which saw British Rail and local authority bus services broken up into competing units.

A 'New Deal' for integrated transport?

The 1990s have witnessed a paradigm shift in transport policy (Dudley and Richardson, 1996). The creation of the DETR has helped to address the mismatch of institutions to problems, but Prescott's determined efforts to craft a sustainable policy have been stymied by the UK Treasury (*The Guardian*, 9 June 1998) and what he termed the 'teeny boppers' in Blair's inner circle. Much to Prescott's annoyance, Blair has intervened on more than one occasion to pacify the anxious car drivers of Middle England, personified by the archetypal 'Mondeo man' who bore him to power in 1997 (*The Observer*, 7 June 1998). The centrepiece of Prescott's strategy is a White Paper entitled 'A New Deal for Transport' (DETR, 1998). Although it undoubtedly represented a sea change in thinking, with new money for public transport, stronger local authority powers and provision for charging on parking and congestion, many of the most difficult issues were removed, devolved to local authorities or require enabling legislation (ENDS, 1998b). Significantly, a parliamentary committee bemoaned the absence of national road-traffic reduction targets to steer the new policy (HC 32-I, Session 1997–1998). It also identified a lack of coordination within government, chiding the DTI for proposing to relax planning consents to enable science parks to be built on greenfield sites. In the past, such developments have served only to fuel the demand for travel.

Energy: Strong or Weak Integration?

Labour's energy policy is to provide secure and diverse supplies of energy at competitive prices. Its environmental policy is to implement sustainable development. Unfortunately, these objectives do not necessarily pull in the same direction. So which one is winning? The DETR has environmental commitments to reduce greenhouse gases and acid emissions. The DTI, which absorbed the UK Department of Energy in 1992, is primarily concerned with supply-side issues, chiefly securing fuel diversity and lower prices in order to achieve economic growth. Then there are a variety of non-departmental government bodies with diverse goals. The Environment Agency's task is to regulate emissions from power stations; the Office of Electricity Regulation (OFFER) oversees the pricing of electricity and has responsibilities for protecting the interests of consumers. The result is not so much a 'policy mess' as an inability to achieve strong EPI.

In order to achieve a genuinely sustainable energy policy Labour must reconcile three conflicting goals:

1   Affordable energy prices: privatization of the energy industry and liberalization of the domestic energy market, two flagship policies of the Conservative government, combined with changes in the worldwide energy market, have led to a steady decline in the electricity price paid by consumers. The DTI regards this as a vindication of its policies and, with OFFER, is promoting further liberalization. However, as prices have fallen, the amount of energy consumed per unit of GDP has increased.

2   Jobs: privatization and fiercer competition dealt a savage blow to the coal industry. As recently as 1990, coal generated two-thirds of the UK's electricity. By 2000, the figure was closer to 20 per cent, compared to over 40 per cent for gas. The recent 'dash' for cheap, relatively clean but finite supplies of gas decimated the domestic coal industry. The Tories allowed market forces to prevail but Blair has stepped in and declared a moratorium on new gas-fired power stations in order to save coal miners' jobs. Nuclear power sits in the political and economic doldrums. By 2015 there are likely to be only a handful of stations still in service.

3   Environmental goals: like transport, energy generates large amounts of the climate-altering gas carbon dioxide (CO_2), as well as other gases that contribute to acid rain. In all probability, the UK and Germany will be the only EU states to attain the climate change targets agreed at the Earth Summit in Rio in 1992. The UK will achieve this feat primarily because of the windfall saving produced by the collapse of the relatively 'dirty' coal industry.

Currently, there are three pressure points at which these different priorities collide headlong into one another. These are described below.

The energy 'mix'
The DTI published the results of a year-long review of fuel sources in October 1998. It tries to square the circle of propping up the coal industry, and maintaining competition in energy supply, by restricting new gas power stations and removing distortions in the energy market which have made coal so unattractive. However, the White Paper predicts that even with these adjustments, coal could end up with just 10 per cent of the electricity market by 2003, with gas taking 50 to 60 per cent. In sustainability terms, the outcome of the review is decidedly mixed, reflecting the allegedly low priority that the DTI gave to the government's environmental commitments (ENDS, 1998c). Gas is a non-renewable resource and at the current rate of extraction, the UK will become a net importer sometime early in the new century. But in environmental terms, any increase in coal burn would push up greenhouse gas emissions, jeopardizing the UK's Kyoto Protocol commitment. The UK should reach its short-term climate target, but problems remain during the period after 2010. By then windfall effect will have dried up as the nuclear industry, a relatively

greenhouse-friendly fuel source, and the gas sector both decline, while road traffic and energy use rise.

Domestic energy consumption

Given the difficulties of reducing emissions from the transport sector, the DETR has decided to focus on the domestic sector in the hunt for the extra cuts in greenhouse gases needed to fulfil the UK's Kyoto target. The main barrier here is the deep contradiction between the DTI's drive to reduce energy prices and promote competition (through which energy suppliers compete to supply as much electricity as possible), and the DETR's campaign to boost energy efficiency and reduce polluting emissions. The fear is that lower prices will produce a 'rebound effect' as energy consumption rises.

Renewable energy production

The gap left by gas and nuclear energy could be filled by renewables. In theory, renewable energy sources (such as solar, wind and hydroelectric power) provide the most sustainable solution to Britain's energy needs, with minimal air pollution. However, renewables have always been the Cinderella of British energy policy. Consequently, they currently account for just 2 per cent of the UK's electricity needs. In opposition, Labour promised to supply 10 per cent of electricity from renewable sources by 2010 (Labour Party, 1994, p25). Today, the main mechanism for achieving this is the Non-Fossil Fuel Obligation (NFFO) Order, which helps commercialize promising new technologies by placing a levy on domestic electricity bills. Progress towards the 10 per cent target is at a snail's pace. Renewables are generally more costly than conventional sources and, given the background of declining prices and tough competition, the big generators are wary of taking up new and uncertain technologies. By 2003, renewables are only expected to generate 5 per cent of UK needs – ca 1000 megawatts (MW) (HC, 1998). Again, genuine EPI is being thwarted by bureaucratic squabbles between the DTI and the DETR. Having investigated the situation, their Lordships concluded: 'the bitter experience ... is of anything but a coordinated and coherent approach either to the making of policy or, in particular, to its crucial delivery' (HL 78-I, Session 1998–1999).

CONCLUSION

There are several lessons that can be learned from the UK's efforts to implement EPI. The first is that even a state blessed with efficient hardware and light green software may still suffer serious coordination problems. What is perhaps most striking about the UK's experience is the continuity of both the hardware and the software of government. Periodic changes have been made to the overall size of the DETR. At the time, these were justified as 'environmental' measures; in practice, they masked deep tensions between environment and transport policy priorities that remain just as stark today. If anything, the conflict between sectoral interests over the overall direction of policy-making is just as deeply institutionalized today as it was in Heath's day. Similarly, thinking about how to achieve EPI through assessment and information-sharing procedures – the software of government – was already well developed in the 1970s.

This leads to a second point. Environmental policy is uniquely cross-sectoral in nature. Given the weak political position of most national environmental departments, the prospects of achieving EPI are likely to remain bleak unless the core executive provides firm backing and clear leadership. What has changed most in the UK in the last 30 years is the *political will* needed by the core executive to plug the software into the hardware. Domestic political pressure, international commitments and new ideas (namely, sustainability) have all played their part. The Conservatives flirted with EPI in the early 1990s, but in the absence of strong political leadership from the centre, the White Paper initiative soon foundered on the rocks of interdepartmental conflict. In this respect, the British experience with EPI powerfully confirms the central finding of Peters' (1998b, p52) study of horizontal government: 'coordination … may be achievable without special mechanisms if there is the will to coordinate, but no mechanism is sufficient if there is an absence of will'.

Thirdly, on paper the means of coordinating policy in the UK are potentially very strong but, paradoxically, the chief advocate of EPI – the DETR – is inherently weak. The DETR struggles to coordinate the tasks that are formally under its charge without adding new burdens such as EPI. The failure of the super-ministry concept in the early 1970s amply demonstrated the folly of trying to achieve EPI by labelling all issues 'environmental' and putting them under the command of a super-sized environment ministry. To the contrary, EPI evidently requires the right mixture of hardware and software. This is why the core executive must share the burden of responsibility for implementing EPI.

Having made ambitious promises in opposition, Labour is beginning to discover the practical difficulties of coordinating policy across the many strands of government activity. Ambitious objectives relating to renewable energy and integrated transport have proved especially hard to deliver; EPI will undoubtedly be a tough nut to crack. Labour has shown a far stronger commitment to achieving EPI than the Conservatives. But in the absence of determined leadership from the centre, many UK departments are evidently finding it all too easy to disown the DETR's sustainable development strategy. Therefore, the fourth and final lesson to be learned from the UK's experience is simply that in the tough world of everyday politics, EPI will only flourish when environment departments fight and win non-environmental departments around to their way of thinking.

REFERENCES

Bjerregaard, R (1995) *Speech to the Royal Society of Arts*, 2 November 1995, Green Alliance/ERM, London

Cabinet Office (1999) *Modernising Government,* Cmnd 4310, The Stationery Office, London

Department of the Environment, Transport and the Regions (DETR) (1997) *Experience with the 'Policy Appraisal and the Environment' Initiative*, DETR, London

DETR (1998) *A New Deal for Transport: Better for Everyone*, The Stationery Office, London

Department of the Environment (DoE) (1989) *Sustaining Our Common Future*, DoE, London

DoE (1991) *Policy Appraisal and the Environment*, Her Majesty's Stationery Office, London

DoE (1994) *Environmental Appraisal in Government Departments*, Her Majesty's Stationery Office, London

Doherty, B (1998) 'Opposition to Road Building', *Parliamentary Affairs*, vol 51, no 3, pp371–383

Draper, P (1977) *Creation of DoE*, Her Majesty's Stationery Office, London

Dudley, G and Richardson, J (1996) 'Why Does Policy Change over Time?', *Journal of European Public Policy*, vol 3, no 1, pp63–83

Dunleavy, P (1995) 'Estimating the Distribution of Positional Influence in Cabinet Committees Under Major' in R Rhodes and P Dunleavy (eds) *Prime Minister, Cabinet and Core Executive*, Macmillan, Basingstoke

Environmental Data Services (ENDS) (1981) 'Government Lukewarm on EEC Environment Strategy', *ENDS Report*, no 69, pp13–14

ENDS (1991) 'UK Launches European Push on Greening of Government', *ENDS Report*, no 194, p3

ENDS (1994) 'Advancing the Sustainable Development Agenda', *ENDS Report*, no 228, pp18–24

ENDS (1998a) 'UK Presidency to Push for Greening of EC Policy', *ENDS Report*, no 276, pp47–48

ENDS (1998b) 'Shades of Grey in Prescott's 'New Dawn' For Transport', *ENDS Report*, no 282, pp21–24

ENDS (1998c) 'Environment Takes a Back Seat in Government's Energy Review', *ENDS Report*, no 281, pp30–32

Haigh, N (1998) 'Introducing the Concept of Sustainable Development into the Treaties of the European Union' in T O'Riordan and H Voisey (eds) *The Transition to Sustainability*, Earthscan, London

Haigh, N and Lanigan, C (1995) 'Impact of the EU on UK Environmental Policy Making' in T Gray (ed) *UK Environmental Policy in the 1990s*, Macmillan, Basingstoke

Hanley, N (1998) 'Britain and the European Policy Process' in P Lowe and S Ward (eds) *British Environmental Policy and Europe*, Routledge, London

Héritier, A, Knill, C and Mingers, S (1996) *Ringing the Changes in Europe: Regulatory Competition and the Redefinition of the State*, De Gruyter, Berlin

Hill, J and Jordan, A (1993) 'The Greening of Government: Lessons From the White Paper Process', *ECOS*, vol 14, nos 3–4, pp3–9

Hill, J and Jordan, A (1995) 'Memorandum from the Green Alliance. In: House of Lords, Select Committee on Sustainable Development' (1995) *Report from the Select Committee*, volume II, Her Majesty's Stationery Office, London

Her Majesty's Government (1990) *This Common Inheritance*, Her Majesty's Stationery Office, London

House of Commons (HC) (1995) *Hansard* (House of Commons Debates), Volume 256, Written Answers, 14 March 1995, The Stationery Office, London

HC (1998) *Hansard* (House of Commons Debates), Volume 317, Written Answers, 19 October 1998, The Stationery Office, London

HC (2000) *Hansard* (House of Commons Debates), Volume 346, Written Answers, 20 March 2000, The Stationery Office, London

House of Lords, European Communities Select Committee (HL) (1980) *EEC Environmental Policy*, Session 1979–1980, Fifth Report, Her Majesty's Stationery Office, London

House of Lords, European Communities Select Committee (1992) *Fifth Environmental Action Programme: Integration of Community Policies*, Session 1992–1993, Eighth Report, HL Paper 27, Her Majesty's Stationery Office, London.

Institute for European Environmental Policy (IEEP) (1992) *The Integration of Environmental Protection Requirements into the Definition and Implementation of Other Policies*, IEEP, London

Jordan, A J (1999a) 'EU Water Policy Standards: Locked in or Watered Down?', *Journal of Common Market Studies*, vol 37, no 1, pp13–37

Jordan, A J (1999b) 'The Construction of a Multi-Level Environmental Governance System', *Government and Policy*, vol 17, no 1, pp1–23

Jordan, A J (2002) *The Europeanisation of British Environmental Policy*, Palgrave, Basingstoke (in press)

Jordan, A and Lenschow, A (2000) 'Greening the European Union: What Can Be Learned from the Leaders of EU Environmental Policy?', *European Environment*, vol 9, pp109–120

Labour Party (1994) *In Trust for Tomorrow*, Labour Party, London

McQuail, P (1994a) *Origins of the DoE*, DoE, London

McQuail, P (1994b) *A View From the Bridge*, DoE, London

Marsh, D, Richards, D and Smith, M (2000) *The Changing Role of Central Government*, Macmillan, Basingstoke

Metcalfe, L (1994) 'International Policy Coordination and Public Management Reform', *International Review of Administrative Sciences*, vol 60, pp271–290

Organisation for Economic Co-operation and Development (OECD) (1996) *Globalisation: What Challenges and What Opportunities for Government?*, Paper OCDE/GD (96) 64, OECD, Paris

Painter, M (1980) 'Policy Coordination in the DoE, 1970–1976', *Public Administration*, vol 58, pp135–154

Pearce, D W (1998) 'Cost-Benefit Analysis and Environmental Policy', *Oxford Review of Economic Policy*, vol 14, no 4, pp84–100

Peters, B G (1998a) 'Managing Horizontal Government', *Public Administration*, vol 76, pp295–311

Peters, B G (1998b) *Managing Horizontal Government: The Politics of Coordination*, Research Paper 21, Canadian Centre for Management Development, Ottawa, Canada

Radcliffe, J (1985) 'The Role of Politicians and Administrators in Departmental Reorganisation: The Case of the DoE', *Public Administration*, vol 63, pp210–218

Rhodes, R A W (1986) *The National World of Local Government*, Allen and Unwin, London

Rhodes, R and Dunleavy, P (eds) (1995) *Prime Minister, Cabinet and Core Executive*, Macmillan, Basingstoke

Richardson, J and Jordan, G (1979) *Governing Under Pressure: The Policy Process in a Post-Parliamentary State*, Martin Robinson, Oxford

Spence, D (1995) 'The Coordination of European Policy by Member States' in M Westlake (ed) *The Council of the European Union*, Cartermill, London

Wallace, H (1997) 'At Odds with Europe', *Political Studies*, vol XLV, pp677–688

World Commission on Environment and Development (WCED) (1987) *Our Common Future*, Oxford University Press, Oxford

Weale, A, Kramme, E and O'Riordan, T (1991) *Controlling Pollution in the Round*, Anglo German Foundation, London

Weale, A (1993) 'Ecological Modernisation and the Integration of European
Environmental Policy' in D Liefferink, P Lowe and A Mol (eds) *European
Integration and Environmental Policy*, John Wiley, Chichester

Wilkinson, D (1998) 'Steps Towards Integrating the Environment into Other EU
Policy Sectors' in T O'Riordan and H Voisey (eds) *The Transition to Sustainability*,
Earthscan, London

NOTES

1   For example, UK economists have helped to pioneer the use of procedures such
as cost–benefit analysis and environmental appraisal to quantify the environmental
impact of decisions (Pearce, 1998).

2   Dunleavy (1995, p310) places the secretary of state for the environment in the
lower third of the Cabinet pecking order.

3   See, for example, House of Lords (1980, paragraph 153 (b); 1992), IEEP (1992)
and Wilkinson (1998). Haigh (1998, p68) remembers British NGOs calling for
EPI and sustainable development to be included in the founding treaties as long
ago as 1980.

4   The treaty did, however, strengthen the reference to EPI in Article 130r (2).

Environmental Policy Integration as a Political Principle: The German Case and the Implications of European Policy

Edda Müller

INTRODUCTION

The political principle of environmental policy integration (EPI) was given full recognition in the programming of German environmental policy from the very beginning, but its realization and implementation was poor. This chapter shows that the difficulties in achieving EPI are not caused by inappropriate programming. However, programmes and instruments to foster environmental integration may not be sufficient to improve actual policy-making. Instead, a number of often underestimated framework conditions should also be given attention. This chapter argues that the distribution of political power, the organizational set-up of ministerial responsibilities and the rules and procedures governing the administrative process of decision-making are important factors in realizing a successful integration strategy.

In the first section of this chapter, an overview is provided of the development of environment programmes in Germany during the last 30 years. This development must not be understood merely as an isolated national process but has been influenced by European environmental policy. In the second section, the impact of the framework conditions on the process of environmental policy-making and integration is addressed. Suggestions are then provided on how to improve the political and institutional framework in view of EPI. Finally, the immediate and potential impact of the recent EU initiatives to enforce the principle of EPI on German environmental policy is discussed.

ENVIRONMENTAL PROGRAMMING AND THE PRINCIPLE OF EPI

Germany has long been known as one of the European Union (EU) pioneers and front-runner states in environmental policy-making (see Skou Andersen and Liefferink, 1997). In particular, German environmental policy was rather successful in reducing air and water pollution, in organizing a proper system of waste disposal and in the handling of waste. But these measures hardly get at the root of environmental degradation because they do not aim to reform those policy fields that are the main contributors to environmental damage.

Examples from transport, agriculture and energy policy may illustrate this point:

- While environmental policy succeeded in drastically reducing the emissions of individual cars, it had no impact on controlling the number of cars and traffic behaviour in general.
- With strict regulations and high investments for cleaning wastewater, Germany could improve the quality of surface water, but it could not curb the risks of groundwater contamination nor avoid further losses in species and biotopes caused by agricultural activities.
- The dilemma of traditional sectoral environmental policy was most evident in energy policy. In the early 1980s, air pollution control policy succeeded in reducing sulphur dioxide (SO_2) and nitrogen oxide (NO_x) from power generation. It could not influence, however, the structure of energy supply and demand. End-of-pipe technologies even favoured the concentration and centralization of power generation in rather inefficient condensing power plants, neglecting the potential of more decentralized, energy-efficient cogeneration and district heating schemes.

This section argues that the failure to 'green' sectoral policies is not due to programmatic deficits. Indeed, Germany's poor performance in EPI seems rather puzzling as it has followed a highly integrated approach in its environmental programming for the past 30 years, and formulated several policy principles to ensure that the environment is taken into account in all public policies. Let us consider the evolution of German environmental policy and its integrative elements before trying to resolve the puzzle of poor implementation in the next section.

As early as 1971, the first German environmental programme contained the objective that environmental concerns should be taken into account in all public and private decision-making processes in 'the same manner as it is the case with regard to economic and social concerns' (Environmental Programme, 1972, p2). Elaborating on this integrative approach, three principles were developed to guide the policy-making process: the polluter pays principle, the precautionary principle and the cooperative principle.

The polluter pays principle implies that polluters should be financially liable for the environmental damage they cause. It was to be operationalized mainly by economic instruments that aimed at integrating external ecological costs in the economic calculations of relevant public and private actors.

The precautionary principle prescribes that environmental policy should work towards avoiding activities which cause environmentally harmful effects, rather than merely reacting to existing environmental pollution and degradation. This has several strategic implications: instead of so-called end-of-pipe solutions, integrated solutions should be found. Policy solutions should have a global and long-term perspective rather than be sectoral and short-sighted. Policy-makers must not wait for absolute scientific certainty and clear evidence of environmental degradation, but policies should be adopted pre-emptively.

Finally, the principle of cooperation has a double meaning. Firstly, all actors concerned – not environmental policy actors alone – should be responsible for the protection of the environment. Secondly, all relevant actors should actively participate in the policy-making process.

On the basis of this ambitious programme, German environmental policy-makers in the early 1970s tried to develop concrete instruments to facilitate EPI. Preparation for an environmental impact assessment act began in 1971. The act was supposed to introduce the legal obligation to conduct an environmental impact assessment (EIA) for all public and private programmes and measures that could be relevant for the environment. The adoption of this act would have implied that the ministry responsible for environmental policy (which was the Federal Ministry of the Interior at that time) was entitled to assess the programmes of other departments and prevent those programmes with negative environmental impacts. Hence, the environment would have gained horizontal influence in a similar manner to finance and constitutional law policy. The Ministry of Finance and the Ministry of the Interior benefit from the provisions in Article 27 of the *Joint Manual of Procedure* of the federal government, which give them veto rights in the interministerial decision-making process. But the act was obstructed at the planning stage.

The reason for this failure was not only the lack of political power and influence of the minister responsible for environmental policy at that time, but – already further down the organizational ladder – the insufficient staffing and institutional status of the unit responsible for developing the instrument. Thus, German environmental policy had to wait until 1990 when the European directive on EIA – restricted to certain projects, not to public programmes – was transposed into German legislation. In fact, even with the external pressure from the EU, Germany was delayed in implementing the directive (Lenschow, 1997).

A similar case of ambitious planning but failure in actual policy-making can be told about the development of economic policy instruments. Already in the 1970s, the environmental policy-makers in the German Department of the Interior were attributing great importance to stimulating the creativity and self-interests of economic actors to develop environment-friendly industrial processes and products. But again, policy outputs remained limited. For instance, when, in 1976, the federal act on a levy for wastewater was adopted, the levy imposed was very low and its effect diluted by long transition periods and numerous exemptions. In the context of the first oil crisis, neither industry nor consumers were willing to carry the costs of wastewater fees and, consequently, local governments backed down from imposing unpopular policies in view of electoral pressures.

Given the strong opposition against economic instruments, federal environmental policy shifted towards the development of regulatory policy, setting emission standards for polluting industrial sites. With the 1974 Clean Air Act, a dynamic instrument for pollution control was introduced by combining the critical load approach with an obligation to reduce emissions according to the best available technology (BAT). It made the precautionary concept palatable for industry in providing significant funds to develop technologies to reduce emissions and to start pilot projects for cleaner plants. Although environmental policy thus contradicted the polluter pays principle, it nevertheless successfully stimulated the development of pollution control technologies that could be made compulsory via legal permits. This strategy proved very successful in reducing pollution; but given the end-of-pipe nature of most of the technologies developed, it increased the costs of non-productive investments in coping with the environmental legal obligations.

As a result, industry temporarily changed its mind regarding the preferred policy instruments and supported economic measures. But this attitude change was short-lived. When environmental policy confronted industry in the late 1980s and early 1990s with proposals on a waste levy and a levy on waste heat, opposition to economic instruments re-emerged. Equally, the proposals for a carbon dioxide (CO_2) levy and an energy tax, both related to the climate policy developed under the lead of the Federal Ministry for the Environment in 1990, were strongly opposed. It was only in 1999 that the new coalition government of Social Democrats and the Green party could begin to turn the tide again and introduce an ecological tax reform. This reform aimed at increasing the price of energy consumption to provide an incentive for the increase of energy efficiency and the promotion of renewable energies.

Despite strong resistance on the part of industry and some members of the general public, four factors made this reform happen. Firstly, there was a change of government and the need to satisfy the Green party as the small coalition partner. Secondly, energy-intensive industries were exempted from the application of the tax reform, and the increase of energy prices for the general public and households was rather modest. Finally, the revenue of the new taxes was earmarked to reduce the social costs of labour for employers and to stabilize the insurance costs of employees.

Generally, during the late 1970s and part of the 1980s, environmental policy was formulated in view of its impact on German competitiveness in European and international markets. Progressive measures were adopted only if they did not raise the production costs of industry or if these costs were distributed evenly in the relevant market. Therefore, Germany invested substantial energy in influencing the European environmental policy in order to harmonize standards. Faced with regular deadlocks on the European arena, German environmental policy-makers returned to investigate the domestic toolbox and started negotiations on voluntary agreements with industry. The first voluntary agreements date from the 1970s – for instance, the agreement on return bottles for beverages and on the reduction of the content of volatile organic compounds in paints and lacquers. These instruments compensated for Germany's incapacity to gain support for legally binding standards. In 1978, Germany introduced the eco-labelling programme the Blue Angel, which produced incentives for the producers of environment-friendly products and took advantage of the relatively high environmental awareness of German consumers.

The fact that these voluntary and procedural instruments in German environmental policy were used defensively, rather than due to a deep conviction of their advantages, became apparent during the 1990s when the EU became active in developing procedural instruments to complement its traditional standard-setting environmental policy. The introduction of the Eco-Audit Directive and the Directive on the Public Access to Environmental Information falls within this period. Interestingly, Germany proved to be a very sceptical negotiator and slow implementer, in both instances (cf Héritier et al, 1996; Knill and Lenschow, 1998). In the end, the EU helped to remove the national bottlenecks that had hampered the search for innovative and integrative policy instruments.

The European and international debate during the 1990s also stimulated the work on target setting and on environmental indicators. The Federal Ministry for the Environment, for instance, formulated a number of headline indicators and related targets that aimed at putting the discussion on the impact of economic development on the environment on a more objective and quantifiable basis. Comparable to the earlier attempt to adopt an environmental impact assessment act, this strategy also intends to enable the Federal Ministry for the Environment to address counterproductive developments in sector policies. The responsible political actors in these sectors may thus be pushed towards formulating sustainable policies, taking account not only of economic and social concerns but also of environmental concerns and shortcomings of previous programmes. To become operational these initiatives will depend upon supportive framework conditions to become effective (see the following section).

The overview of the EPI principle in German environmental policy programming and implementation would be incomplete without mentioning the special strategies related to waste and climate policy. Waste policy developed a number of instruments to influence waste generation at the source instead of handling it afterwards. With the amendment of the Waste Management Act in 1986, the principle of the producer's product responsibility was legally introduced. This principle was further operationalized in the so-called 1996 Cyclic Economy and Waste Act. With the introduction of the obligation to return products after their use to the producer, and the possibility of introducing deposits on the sale of one-way products, environmental policy hoped to influence product design already at an early stage of production. The idea was that producers would realize a self-interest in developing long-life goods and products with a smaller diversity of materials and with less harmful components. Furthermore, priority would be given to avoiding waste and to recycling resources.

The formal implementation of these principles was difficult. Only some ordinances, such as the one on the return of transport package, of packing material for household products and of batteries, were realized domestically. For other products, the impact of national regulation on the competitiveness of its producers stood in the way of easy implementation. In the meantime, however, the European Commission has taken the lead in 'greening' the waste issue. The example of the Directive on End-of-Life Vehicles shows, however, that strong economic players such as the German car manufacturers may be equally able to postpone and dilute European directives – especially if supported by a powerful political actor such as German Chancellor Gerhard Schröder, who used to be chairman of the board of Volkswagen (VW). But the final approval of the Directive on End-of-Life Vehicles also proves that German environmental policy may benefit from the European level in overcoming strong domestic opposition against implementing progressive programmes – in this case, the principle of the producer's product responsibility and the obligation to return products after their service to the producer.

Climate policy is another example where pressure from above may be crucial for further progress – this time despite relatively favourable domestic conditions. When, during the late 1980s, the international climate policy discussion started, it was welcomed mainly by those units in the German Federal Ministry for the Environment that were responsible for cross-sectoral issues and had faced numerous problems in their interaction with energy and transport policy-makers in the past. Retrofitting and end-of-pipe technologies do not work for the major greenhouse gas, CO_2. Solutions to reduce CO_2 were therefore mainly sought in measures to increase energy efficiency, to save energy and to substitute fossil fuels by CO_2-free energy sources such as renewables. Hence, the climate change problem was perceived as an excellent opportunity to successfully question the unsustainable structures of, primarily, energy and transport policy, but also of agriculture and product policy.

In no small measure due to international climate policy activities, Germany's domestic climate-change strategy turned out to be successful in the initial stage. The German Federal Ministry for the Environment was given the responsibility for preparing a government decision on a German target for CO_2 reduction and for formulating and coordinating the necessary programme to implement this target. In June 1990, the German government approved a 25 per cent reduction target until 2005 compared to 1987 levels, which was upgraded after unification to a 25 per cent reduction target compared to 1990 levels. A programme was also adopted identifying all policies and measures necessary to implement the target.

However, the success story ends at the programming stage. Implementing the programme is difficult because the initiative of executing most of the measures that were foreseen in the climate change programme must be taken by those departments that are responsible for the sectors and economic activities that are the main greenhouse gas emitters – namely, energy and transport. For reasons that are elaborated in the section below, this is not easily forthcoming. International and European climate policy may therefore be extremely important in helping Germany to surmount its domestic bottlenecks and to keep climate policy going. Such pressure from above might compensate for the lack of procedural instruments and direct responsibility of environmental policy to frame the policies and measures needed to implement the politically agreed targets and programmes. At the very least, such pressure might actively guide the political debate on concrete proposals to achieve change.

In summary, this brief sketch of the past 30 years of German environmental policy-making shows that Germany may carry the label 'pioneer' with some justification with respect to developing strategies for EPI. Like most other industrialized countries, it did not, however, fully implement these strategies. The following section describes the framework conditions, potential barriers or support factors for progress in EPI.

FRAMEWORK CONDITIONS FOR SUCCESSFUL EPI

This section argues that in the German case (and in other cases) EPI will only progress in the 'right' constellation of political power and the right setting of institutional and procedural framework conditions. It is doubtful whether an 'ideal world' that recognizes long-term environmental objectives in all sector policies can exist without conflicts resulting, at least temporarily, in winners and losers. Rather, piecemeal and incremental policy-making will further govern environmental policy no less than it governs decision-making in other policy fields. This is even more likely since national and European policy will increasingly only have limited power and influence to control developments driven by the globalization of economic and financial markets, and by the somewhat unforeseeable environmental impacts of future technological innovation.

Nevertheless, because of the incremental character of policy-making it is worthwhile to redress and improve the structures to facilitate not only the development of integrative programmes, but also the subsequent coordination, negotiation, approval and implementation processes that take account of the environment.

The political power dimension looks at the role of environmental policy in the internal governmental decision-making process and in the bargaining process with opposing interest groups in society. While, over the past 30 years, the general acceptance and awareness of environmental policy in the general public and media were rather high, this diffuse support was never equally reflected in the party system and the political competition for votes. These power structures played an important role in the ups and downs of German environmental policy-making. Furthermore, the institutional and procedural framework conditions influence whether the preparation of environmental political decisions will be more or less successful. Significantly, political and institutional factors interact with one another. For a short period, a favourable political constellation may compensate for barriers posed by the institutional and procedural framework. If the political support for EPI is lacking, however, institutional and procedural factors are crucially important in facilitating the consideration of environmental concerns in sectoral policy-making vis-à-vis conflicting political, economic and social interests (Müller, 1995, p484).

The Political Power Dimension

In the current debate, the concept of EPI is embedded in the sustainability paradigm, which communicates a vision of the possibility of balancing economic, social and environmental goals in the short and the longer term if only the right programmes, targets and political instruments are used. As a vision, it has a remarkable potential of consensus. However, this consensus very often breaks down when it comes to concrete decisions that are affected by ongoing power struggles.

Not all environmental objectives can be realized without conflicts with short-term economic and social interests. The integration of environmental objectives in economically and socially relevant decisions may cause problems for employment at the regional level or for certain social groups. Whether the pursuit of environmental objectives can be sustained during the transition period until the economic and social benefits of environmental policy measures can be reaped depends exclusively upon the emphasis the environmental agenda receives in the political power play.

The German case shows that conflicting interests in society during the bargaining process are not constant. They change over time and depend upon the general economic, financial and social situation in a country, as well as upon political constellations with regard to voter support and the place of environmental issues in the agendas of political parties.

German environmental policy went through good and bad political conjunctures (Müller, 1995, p45), and not all were economically determined. For instance, the decision in the early 1980s to phase out lead in gasoline and to gradually introduce the catalytic converter for passenger cars imposes significant costs on the car industry and, indirectly, on the consumers. Similarly, the adoption of the large combustion plant ordinance in 1983 and the strengthening of the technical guidelines related to air-polluting plants in 1986 (TALuft) imposed on German industry more than 20 billion Deutschmarks (DM) of investment at a time when German industry was beginning to recover from a recession period due to the second oil price crisis (Müller, 1995, p271ff). The reason for the rather weak bargaining power of German industry during that time was the arrival of the Green party on the political arena, which led to a strengthening of the environmental wings within the established party system. In addition, at a time of rising unemployment, investments in the 'improvement' of the environment were perceived as measures to stimulate industrial activities and thus create additional employment.

During the entire period of environmental policy in Germany, environmental policy-makers were fully aware of power politics and the importance of alliance building. During the past 30 years, all ministers responsible for the environment tried – regardless of their party affiliation – to win the support of the general public by stimulating environmental awareness and by strengthening the ecological movement, primarily by funding some of their activities. In 1972, for instance, the Federal Ministry of the Interior paid the travel expenses of the founders of the BBU – the first modern environmental NGO in Germany (Müller, 1995, p88). Part of this strategy to gain public support was also the integration of public participation procedures in environmental legislation. When this legislation was amended again, and public participation reduced under the conservative government, this marked a defeat not only of environmental policy in general, but also of the conservative environment minister in his continuing support-building attempts.

Since the 1990s, environment policy got new allies among business actors representing the 'winner industries' of successful EPI, such as the providers of more energy-efficient technologies. Even though the structural conservatism of the existing industrial lobbying institutions made this attempt rather difficult, the recent creation of special associations of the winner industries, such as the European Business Council on Sustainable Development, may lead to more diversity in voicing economic interests.

The emergence of the Green party in the late 1970s strengthened the position of environmentalists in all traditional and major parties. Ironically enough, this effect became weaker the more successful the Green party became in elections and in assuming government responsibility in several states and now at federal level. At present, party politics has ceased competing for votes on an environmental agenda. The other parties appear to have accepted that there is a rather limited electorate of about 5–8 per cent of the votes that support the Green party; as a result, other parties have stopped competing for this group with a progressive environmental agenda, much to the disadvantage of integrated policy-making.

The fact that Green party participation is not a guarantor for integrated policy-making was evident only recently in the domestic struggles about the already mentioned EU Directive on End-of-Life Vehicles. The fact that the German chancellor intervened in the process and made his environment minister look like a fool is partly explicable by Social Democratic attempts to clip the wings of its small coalition partner. They benefited from the fact that the Green party had just lost some public support by advocating a significant increase in the price of gasoline and by introducing a speed limit on German motorways.

In conclusion, the strategies of environmental policy-makers to enhance their relative power in the game have been fragile. This increases the importance of the right institutional setting for the framework conditions of environmental policy-making.

Institutional Framework

With regard to EPI, the importance of the organizational set-up of environmental competencies within the governmental institutional structure is twofold:

1 It determines the agenda-setting and right of initiative of environmental policy, its competence in defining problems and the need for coordination at the interministerial level.
2 It influences the weight and visibility of environmental policy at the decision level of the cabinet.

In deciding on the institutional setting for environmental policy, the main question was: should environmental competencies be concentrated in one ministry, holding sole responsible for this policy area? Or is it advantageous for integrated policy-making to have sectoral policy ministries deal with the relevant environmental issues (Müller, 1995)? Hidden behind this institutional choice was always an element of symbolic and power politics. Should environmental policy be tackled within an important traditional ministry, or should it be given to a new ministry that must find its place in the unwritten hierarchy and ranking of the ministries?

Turning to the German situation, the institutional framework of German environmental policy was set up in the early 1970s. The jurisdiction for the specialized and technical sectors of environmental policy was given to the Federal Ministry of the Interior. Nature conservation remained within the jurisdiction of the Federal Ministry for Agriculture. The Federal Ministry of the Interior was also given a coordinating role for the overall planning of environmental policy. Environmental policy thus was assigned to a strong ministry under the lead of a minister from the small liberal party in the ruling coalition. Importantly, from the perspective of power politics within the coalition, the liberal party also disposed of the important competency for constitutional law.

This early institutional make-up proved helpful to set up the legal framework for environmental policy-making in the German federal system. During the beginning of the 1970s, changes in the constitution with regard to the repartitioning of legislative competencies between the federal and the state level were approved. For most technical sectors of environment legislation, full competencies were allocated to the federal level; however, with regard to nature conservation and water, the federal state was (and continues to be) restricted to framework legislation. Thus, the Federal Ministry of the Interior received the main legislative tools at hand to develop full legislation for its own environmental responsibilities, whereas the Federal Ministry for Agriculture was restricted to framework legislation with regard to its nature conservation responsibilities.

The fact that the Federal Ministry of the Interior was responsible for the overall planning of environmental policy also helped to develop the instruments for environmental policy – for instance, the drafting of the 1971 environment programme. The Federal Ministry of the Interior has no special clientele interest to defend and could therefore play a more central and independent role in formulating programmes. In addition, this role was welcomed by the minister of the interior, who actively seized the opportunity to provide his liberal party with an innovative future-oriented image (Müller, 1995, p58).

Nevertheless, these rather favourable organizational and political framework conditions did not turn out to be strong enough to successfully integrate environmental policies within the programming and decision-making of sector policies. To resolve this puzzle, we must move up the institutional ladder to the cabinet level. Here, the coordinating role of the Federal Ministry of the Interior was 'complemented' by two institutions that aimed at integrating environmental concerns in the other policy fields: a Committee of the Cabinet and a Permanent

Committee of the Directors-General of different ministries. Under the leadership of the chancellor, the Committee of the Cabinet had the sole task of discussing and agreeing on the guidelines and the scope of environmental policy in relation to concerned sector policies. Its decisions, in turn, were prepared by the Permanent Committee of the Directors-General. Neither institution ever fulfilled its function of integrating environmental concerns within other policies. On the contrary, they practically served as a watchdog, controlling the actions of the Federal Ministry of the Interior and later the Federal Ministry for the Environment, preventing them from intruding into sectoral policies with ambitious environmental measures. Coordination turned out to be a one-way exercise aimed at minimizing environmental 'noise'.

The specific constitutional relationship between the federal and the state level (the German *Länder*) further complicated the task of integrating environmental concerns within other policies. The German federal system is characterized by a mutual dependence in which most federal legislation and actions require the consent of the states and, for their implementation, the cooperation of the state administrations. Therefore, the vertical coordination processes between the federal and the state governments are of major importance. For the coordination of environmental policy, a permanent Conference of the Federal and the State Environment Ministers was established. Similar ministerial conferences exist for other policy areas, such as transport, economic affairs or agriculture. However, there is a significant difference between the decision-making process in these sectoral conferences and the conferences of environment ministers. Before meeting with his or her colleagues from the state ministries, the federal environment minister is obliged to coordinate the conference agenda in the Permanent Committee of the Directors-General of the federal government. Here, every ministry has the chance to object to environmental initiatives. The other federal ministers are not bound by a firm institutionalized procedure. Most of the time, they decide that the environment is not relevant and therefore should not be involved in any coordination attempts. Thus, most sectors are able to build up a vertical alliance at an early stage of policy formulation. Environmental policy actors get involved later in the decision-making process and find it difficult to successfully influence or even stop these pre-negotiated policy decisions, even though they may be harmful to the environment.

The pattern of vertical coalition and alliance building, as opposed to horizontal coordination, is well known in the German political system (Ellwein and Hesse, 1989). The most prominent example is agricultural policy. The green agrarian coalition that crosses party lines and government levels has succeeded, until recently, in protecting its special interests against any attempt of integrating environmental or even financial considerations into agriculture policy. This pattern also continues to play a role in transport policy. The formulation of an integrated transport policy – for instance, with regard to the modal split between road and railway traffic or between individual and public means of transport – was always hampered by the strong vertical alliance of the administration for road construction in the *Länder* and the corresponding units of the Federal Ministry for Transport.

With the growing importance of EU policies and regulations, the phenomenon became even more prevalent due to the sectoral pillar-structure of EU policy-making (cf Armstrong and Bulmer, 1998). Sectoral policy coalitions between national European-specific policies were common, given the organization and mechanisms of the European policy-making process. The specialized Directorates-General (DGs) of the European Commission prepare decisions that are finally, after coordination at the national level, negotiated and adopted by the corresponding Councils of Ministers. EPI suffered particularly from this phenomenon. The initiatives during the early 1990s to deal with EPI in joint councils of the related policies – the joint Council of Environment and Transport Ministers and the joint Council of Environment and Energy Ministers – were therefore very much welcomed. This issue is referred to later in the chapter.

The establishment of the Federal Ministry for the Environment in Germany in 1986, following the Chernobyl catastrophe, was perceived as a major improvement of the institutional framework for environmental policy. For the first time, environmental policy could put the weight of cabinet rank in the interministerial negotiating process. Because of the transfer of the jurisdiction for nature conservation to the Ministry for the Environment, the ministry was also able to formulate comprehensive environmental programmes without prior interministerial coordination.

The concentration of these competencies in a more visible federal environment ministry was expected to mobilize public and political support for environmental policy. Whether the new institutional setting helped environmental policy to better integrate its concerns in other policy sectors is questionable, however. It appears that when environmental policy ranks relatively highly on the political agenda of several political parties, the greater visibility of an environment minister and the exclusive representation of environmental interests in the cabinet are powerful resources that help to initiate cross-cutting programmes, such as the climate protection programme. It also ensures that the same emphasis on environmental policy will take place in the parliament. The structure of the committees in parliament is normally organized in tandem with governmental departments. A non-negligible effect of a special environment committee in parliament is the provision of career opportunities for politicians who can expect that a successful leadership of the environment committee will be a valuable entry ticket for a ministerial or secretary of state position in the government. In less favourable times, such as today, the potential of EPI may even be weakened by the present arrangement. The Ministry for the Environment forms the target for a discontented public and critical NGOs, who hold the environment minister responsible for any sectoral policy that harms the environment, even though his or her influence on other policies may have been negligible. However, a special ministry for the environment is never sufficient to foster environmental integration. To be effective even in difficult political situations, it needs to be equipped with procedural rights. This is where the mechanism of administrative policy preparation is relevant.

Administrative Framework

The importance of the administrative framework is primarily due to specific mechanisms and rules in preparing political decisions, which tend to favour special purpose and departmental policies compared to cross-cutting, intersectoral issues. The German ministerial organizational structure has evolved out of the common continental pattern of five classical ministries of war, foreign affairs, finance, justice and domestic affairs. Other new ministries have mainly been created to serve special purposes or special interests such as economic affairs, transport, labour or agriculture (cf Ellwein und Hesse, 1989). They often have a dominant clientele orientation and define their own role as protectors of these interests. In order to investigate the mechanisms through which ministries pursue their clients' interests, this section analyses the rules and procedures governing the administrative process of preparing political decisions. A number of simple questions will guide this analysis:

• Who has the right to elaborate a proposal and to set it on the interministerial agenda for negotiation and coordination?
• Who is entitled to have control regarding the procedures for coordination, the scope of the negotiation and the timing of the negotiating process?
• At what level is a decision taken to solve controversial issues?

The jurisdiction of a ministry defines precisely the scope of action and the rules for action. Only the competent ministry has the right of agenda-setting in a given area. It shapes the process of problem definition and, on that basis, prepares the first draft of a proposal. The rules for negotiating and coordinating the proposal with other departments that may be affected by it are set up in the *Joint Manual of Procedure of the Government* and the *Joint Manual of Procedure for Interdepartmental Cooperation*. Accordingly, the Ministry for the Environment can only initiate and negotiate under its own leadership those items that are within its jurisdiction. It cannot oblige, for instance, the Ministry for Economics to discuss a draft amendment of the energy act prepared by the environment ministry. The only way to integrate environmental concerns into the programmes and measures of other departments is to wait until the competent ministry has invited the Ministry for the Environment to a ministerial meeting where a policy is negotiated and coordination takes place.

It is obvious that a number of seemingly trivial facts are decisive if the Ministry for the Environment will be able to significantly improve the environmental 'friendliness' of a proposal, most notably the availability of time and human resources to analyse a proposal and to prepare amendments. Time and resources are also major bottlenecks to conducting negotiations in a manner that urges the lead department and other involved departments to seriously consider satisfying responses (cf Müller, 1999). These factors are, unfortunately, not given full attention in the staffing of environment ministry units, although lessons could have been learned from experiences in the Federal Ministry of the Interior during the early 1970s.

To compensate for lack of time and resources, the power and reputation of the Ministry for the Environment is of utmost importance. Negotiations at the working level can easily be stopped and transferred to the next hierarchical level. However, experienced officials will only do this if they are convinced that negotiations will be successful.

This normal process of coordination is well characterized by Scharpf, who introduced the term 'negative coordination' (Scharpf, 1973, p89). Because the other 'non-responsible' departments are involved at a very late stage of policy preparation, alternative problem perceptions and solutions are rarely discussed. Suggestions for amendments that are voiced at this late stage in the game are normally limited to details of the existing draft that directly impinge upon the specific interests of the respective other departments; they do not question the fundamentals of the draft.

To illustrate this process, this section provides a personal anecdote about the coordination of a sub-report of the Federal Ministry for Economic Affairs that was going to be part of the German federal government's CO_2 reduction programme. The draft cabinet decision on the programme had to be prepared by the staff of the Ministry for the Environment and negotiated under the leadership and responsibility of this ministry. According to the rules of procedure, the ministry could not set its draft on the agenda for the final interdepartmental coordination meeting and submit it to the cabinet before the sub-report of the Ministry for Economic Affairs was coordinated and approved by all departments involved. As a result, the Federal Ministry for Economic Affairs invited the other departments to a coordination meeting two weeks before the environment ministry's not yet negotiated comprehensive programme was scheduled on the cabinet agenda. This occurred on a Friday at 2 o'clock in the afternoon.

Against the protest of the representatives of the Federal Ministry for the Environment, who had prepared a long list of objections and amendments, the officials of the Federal Ministry for Economic Affairs made use of their control over the rules of negotiation. They insisted that the draft sub-report should not be negotiated page by page, which would have been the usual procedure, but ministry by ministry according to the official mailing list of the government. Thus, they started with the Ministry of Foreign Affairs, and the Ministry for the Environment was among the last to intervene: due to its late establishment it ranks at the end of this list. In a relatively short time most of the ministerial representatives were satisfied, their minor amendments were accepted by officials of the Ministry for Economic Affairs and they left the meeting to enjoy an early weekend. When the representatives of the Ministry for the Environment had the floor, they were more or less alone with the economic ministry's staff. In this situation they could either insist on properly negotiating their amendments, in which case the representatives of the Ministry for Economic Affairs would have had to convene a new meeting, or accept the dissatisfying draft of the sub-report in order to avoid a postponement of the cabinet decision. They chose the second option and therefore could negotiate the final draft and summary of all sub-reports under their leadership and according to their rules of procedure.

In the end, this strategy proved rather successful since the most counterproductive proposals of the Federal Ministry for Economic Affairs could be deleted in the final draft of the cabinet's decision. Nevertheless, the story shows how the administrative framework structures the power struggles among different ministries and how it does not invite constructive coordination at all.

Improving the Framework Conditions for EPI

If the political principle of environmental integration were given full recognition in all sector policies, the role of a specific ministry responsible for the environment would be obsolete. In the real world of environmental policy, this stage has certainly not yet been reached. A minister for the environment, supported by an effective administration, is therefore still required. A ministry such as this does not only have the role of articulating environmental objectives and interests. It should also strive to integrate environmental objectives at an early stage of policy formulation and to gain the necessary political power at cabinet rank to successfully deal with controversial issues. As seen in the section above, the problem lies in institutional and procedural structures that circumscribe political power and visibility. It is difficult to make use of either if you do not have jurisdiction over problem definition or the right of initiative or control in defining the negotiating rules.

A strategy to improve the successful implementation of EPI should therefore be twofold. It should work towards:

1 changing the institutional setting and the organization of responsibilities within the government; and
2 strengthening the Ministry for the Environment and its administration with regard to procedural rights and rules relevant for the interministerial coordination and problem-solving process.

With regard to improving the repartition of jurisdiction within the German federal government and rearranging its organizational setting, this author suggests that the jurisdiction for nature conservation should be handed to the Ministry for Agriculture. The Ministry for the Environment, in turn, should have responsibility for energy policy. Compared to the 1970s and 1980s, agricultural policy today is in a much more difficult economic and financial situation. Due to the General Agreement on Tariffs and Trade (GATT) and World Trade Organization (WTO) pressure, as well as the financial constraints of the European Common Agricultural Policy (CAP), the traditional subsidizing of environment-unfriendly agricultural activities is challenged. However, actual reform may depend upon the construction of win–win scenarios. The reorganization of competencies may provide for such solutions because agricultural policy may move towards a more favourable attitude to nature conservation if the financial transfers benefit farmers who are hurt by subsidy cuts elsewhere. As described above, the risk of 'negative coordination' increases when programmes have to be coordinated and negotiated across departmental borders. Conversely, the chance of 'positive coordination' will be facilitated if comprehensive programmes can be developed in the internal ministerial process.

The allocation of responsibilities for energy policy to the Federal Ministry for the Environment, on the other hand, would significantly increase the weight and influence of the environment ministry in the interministerial context. Such weight seems a necessary precondition for putting economic and environmental concerns on equal footing and, in due course, for advancing innovative thinking on mutually profitable solutions. Energy policy in itself is a cross-cutting issue. Energy fuels the entire economy. It influences production processes and product design, it structures settlements and the related need of mobility, and it has an impact on the quality of buildings and on agricultural methods and marketing strategies. Unsustainable patterns of energy supply and demand in the past have been the source of most air pollutants, as well as negatively effected land use and the sprawl of cities. With jurisdiction for energy policy, the environment ministry would have the right of initiative and the lead function to develop and negotiate innovations where both economy and environment would profit. In particular, it would be in a better position to implement the climate change targets that primarily demand measures related to an efficient use of energy resources and the transition from the dominant use of fossil fuels to a broader use of renewable energies.

Finally, the concept of EPI will only have a chance to demonstrate progress when the environment ministry and its administration dispose of the tools and procedural rights that are similar to those used by traditional ministries. Two procedural instruments are important in this author's opinion: the agenda-setting right and the veto position in the cabinet. Both instruments are not new and do not call for a revolutionary change of the *Joint Manuals of Procedure of the Government* and for interdepartmental cooperation; they can be adopted by a simple government decision. The right of initiative and agenda-setting by a ministry other than the one formally considered competent has already been introduced for problems with a gender dimension. In the environmental field, the right of agenda-setting would hinder sector policy departments in blocking the implementation of politically agreed programmes, such as the climate change programme. These departments could no longer rely on a 'wait and see' strategy when responsible for developing operational solutions to implementing environmental targets. This is because the environmental ministry may push the agenda from the outside. Whether the result would be positive for the environment will depend upon the support of environmental objectives in the political power play, the general public and the weight both will give to conflicting economic and social interests.

The veto right already exists for the finance department with respect to measures with a financial impact and for the Ministry of the Interior for matters related to constitutional law. Practice shows that the veto right is rarely used in the interministerial process. However, it produces an anticipatory effect and the same is expected in the case of environmental policy. Nevertheless, compared to the agenda-setting right, the veto right seems of lesser importance. Veto rights in the cabinet normally only have the ability to suspend measures unless external veto actors play a role (for example, the German Supreme Court for decisions related to constitutional matters). A veto right would, however, strengthen the role of the environment ministry in the interministerial coordination process. Sector policy departments would no longer wait to involve the environment ministry until the latest stage of policy formulation and would be more careful when coordinating their proposals with the ministry. The objectives of the representatives of the environment department would be taken more seriously and have a greater impact, in order to avoid a later veto. Ideally, the veto right should be linked to the legally required environmental impact assessment of public programmes already foreseen in the environmental programme of 1971. Perhaps European environmental policy would help to make this possible.

IMPLICATIONS OF EUROPEAN ENVIRONMENT POLICY

The history of German environmental policy, particularly its struggles with the EPI principle, has provided some evidence that the EU level has served on several occasions to break domestic political bottlenecks. EU legislation – once agreed upon – may impose rules that could never be adopted in the Member State due to strong opposition from industry, bureaucracy or important (from the perspective of vote-seeking parties) societal actors. In the context of the EU, governments may be able to shift the blame for unpopular measures (see, for example, Smith, 1997). The Eco-Audit Directive and the Directive on Public Access to Environmental Information, both aiming at raising awareness of the environmental impacts of seemingly non-environmental activities, are measures that were adopted against strong opposition in Germany and would not have passed the German policy-making process.

But Germany also influenced European environmental policy and attempts to develop tools for policy integration. The concept of best available technology (BAT) as applied in the Directive of Integrated Pollution and Prevention Control deserves special mention. This concept is the most misunderstood and misinterpreted achievement of German environmental policy. It was opposed by proponents of the critical load concept – primarily in the northern part of Europe – which theoretically addresses directly the level of protection needed to save vulnerable ecosystems. In practice, however, this concept is weak because it requires a scientific consensus on the carrying capacities of ecosystems, human health and other endangered goods such as materials (for example, damage caused by acidification or salinization due to the corrosion of bridges, roads or buildings). The BAT concept, by contrast, supports the precautionary principle. BAT must even be used if the state of the environment is not endangered. Furthermore, it must, by definition, be both economically and ecologically practicable.

This section now addresses the question of how the recent initiatives of European policy with regard to EPI may affect German environmental policy in the future. In brief, the recent attempts and initiatives of the EU Commission and several councils to highlight the need of EPI may support national environmental policy-makers in their attempt to improve the environmental quality of sector policies.

From a political point of view, the initiatives at the level of European councils, such as the Cardiff, Cologne and Helsinki councils, to publicly commit to European policy in order to integrate environmental concerns in sector policies such as energy, transport, industry, internal market and tourism are helpful. Monitoring progress towards such integration will be important, and criteria for this developed by the European Environment Agency (EEA) cover institutional, market and managerial tools needed for successful integration (EEA, 1999a).

Supported by these initiatives, but also from an institutional point of view, the convening of joint councils (for example, for transport–environment and energy–environment issues) may be equally helpful because these councils ensure that sectoral programmes are coordinated with the actors responsible for environment policy and also make the results visible to the general public. Today, the occurrence of sectoral policy-making processes at the German (and Member State, in general) and European level favours the building-up of vertical sectoral alliances in the same way as described in this chapter for decision-making in the German federal system. Until now, these structures helped to protect sectoral policies against environmental interference. Whether the political publicity of joint councils may help to avoid the 'building up' of these vertical and sectoral alliances at an early stage, and whether the need to coordinate will be acknowledged by the entire European and national administrative system, will certainly depend upon radical change in the institutional and procedural structures of the European process.

Interestingly, the Prodi Commission has decided to make use of institutions that German environmental policy employed in the early 1970s. A number of Commission working groups (Commissioners' Group) have been installed, among others a Commissioners' Group on growth, competitiveness, employment and sustainable development (CECb, 1999). Thus, the Commissioners' Group for the Environment is given the chance to promote environmental objectives and to address conflicts at a high level. It will be interesting to see if this opportunity is more successful than in the similar German situation.

Past experiences in approaching the issue from the 'bottom up' have not always been successful, however. The EEA, for instance, was established to provide relevant information to European environmental policy-making and, in particular, to support environmental integration. Its budget is negotiated as part of the environment budget of the Environment DG and has proven insufficient in dealing with EPI matters. To be able to work on issues such as indicators for the impact of transport on the environment, the agency needs to address the Energy and Transport DG for additional funding. It is questionable that this sector policy department is willing to sufficiently sponsor activities that may oblige it later to reconsider its policy.

For the execution of these initiatives and efforts, the development of indicators and target setting plays an important role. Until now, concrete results are difficult to detect (cf EEA, 1999b). Interestingly, the most advanced of the new sector reporting mechanisms for transport (TERM) was the initiative of the EEA and the UK presidency. In April 1998, the Joint Environment and

Transport Council overcame the normal vertical resistance of the transport sector to promote, from the top down, the need for new indicators that cover the driving forces of planning and prices, as well as technical issues such as fuel efficiency and vehicle use (see EEA, 1999b). Progress with new sectoral environment-monitoring mechanisms on energy and agriculture is not as well developed, but the development by the EEA of a generic framework for monitoring could help (EEA, 2000).

The proof of progress in environmental integration will depend largely upon the results of some cross-cutting environmental programmes that have the potential to direct economic activities in a more sustainable direction. The following four programmes are relevant in this respect:

1   The Climate Change Programme.
2   EU waste policy.
3   The Directive on Integrated Pollution and Prevention Control.
4   The programme related to chemical substances.

In all four programmes, technological innovation plays a major role. The ambitious European Climate Change Programme and the capability of the EU to comply with the obligations of the Kyoto Protocol target will, to a large extent, depend upon policies and measures aimed at successfully implementing energy efficiency and renewable energy technologies in all EU Member States. These measures have the potential to provide win–win solutions for the protection of the environment and for the sake of economic development and employment in the Member States.

Waste policy is another interesting field in terms of implementing the goals of sustainable development. Numerous examples show that recycling strategies and strategies to minimize the need for resources and the diversity of materials used in the production, design and packaging processes do not only have a positive effect on the environment but are also beneficial in micro-economic terms.

A cornerstone for successful EPI will be the implementation of the Directive on Integrated Pollution and Prevention Control. The directive introduces the concept of BAT. It is here that technological innovation plays a major role. But the dissemination of information on best practices and bench-marking will also be important in order to make best use of the directive.

Finally, the policy on chemicals will be important to assess progress in EPI in major industrial sectors, and with regard to the marketing of products. In this context, European policy on environmental liability would be most relevant. Initiatives are under way to not only improve liability of economic actors for environmental damages (CEC 2000), but also to examine a substantial revision of the product liability directive (CEC 1999a), which does not yet cover environmental damage. These initiatives are very interesting for the integration of environmental objectives in product design and the use of hazardous substances. Environmental policy will be unable to, and should not aim to, control in detail the development and the use of chemical substances. But it has the obligation to introduce instruments which will oblige economic actors to seriously consider the possible effects and impacts that the production of potentially harmful chemical substances has on the environment, before they decide on investing in new production and product lines.

The scope and impact of these measures remains uncertain and also depends upon the jurisdiction of the European Court of Justice and the support of the EU Parliament for EPI. However, speculation regarding this issue clearly exceeds the scope of this chapter.

In conclusion, European policy with regard to EPI is most relevant in terms of its agenda-setting function and role of initiating public debate. The EU has proven in the past that it is successful in promoting paradigms and ideas (Wallace, 1996, p150). Institutional arrangements, concrete programmes and measures may follow as a consequence of a dynamic, which is driven by ideas. The Commission – as the main promoter of new ideas and expert knowledge (cf Héritier, 1993) – should not be underestimated.

Together with the political dynamic of European policy, the agenda-setting functions of the European debate on the need for EPI may be helpful if German environmental policy is to achieve EPI in domestic sector policies. Until now, Germany's objectives and initiatives remained mainly conceptual. However, the economic rationale pushing for economic growth, trade and transport may be stronger and faster than the successes of EPI on the EU level and in the Member States (EEA, 1999c). At present, it is questionable whether the European environmental policy-making process will be able to successfully implement and make use of the support provided by general programmes and politically agreed objectives – not least because European environment policy faces a challenge similar to national environment policy. This challenge is that it depends upon changes in the institutional and procedural framework of decision-making in order to move on an equal playing field with the partners representing economic and social interests and policies.

REFERENCES

Armstrong, K and Bulmer, S (1998) *The Governance of the Single European Market,* St Martin's Press, New York

Commission of the European Communities (CEC) (1999a) *Green Paper on liability for defective products,* COM, 28 July 1999, 396 final, Brussels

CEC (1999b) *Groups of Members of the Commission,* SEC, 16 September 1999, 1483, Brussels

CEC (2000) *White Paper on Environmental Liability,* COM, 9 February 2000, 66 final, Brussels

Ellwein, T and Hesse, J J (1989) *Das Regierungssystem der Bundesrepublik Deutschland,* Westdeutscher Verlag, Opladen

European Environment Agency (EEA) (1999a) *Monitoring Progress Towards Integration: A Contribution to the 'Global Assessment' of the Fifth Environmental Action Programme of the EU,* 1992–1999, near-final draft, Copenhagen

EEA (1999b) *Are We Moving in the Right Direction? Indicators on Transport and Environment Integration in the EU,* final draft, 1 December 1999, Copenhagen

EEA (1999c) *Environment in the European Union at the Turn of the Century*, Environmental Assessment Report No 2, Copenhagen

EEA (2000) *Environmental Signals 2000*, European Environment Agency Regular Indicator Report, Environmental Assessment Report No 6, Copenhagen

Environmental Programme of the Federal Government, 1971 (1972) *Umweltschutz: Das Umweltprogramm der Bundesregierung*, Mit einer Einführung von Hans-Dietrich Genscher, Stuttgart, Berlin, Köln, Mainz

Héritier, A (1993) 'Policy-Netzwerkanalyse als Untersuchungsinstrument im Europäischen Kontext: Folgerungen aus einer empirischen Studie regulativer Politik', in A Héritier (ed) 'Policy-Analyse: Kritik und Neuorientierung', *Politische Vierteljahresschrift Sonderheft 24*, Westdeutscher Verlag, Opladen, pp432–447

Héritier, A, Knill, C, Mingers, S (1996) *Ringing the Changes in Europe*, Walter de Gruyter, Berlin

Knill, C, Lenschow, A (1998) 'Coping with Europe: the impact of British and German administrations on the implementation of EU environmental policy', *Journal of European Public Policy*, vol 5, pp595–614

Lenschow, A (1997) 'The Implementation of EU Environmental Policy in Germany', in C Knill (ed) *The Impact of National Administrative Traditions on the Implementation of EU Environmental Policy*, Interim Research Report, European University Institute, Florence

Müller, E (1995) *Innenwelt der Umweltpolitik*, second edition, Westdeutscher Verlag, Opladen

Müller, E (1999) 'Impressionen zum Thema Zeit in der Umweltpolitik', in W Jann, K König, C Landfried and P Wordelmann (eds) *Politik und Verwaltung auf dem Weg in die Transindustrielle Gesellschaft*, Nomos, Baden-Baden, pp297–308

Scharpf, F W (1973) 'Komplexität als Schranke der politischen Planung', in F W Scharpf, *Planung als politischer Prozess. Aufsätze zur Theorie der planenden Demokratie*, Campus, Frankfurt/Main, pp73–113

Skou Andersen, M and Liefferink, D (1997) *European Environmental Policy: The Pioneers*, Manchester University Press, Manchester and New York

Smith, M (1997) 'The Commission Made Me Do It: The European Commission as a Strategic Asset in Domestic Politics', in N Nugent (ed) *At the Heart of the Union: Studies of the European Commission*, Macmillan, London, pp167–186

Wallace, H (1996) 'Die Dynamik des EU-Institutionengefüges', in M Jachtenfuchs and B Kohler-Koch (eds) *Europäische Integration*, Westdeutscher Verlag, Opladen, pp141–163

5

Environmental Integration: Is a Green Government Enough? Some Evidence from the Italian Case

Rodolfo Lewanski

INTRODUCTION

Environmental policy in Italy developed with considerable delay when compared to other industrialized countries. A simple analysis of the dates in which ad hoc institutions were set up and principal legislation was passed evidences that, all in all, such delay amounts to some 10 to 15 years until the end of the 1980s (Lewanski, 1997). Over the last decade or so, however, environmental policy has gathered momentum, allowing Italy to 'catch up' with most advanced countries in terms of its legislative and institutional toolbox. Being a latecomer need not be a negative fact per se; actually, it could represent an effective strategy to avoid mistakes and take short cuts. However, looking at the Italian situation up to the mid 1990s, policy actors appeared to be hardly affected by the examples set by more advanced countries in adopting innovative targets, approaches and instruments in order to increase policy effectiveness. The policy institutionalization process in that period remained 'shallow' (Jänicke, 1991, p12) and some of the elements of the ecological modernization paradigm, of which integration represents an important element (Hajer, 1995, p26), had not yet permeated the political–administrative culture.

Such delay is especially evident in the aspect under consideration in this chapter. In 1994, the Organisation for Economic Co-operation and Development (OECD) reported that although in Italy 'serious efforts are being made to better co-ordinate policies and production and consumption patters in the various sectors of the economy in order to avoid damaging the environment … the Ministry of the Environment still has a long way to go to integrate its action with that of the other ministries and insert the environmental dimension in their projects' (OECD, 1994, pp91, 114).

Shortly after this critical assessment, a major change occurred. In May 1996, a centre-left government, also including a relevant 'green' component, was formed for the first time in Italy. Significantly, the latter was represented not only by the presence of the Green party in the new government but also to a 'greened' agenda of some of the other coalition parties – especially the leftist ones. Thus, the analysis of the Italian case offers an interesting opportunity to test to what extent environmental policy integration can be fostered by the government's political orientation. More specifically, two factors might play favourably in the direction of environmental policy integration (EPI) within a coalition government. Firstly, the 'green' components of the coalition may foster integration to enhance environmental protection objectives more effectively. Furthermore, EPI may result from a dynamic within the coalition. The consensus-seeking process among the different constituencies may present a way to reconcile economic growth targets – a necessary source of legitimacy for any government – with the environmental protection goals advocated by the coalition's 'green' constituency.

In order to empirically verify the extent to which EPI has become relevant in governmental policies, the analysis focuses on the legislative provisions (such as laws and decrees) produced by parliament and governments over a four-year period, from May 1996 (when the centre-left coalition won the general elections and Romano Prodi became prime minister) until April 2000 (when his successor Massimo D'Alema resigned following the poor results his coalition obtained at the regional elections).[1]

This chapter first offers an overview of the development of environmental policy in order to give the reader an appreciation of the specific features of the Italian case during the 30-year period that spans its inception to 1996. It then analyses the elements of integration that are found in national legislation passed by the Prodi and D'Alema governments in the four-year period of 1996–2000. Finally, the chapter attempts to offer an evaluation of policy integration accomplished by the centre-left government, as well as an analysis of the factors that have hindered or enhanced EPI.

THE DEVELOPMENT OF ENVIRONMENTAL POLICY IN ITALY UNTIL 1996

The beginning of environmental policy in Italy dates back to the mid 1960s. The first explicit piece of legislation attempting to tackle a problem, namely air pollution, specifically in *environmental* terms (rather than for its health consequences or for its spillover on particular economic activities such as fishing and navigation) is Act 615, passed in 1966. The aim of this and other similar laws of the same period was to clean up geographically limited problem areas. The actual implementation and enforcement of air-pollution control policies, however, began only in the early 1970s and was limited to a few areas of northern Italy. In the mid 1970s, policy addressed water pollution; solid waste became the main issue of the early 1980s. Other legislative efforts that dealt with issues ranging from sea protection to the biodegradability of detergents, drinking water, parks, air quality standards, landscape protection, prevention of accidents by hazardous industrial plants, impact assessment, noise pollution, and soil protection against hydraulic risks were added to the policy toolbox during the 1980s, largely under the influence of EU directives and the example of other more advanced countries.

The institutional capacity in the environmental field grew slowly until the 1990s. Regions, just created in the early 1970s, were given considerable powers by environmental legislation that started to develop during the same period. Important institutional actors were also created at the sub-national level in the early 1980s, such as the local health units (*unità sanitarie locali*). The establishment of the Ministry of the Environment in 1986 formally marked the upgrading of the status of environmental policy vis-à-vis other sectoral policies.

Environmental issues initially suffered from low visibility until the Seveso accident of July 1976 caught the attention of the media. Environmental emergencies and disasters occurring throughout the world and in Italy were widely reported by the media, and the emergence of the nuclear issue further contributed to growing public awareness and stimulated public demand for environmental quality. While the environmental movement was initially quite weak, by the end of 1995 associations active in this field had a total membership of more than 900,000 (Ministero dell'Ambiente, 1997, p349) and their capability to influence policy-making gradually increased during this period.

Nevertheless, the political system was slow in giving attention to an issue that was of little or no relevance for inter- and intra-party power relations; notwithstanding the growing awareness of the public, environmental issues were perceived by most politicians as offering very little payoff in electoral terms. Only the relatively good results obtained by the Greens in local and national (2 to 3 per cent) elections induced other parties gradually to acknowledge the existence of the issue and to incorporate some of the themes of the environmental movement, although such reorientation sometimes clashed with traditional 'productivist' cultures, as in the case of the Communist party (now Democratici di Sinistra – Democratic Left).

Financial resources allocated to deal with environmental problems were insufficient until the end of the 1980s, when total expenditures concerning environmental issues by central, regional and local authorities finally reached 1 per cent of gross national product (GNP) (Ministero dell' Ambiente, 1992, pp332–337), a level considered by international experts to be the minimum for a developed nation, but still lower than the EU average of 1.2 per cent (OECD, 1994, p94). Furthermore, a high ratio of the allocated resources was regularly used to cope with environmental disasters (such as floods and landslides) that were often caused by environmentally unsound policies (for example, unauthorized building and the construction of disrupting projects) or due to delays in cleaning up heavily polluted areas. As a result, the Italian environmental budget did not target the systematic *prevention* of further pollution.

Until 1992, the development of environmental policy took place in a relatively stable political context in which governments were typically formed by a coalition including the Catholic and Socialist parties jointly, with varying other smaller moderate political partners. With the disclosure of extended corruption within the governing parties and the administration (*Tangentopoli*), the Italian 'First Republic', born after World War II, came to an end. The two main parties disappeared from the political scene, whereas new parties (such as Forza Italia) emerged and other parties, to the right and to the left (such as Alleanza Nazionale and the Democratici di Sinistra), that had previously been kept out of the governing coalitions started to play an important role in the political game. The crisis opened a period of great uncertainty from which a new political order has yet to emerge.

Under such circumstances, environmental issues were hardly a priority. During the Berlusconi government (1994–1995), the Ministry of the Environment was headed by a representative of the extreme right who showed no interest in environmental protection and openly claimed to be in favour of nuclear energy, highways and hunting in national parks. In the following 'technical' Dini government (1995–1996), environmental issues received greater attention, although the fact that the minister of public works headed the Ministry of the Environment met heavy criticism from the environmental movement.

First attempts in this period to encourage integrated policy-making remained half-hearted. The attempt to coordinate the activities in the environmental field in the context of three-year environmental management programmes, which define expenditure priorities (Ministero dell'Ambiente, 1992, p416), was targeted only at the coordination of fragmented fund allocation rather than at intersectoral policy integration. These programmes were recently abolished[2] after it was recognized that fund allocation followed criteria such as regional surface rather than strategic choices of the administration or actual environmental needs (and indicators). Furthermore, the programmes did not accelerate the expenditure process (on the contrary, some authorities delayed the entire process), they did not mobilize additional local resources (Malaman, 1994) and they did not improve spending capacity (in 1993 less than one third of the funds allocated in the Triennial Programme of 1988–1991 were spent; Cesaretti, 1995, p43).

As far as the choice of policy instruments is concerned, there was some evolution in Italian environmental policy-making. The field was, for a long period, dominated by a regulatory 'command-and-control' approach – featuring an exasperated formalism and uniform standards covering the entire national territory[3] – based on emission, process (for example, combustion) and product standards (for example, detergents and fuels) and, somewhat later, on ambient quality standards. Since the end of the 1980s, the Ministry of the Environment has also resorted to less traditional regulatory approaches, such as the creation of compulsory consortia set up to promote the recycling of selected materials (such as glass, plastic, wood, paper, aluminium, steel, mineral oil and car batteries) (Malaman and Ranci, 1991; Ministero dell'Ambiente, 1998, p27) and voluntary agreements (Amadei et al, 1998). Although proposals to introduce eco-taxes initially met opposition from environmentalists, business and most ministries, in defence of their respective constituencies (Gerelli, 1990, p197), a number of such taxes have been introduced in Italy. These taxes cover discharges into water, urban waste, plastic bags (subsequently changed into a tax on polyethylene plastic film), plastic and glass liquid containers, unleaded gasoline, aircraft noise, used car batteries and motor oil. It must be noted, however, that the taxes did not gain acceptance because of their environmental objectives but, primarily, because of the need to cut the high levels of debt within the public sector. In all, environmental taxes in 1994 generated an income of 6840 billion lire (Ministero dell'Ambiente, 1997, p341). If one considers all environmental taxes in a wider sense (including taxes on energy and vehicles), however, the total revenue amounted to 51,700 billion lire in 1995, equivalent to 11.4 per cent of total tax revenues (3 per cent of GNP) (Legambiente, 2000, p282).

In conclusion, it can be said that by the mid 1990s Italy, which had been a latecomer in the environmental policy field compared to other industrialized countries, had essentially caught up as far as legislation, institutional capacity and resource allocation were concerned. Nevertheless, poor implementation by the administrative system impinged on policy effectiveness. Apparently strong and stringent regulation was typically not enforced, prompting commentators to characterize the Italian case as 'regulation without rules' (Giuliani, 1992, p89).

Another feature to be noted is that Italian policy appears to be highly 'reactive' in the sense that, to a large extent, policy measures in this field have been directly triggered by two types of stimuli: firstly, by environmental emergencies and disasters and, secondly, by inputs exogenous to the domestic polity – namely, international environmental obligations and, especially, policy measures taken at the EU level. There is little doubt that much national environmental legislation would not have come into existence without the pressure of having to comply with EU directives.

As far as integration is concerned, only traces can be found in policies enacted during this period. The case of water management provides a good example. Recurring landslides, soil erosion and floods are due to a high level of geological instability, but are also a result of sectoral policies that do not take environmental aspects into consideration, often resulting in heavy damage and loss of lives (Legambiente, 1997, p187).[4] This is evidenced in the extensive construction of buildings and roads, excessive excavations, the exploitation of mountainous landscapes and inadequate maintenance of water drainage systems. The flooding of Florence in the 1960s, imperilling unique art treasures, made the world aware of the problem, but in Italy itself hardly any policy measures ensued. However, a committee (called De Marchi after the name of its chairman) was set up, and on the basis of its proposals, Act 183 was passed in 1989.

The law represents a first attempt to introduce an integrated management approach involving the entire water cycle, based on the hydrographic basins, and with the aim of protecting land from water. The hydrographic plan drafted by the water authorities represents the main policy tool that all other sectoral (agriculture, forestry) and land-use plans, as well as administrative activities, are supposed to respect. Ten years later, however, a number of such authorities have yet to be created.[5] The subsequent Act 36 of 1994 aimed at integrating the stages of water provision from supply to depuration within territorial areas to be defined. The objective was to optimize the quality of service and to reduce costs. It also aimed at reducing consumption and at promoting the reuse of the resource. Although it is too early to evaluate its performance, there are already obvious delays in implementing the provision, especially in terms of singling out optimal areas and unifying the agencies that manage water services.

Thus, the weakness of integration in Italian environmental policy, at least until the mid 1990s, can be explained by a number of factors: the low internal demand for environmental quality; the lack of interest in the political system; the late development of environmental policy in general; its reactive character; and the generally poor performance of the administrative system. These are all factors that could hardly encourage innovative approaches, such as EPI.

1996–2000: THE FIRST TIME FOR ENVIRONMENTALISTS

The national elections held in April 1996 were won by the 'Olive' (centre-left) coalition, headed by Romano Prodi. Somewhat paradoxically, the Greens, while obtaining one of their worst results yet (2.5 per cent – 937,000 votes), were rewarded with the largest number of representatives in the lower governmental chamber ever obtained (from 18 to 28 seats) thanks to the pre-electoral agreements stipulated among the parties of the coalition. The environmental movement was also assigned a number of relevant posts. The Green party obtained the post of the minister of the environment (Edo Ronchi) and that of under-secretary within the Ministry of Public Works. Several members of environmental associations were assigned to important positions within public agencies such as the National Electricity Board (ENEL) and the state-owned railway company (FS). Furthermore, the environment represents an important concern on the agenda of the major party of the coalition: the Democratici di Sinistra. In October 1998, a reshuffling of the government took place as the coalition's centre of gravity shifted rightwards and Massimo D'Alema replaced Prodi as prime minister. Nevertheless, the new government showed strong traits of continuity compared to the previous one. The coalition supporting it remained, by and large, the same (though the extreme left exited the coalition, and its place was taken up by a small centre party) and many ministers kept their posts, including Minister of the Environment Edo Ronchi.

The D'Alema government ended on 19 April 2000 after poor results in the election of the new regional councils and presidents. A new cabinet, headed by Giuliano Amato (previous member of the Socialist party) was formed with the votes of the same coalition as the former government.[6]

Notwithstanding this very new political situation represented by the first Italian government to include a relevant 'green' component, environmental issues initially were hardly among the government's priorities. Economic (inflation, employment, public debt and especially entering the European monetary union) and institutional (federalism, electoral rules) issues were at the forefront of the government's concerns. In order to boost employment and the economy, and to gain consensus, the government was often tempted to bring back in traditional 'recipes', such as public works policies (especially new roads and highways, with the argument that poor transportation negatively affects Italian competitiveness on international markets). Environmental issues, however were soon recalled, especially after the disaster that occurred in the Campania region in May 1998 when a huge landslide of some 3 million tonnes of mud overran several small towns in the provinces of Salerno, Avellino and Caserta, killing some 250 people and severely damaging houses, farms and industries. In the context of this disaster, environmental policy acquired legitimacy in policy terms and a considerable public profile.

Increasingly, references to environmental aspects and to the necessity of integrating environmental goals within sectoral policies are found in legislation and policy documents issued during this period. For example, the National Health Plan for the period of 1998–2000 states among its main targets the improvement of the quality of the environment as a means to enhance the health of the population and points out a number of areas in which measures are to be taken in order to reduce pollution (such as urban traffic). Thus, the plan appears to call for very broad cross-sectoral policy integration in order to reach the targets it sets out. Explicit references to the environment have also appeared in provisions defining the powers of specific ministries, as in the case of the ministries of treasury, foreign affairs, defence and foreign commerce, signalling a stronger consideration of environmental aspects within their respective policy areas. Also, recent legislation[7] enacting EU Directives 91/271 – concerning treatment of wastewater – and 91/676 – concerning protection of water from pollution caused by nitrates of agricultural origin – follow a new integrative direction.

In the context of institutional reform, however, the political struggle that is implied in EPI becomes quickly apparent. The organization of land and soil management may serve as an illustration. As mentioned above, the Dini cabinet had entrusted the two ministries of environment and public works to the same person. Prodi subsequently decided to keep the two ministries separate and hence acted against the Greens' proposal to join functions concerning land use, public works and pollution control in a unified Ministry of the Environment and Territory.[8] His decision was led by political, not environmental, considerations because he hoped to widen the support for the government (the post was initially assigned to Antonio Di Pietro, the popular *Tangentopoli* judge). The disaster in the Campania region renewed the debate, and the Green party proposed to transfer the powers concerning land management and protection to the Ministry of the Environment. During this round, the political context changed due to the wider process of 'federalization' of the Italian institutional system (on the basis of the 1997 Act 59). As a result, the Ministry of Public Works lost an estimated 70 per cent of its powers to the regions, thus providing the opportunity for reorganizing central ministries. In 1999, the number of ministries was cut from 18 to 12 and the decision was taken to transfer powers in the field of land management and planning to the Ministry of the Environment.[9] However, the provision will apply only to the next government and not to the present one; thus, an evaluation of the actual impact of the reorganization will depend from the policies adopted by the new centre-right government elected in May 2001.[10] This story indicates that progress towards EPI remains highly coincidental.

Nevertheless, substantive policy does indicate change. The following analysis focuses on three policy areas of major relevance: transportation, energy and production and economic policies. These cases present clear evidence of a 'greening' process.

Transportation

Mobility in Italy is largely based on road transportation; this is true to an even greater extent than in other European countries. There are more private vehicles in relation to the population than in any other EU country, with the only exception of Luxembourg (Legambiente, 1996, p104). The share of road transport is at present one of the highest in OECD countries. This situation, caused by the lack of adequate policies favouring other modes of transportation during the past decades, gives way to especially dramatic consequences in two areas: freight transportation and urban mobility.

While total freight traffic has grown by 150 per cent, the share of freight transportation by road has risen even faster (from 65 per cent of total traffic in 1980 to 72 per cent in 1993), whereas transport via rail and water has constantly lost ground (ISTAT, 1996, p248). Thus, recent policy in this area has aimed at balancing various modes of transportation and, more specifically, at promoting combined intermodal forms of freight transportation (rail, sea and internal waterways, with only the initial or final part of the journey carried out by lorry).[11] The National Transportation Conference held in 1999 and the General Transportation Plan, both jointly promoted by the ministries of transportation, public works and environment, have recognized the need to implement a strategy capable of reducing the negative externalities caused by mobility (Legambiente, 2000, pp74–75). Considerable funds have been allocated for modernizing ports, in order to promote the transfer of freight transportation from lorries to seaways (Minella, 1999),[12] and to allow navigation along waterways of the Po Valley.[13]

As far as urban mobility is concerned, along with congestion, pollution has emerged as a major problem in urban areas since the early 1990s, and has become even more critical in connection with the obligation to respect air quality levels established by the EU. In this area, a variety of measures have been initiated, including: air quality monitoring and smog alarms; improvement of fuel quality;[14] the use of electronic devices for controlling access to parts of inner cities; modification of gasoline pumps in order to avoid dispersion of vapours;[15] measures to reduce the use of private vehicles in commuting to and from work;[16] changes in opening and working hours of both public and private activities;[17] and consideration of pollution and traffic implications by local authorities within policies concerning commercial activities.

Two policy measures are of special interest for the purposes of this discussion. Firstly, substantial financial resources (some 2200 billion lire[18]) have been allocated to the construction of mass transportation systems in larger cities (at present there are only 122 kilometres of underground, mainly concentrated in Rome, Milan, Naples and Genoa, one of the lowest figure in Europe) with the explicit intent of reducing air and noise pollution (also with specific reference to the greenhouse effect), as well as traffic accidents and to save energy.[19] Secondly, since 1996 the diffusion of less polluting vehicles (catalysed vehicles still comprised only 0.1 per cent in 1991) has been fostered by incentives for turning in old motorcycles[20] and automobiles.[21] The system finished in 1998 for cars and by the end of 2000 for motorcycles.[22] A further incentive to rejuvenate the existing fleet, and to periodically control emission levels, is likely to emerge from enacting EU Directive 94/23 that compels vehicle owners to undergo a check-up after four years (for new vehicles) and then every two years.[23] Furthermore, a governmental decree issued in 1998 compels public administrations to buy low-emission (such as methane, electric and hybrid) automobiles as a means to create a market for such vehicles (5 per cent of new vehicles in 1998; 50 per cent by 2003). Further funds (40 billion lire) for buying low environmental impact vehicles have recently been made available by the central government,[24] which also decided to promote the collective use or forms of shared property of low-emission vehicles. The government also allocated sums in favour of local transportation authorities to buy new means of public transportation with low environmental impacts.[25]

Energy

Notwithstanding Italy's high dependency on imported energy sources, energy-saving policies were extremely weak until the early 1990s.[26] Sales of insulation materials, for example, are among the lowest in Europe (5 million metric tonnes per year, which is 50 per cent lower than in Spain). Italy produces less energy from wind (28 megawatts – MW – in 1995) than many other European countries, including Greece and Spain. Its record is somewhat better as far as photovoltaic energy is concerned (Legambiente, 1997, pp98–99). Between 1990 and 1997, energy produced from renewable sources (excluding hydroelectric) has increased only by 20 per cent (Legambiente, 2000, p5). Legislation during the 1990s was directed at rectifying this picture. It included such measures as the introduction of energy managers in large firms (consuming more than 1000 petroleum equivalent tonnes per year), compulsory energy certification for all new buildings, the adoption of a local energy plan by all municipalities with more than 50,000 inhabitants, information campaigns, incentives for energy saving, and energy labelling for equipment. Actual funding of this legislation, however, turned out to be insufficient and even spending available resources has been difficult.

The obligations derived from the Kyoto Protocol agreement (the reduction of CO_2 emissions by 6.5 per cent by 2008–2012, compared to 1990 levels[27]) represent a new incentive to promote energy-saving measures and energy sources that do not emit greenhouse gases. The *National White Book on Renewable Sources* adopted by the government in 1999 indicates the target of 7600 MW to be generated from such sources by the year 2010 (Legambiente, 2000, p95). However, the present privatization process of the Italian electricity market due to EU policies in this field poses some difficulty in further supporting such measures. A governmental decision in 1992 (called CIP 6), which forced the monopolist ENEL to buy excess electricity generated by private producers at a high price, had promoted renewable energy sources or alternative sources.

However, privatization of the energy sector brought such a device to a halt (Legambiente, 1997, p99). As an alternative, beginning in 2001 all electricity companies producing more than 100 gigawatt hours (gigawatts/hour) are required to produce a portion of their electricity from renewable sources (initially established in 2 per cent of the production exceeding 100 GWh).[28] Taxes levied on renewable sources have been reduced[29] and a CO_2 tax introduced in 1999[30] has increased the cost of electricity produced by means of fossil fuels.

Energy efficiency, reduction of consumption and promotion of renewable sources, jointly with reduction of CO_2 emissions in order to meet Italy's Kyoto commitments, are also objectives of other policy sectors, such as agriculture (together with the objective of cutting production costs).[31] Several programmes promote the use of agricultural produce for energy production purposes and the production of organic fuels.[32] National provisions issued in 1998 and 1999 enacted a number of EU directives in the field of energy saving, such as labelling of electric appliances, certification of construction materials and heating equipment. The government set up a 'Osservatorio' responsible for monitoring policies and measures indicated by the *National White Book on Renewable Sources*.

Production

Though there has been considerable growth of the eco-industry over the last 15 to 20 years.[33] It has suffered from competitive disadvantages vis-à-vis other countries where environmental policy has started earlier and has been pursued more strongly than in Italy. Furthermore, industry still primarily focuses on the production of add-on devices, rather than on the modification of the production processes. Recent national legislation (Decree 372 of 1999) enacting Integrated Pollution Prevention and Control (IPPC) Directive 96/61,[34] with the explicitly stated objective to foster an overall and integrated consideration of all environmental aspects (such as air, water, waste and noise), as well as to pursue an effective use of energy upon releasing or renewing permits to existing plants, might finally bring about a change in this respect. A similar change might be fostered also by recent legislation enacting EU Directive 96/62 concerning ambient air quality, asserting that authorities should adopt measures in pursuance of the law's objectives according to an integrated approach capable of protecting air, water and soil.[35]

Today, there is a growing awareness that the competitiveness of Italian firms on international markets depends also upon their ability to develop environmentally compatible goods and services,[36] as well as to promote the recycling of solid waste and to reduce energy consumption and pollution. ENEA (*Ente per le Nuove Tecnologie, l'Energia e l'Ambiente*), the national agency for energy and the environment, was recently entrusted with tasks in the field of research and technological innovation. The aim was to promote sustainable development, competitiveness of the economy and employment jointly with environmental protection, especially in favour of small and medium-sized firms that represent a significant portion of Italian industry.[37]

In addition, the idea that good environmental conditions represent a relevant resource for tourism is taking root. The government has promoted a policy for demolishing buildings that were constructed illegally within parks and areas of special scenic beauty (such as the coast of Amalfi),[38] and is trying to combine the construction of new tourist ports according to environmental protection standards.[39] A considerable number of national land and sea parks and protected areas have been instituted. Interestingly, such policy aims not only at preserving natural resources, but also at promoting both new and traditional economic activities deemed compatible with the parks themselves.[40]

Environmental aspects are receiving increasing attention within agricultural policy. The most interesting example is represented by the introduction of a 1 per cent tax on a number of pesticides and livestock foodstuff; the income obtained from such tax will form a fund for promoting biological agriculture and food quality.[41] Furthermore, financial assistance is granted for investments aimed at reducing negative environmental impacts (with explicit reference to EU provisions). A Code of Good Agricultural Practice that explicitly focused on nitrate pollution, implementing EC Directive 91/676, was introduced in 1999. Some initial, yet interesting, measures build on the connection between environmental protection and the conservation of traditional agricultural practices and products in the hope of creating a specific market niche for high-quality traditional products versus 'industrialized' foodstuff.[42] Financial resources have been allocated to tackle some of the most serious environmental problems caused by agriculture and are aimed at, for example, water saving and reuse[43] or at introducing new technologies capable of reducing pollution caused by animal breeding.[44] However, the EU programmes to protect the environment from agricultural practices do not appear to be very successful in Italy. In 1995, requests from farmers for funds for five-year set-aside measures concerned only 245,000 hectares, whereas the 20-year set-aside concerned only 170 hectares. EC Regulation 2078/92 (concerning agricultural production methods compatible with environmental protection) concerned 98,000 hectares (0.6 per cent of total agricultural land) and Regulation 2080/92 on reforestation involved only 50,000 hectares. For the latter, expenditures were only some 80 billion lire out of the 3000 available (Valentinelli, 1998, pp72–73; see also Chapter 6 in this book for a general overview).

EXPLAINING INCREMENTAL PROGRESS

On the basis of the evidence presented above, there is considerable progress in integrating environmental policy within sectoral policy. References to environmental aspects have become increasingly frequent over the last four years. Yet, there are also more 'green' declarations than 'green' operation and implementation. In this section, the factors hindering EPI and those supporting it are highlighted.

The Bottlenecks

The economic–environmental balance

Environmental policy was long perceived as existing in a trade-off relationship with economic objectives. However, the Italian case shows evidence that so-called environmental policy may be adopted to serve primarily economic objectives. The environmental discourse may be used to justify measures that are actually traditional policies 'in disguise'. At least some of the recent policies in Italy are aimed at boosting the economy and reducing unemployment, whereas environmental aspects serve to secure the support of green coalition partners and of the 'environmentally aware' public opinion.

Such conclusion is exemplified by the CO_2 tax that explicitly aims at a 'double dividend' – that is, collecting resources to promote less polluting and more energy efficient behaviour, on the one hand, but also fostering employment on the other (by cutting various forms of social security contributions on wages paid by employers in order to reduce labour cost). The policy aimed at promoting the substitution of old automobiles and motorcycles illustrates this point even more clearly. Although environment – and road safety – will certainly benefit from the turnover, it is quite clear that the government was, first of all, looking for a way to boost the economy in a period of poor performance, which is evidenced by the fact that part of the policy is contained within a wider provision titled 'Urgent Measures for the Economy'.[45] In fact, in its first year, the measure produced an increase in the GNP estimated at 0.4 per cent. It is also worth noting that the cost of the measure for the state turned out to be very low since it brought fiscal resources deriving from additional sales. This economic success convinced the government to extend the approach to other sectors, such as agriculture and freight transportation.[46]

So far, these measures have accomplished very little in terms of improving the situation of air pollution, especially in urban areas; this would require an overall reduction in the use of private transportation. Nor were they successful in eliminating non-catalysed vehicles (in fact, Italy was one of the few EU countries who required a prorogation of the deadline for banning leaded gasoline).[47] Similarly, measures aimed at stimulating the economy by means of incentives (in the form of tax deductions) granted for construction or restoration work of residential buildings hardly succeed in reducing noise pollution or energy consumption; their main goal is to promote the slumping building sector.[48]

Similar considerations apply to a number of provisions to reduce unemployment. Unemployed persons are offered low-salary, 'socially useful' jobs, including activities related to environmental protection, such as nature conservation, waste treatment, water management, improvement of the urban transportation services and biological agriculture.[49] Several provisions allocate funds for the construction of 'environmentally friendly' infrastructures, such as wastewater collection and treatment plants.[50] Act 344 of 1997 aims at promoting employment in the environmental field by means of training and education. Other new jobs are being created by promoting the diffusion of solar energy and the recycling of harmful products, such as chlorofluorocarbons (CFCs) in old refrigerators. Policies aimed at restoring abandoned industrial areas (such as Bagnoli near Naples and Sesto San Giovanni near Milan) attempt to couple the creation of jobs and the setting up of new small firms capable of respecting environmental standards with the depollution of soil and water and the recreation of pre-existing environmental conditions (Zanelli, 1999).[51] Furthermore, opportunities for employment in activities connected to nature and environmental protection are favoured by new fiscal rules concerning non-profit organizations, including those operating in environmentally related fields.[52]

Obstacles in the implementation process

So far, this chapter has been concerned only with formal provisions and has neglected the actual implementation of EPI measures. Here, several obstacles have hindered the efforts by the government to introduce an integrative approach.

Italian administration is characterized by the legal-formalistic policy style coupled with the lack of a problem-solving (Aberbach et al, 1981, p52) and result-oriented culture (La Spina and Sciortino, 1993, pp217–220) in the public bureaucracy . This is an unfavourable condition for policy innovations in general. Furthermore, technical competence – particularly relevant for environmental policy – is not widespread within the administration and enjoys low status in the eyes of the political and administrative actors.

Besides such evidence of missing capacity, patterns of departments protecting their own 'turf', though certainly not a phenomenon unique to the Italian case, also hamper integration. Only recently, the minister in charge of bureaucratic reform, Bassanini, complained of the obstructionism within the civil service against the reforms passed by government and called for a turn-over of the top management (*La Repubblica*, 19 June 1998, p26). Phenomena of bureaucratic obstructionism can be expected also in relation to measures of procedural integration: simplification and consolidation of existing procedures might well be perceived as loss of power, if not a threat to the survival of a specific office or administration. The high degree of fragmentation of powers among a vast array of national ministries and agencies, as well as among authorities at different levels of government, raises the challenge even further. Furthermore, the Ministry of the Environment is required to seek the opinion and secure the agreement of other interested ministries (such as industry, public works and health) in a number of matters. It would, however, be a mistake to consider this as a device aimed at fostering integration; in fact, it assures such ministries – and their constituencies – considerable control over the decisions of the Ministry of the Environment, severely hampering its capability for action (see Chapter 4 for similar experiences in Germany).

Even considering the Ministry of the Environment alone, its organizational structure, focused on single media, evidences that even cross-media integration is difficult to pursue. The ministry was initially set up much along the traditional bureaucratic model, and structured along six departments, including:

- ARS (water, waste, soil);
- VIA (impact assessment, citizen information, reports);
- IAR (air and noise pollution, hazardous industries);
- CN (nature conservation).

The remaining two deal with personnel management and internal organization of the ministry (Frey, 1993, p11; Salvia, 1989, p37).[53]

Political will

Political difficulties should not be neglected. In Chapter 3 of this book, Jordan pointed to the crucial factor of political will in achieving EPI. Coalition governments face an even higher challenge since they depend upon a certain consensus within the government. At the same time, each party strives to ensure its influence in the cabinet and its control over sections of the administration. Any shift of powers from one ministry to another or, even worse, the proposal to merge ministries can weaken the coalition; even attempts to integrate sectoral policies can be easily perceived as a subtraction of powers, rather than as a positive sum game. The earlier example of the merger of land-use policy with the protection of the environment must be seen in that context because the two ministries involved (public works and the environment) 'belonged' to different political factions in the coalition. The Democratici di Sinistra and most of the Green party supported the minister of the environment, whereas the Catholic Partito Popolare supported the minister of public works.

The limited reach of different policy instruments

A final aspect concerns the instruments used to produce integration and their effectiveness. Traditional environmental policy in Italy and the EU is mainly based on 'command-and-control' regulatory policy instruments. Implementation reports of the EU show a very poor record, particularly in Italy (European Commission, 1996). Hence, we witness a new interest in 'softer' and 'bottom-up' approaches in environmental policy-making, ranging from economic instruments such as taxes to participatory, reporting or monitoring requirements (Knill and Lenschow, 2000). However, these are not always capable of living up to their promises. For example, airport taxes,[54] which were imposed to reduce noise during take-offs and landings, do not seem to be effective since practically all Italian airports present noise levels above legal limits, according to a recent report.[55] On the other hand, new regulatory instruments such as environmental impact assessments (EIAs) also seem to be hardly capable of ensuring due consideration of environmental aspects, as demonstrated by the continuing protest movement of the populations living around the new Malpensa airport (where an EIA was carried out).

Two types of approaches are worth mentioning for their potential to change public attitudes and capacities in the longer run:

- Information and public awareness: the Ministry of the Environment, for example, launched the idea of one 'car-free' Sunday a month (*Domeniche senz'auto*) – the use of private vehicles would be banned in city centres as a way to reduce both gasoline consumption and air pollution. The idea was initially criticized, but eventually managed to attract more than 180 towns and cities, and, according to polls, met the favour of more than 80 per cent of Italians and the interest of many European administrations. Another example is offered by the national energy authority. It recently compelled electricity companies to provide information to their customers that will allow them to be informed of their average daily electricity use, with the explicit aim of saving resources and reducing emissions.

• Efforts have begun to build new professional skills: public policy focuses on training specialists in fields related to the environment.[56] One specific measure is the training of so-called 'mobility managers' – medium- and large-sized firms and administrations are required to designate individuals responsible for reducing the use of individual vehicles in favour of collective transportation in order to limit congestion.[57]

Enhancing Factors

A political factor, namely the presence of a strong 'green' component within the governing coalition, partly accounts for the 'greening' of public policies, as described above. Three further factors, however, also seem to be of relevance in the Italian case.

Administrative reform

EPI appears to be favoured by a window of opportunity represented by processes of administrative reform that currently are under way in Italy, as in other developed countries. For the centre-left governments in power during 1996–2000, administrative reform such as the transfer of powers from the central state to local and regional authorities, or the streamlining of administrative procedures and the elimination of red tape, represented a priority in their attempts to increase popular support and to deal with a diffused anti-state mood. For the Prodi–D'Alema governments, this effort was also tied, once again, to the goal of fostering economic growth and employment. The integration of European and global markets and, hence, greater competitive pressures demand administrative effectiveness and efficiency. This is because the public sector must increase its capability to produce added value for society and the economy (for example, by creating the conditions that attract investments), while facing a reduction in revenues. In other words, political and economic crises have contributed to a reform movement that may produce institutional structures conducive to environmental integration.

Authorization procedures for production activities are traditionally very cumbersome in Italy. For example, it always took a long time to open new industrial plants or substantially modify existing ones because a number of permits had to be obtained from different offices of the same administration (such as the region) or from different public authorities at various levels of government (from local to national). In the environmental field alone, five separate permits were required for siting a new industrial plant (air, water, waste, soil and cultural heritage).[58] In an attempt to improve the situation, in 1998 a simplified permit procedure was introduced: requests for authorizations are presented to a *sportello unico* (a 'sole counter') that in turn is responsible for collecting all the necessary permits, thus reducing the burden previously put on business.[59] Such changes seem to match well with the trend under way in environmental policy. Furthermore, the provision enacting the European IPPC directive was passed during a period of substantive modifications in the Italian administration. The two processes appear to mutually reinforce each other.

International and European commitments

International commitments or, more frequently, EU directives represent a further enhancing factor of special relevance to the Italian case, especially since Italy often appears to respond to international inputs. International agreements have no doubt contributed to promoting the necessity of 'integrating the environmental dimension' within policies in such sectors as energy, tourism, industry, agriculture and transportation in order to tackle the environmental issues (for example, in relation to two especially sensitive areas for the Italian peninsula, namely the 1991 Alps Convention for the protection of the Alps[60] and the 1995 Mediterranean Act of the Plenipotentiaries Conference on the Convention for the Protection of the Mediterranean Sea from Pollution[61]).

The agreement that until recently seems to have the greatest potential for integration is the Kyoto Conference on Climate Change (see Chapter 9 for an overview). The minister for the environment has been especially interested in exploiting this agreement to foster environmental concerns, as well as his own position within the coalition. Projects were passed in such fields as energy generation, alternative energy sources (for example, from agricultural produce), energy efficiency in buildings and in productive activities, transportation and research. These projects involve costs of some 90,000 billion lire for the next 13 years. A National Conference on Energy and Environment held at the end of 1998 developed strategies aimed at economic growth (also by creating competitive eco-compatible products and technologies), as well as maintaining the availability of energy while reducing greenhouse emissions. Most recent measures in the field of energy saving (such as eco-labels for electric appliances and renewable energy sources) explicitly refer to the Kyoto CO_2 reduction targets and the related EU policy decisions (such as the Commission's communication on 'Climate Change – Toward an EU post-Kyoto Strategy').[62]

Cognitive dimension

This section notes the effects of a new environmental discourse – or paradigm shift – in Italian politics. The international and European discourse may change the general belief systems of policy actors and hence, the cognitive approach to policy problems (Sabatier and Jenkins-Smith, 1993). In the Italian case, learning capacity, traditionally low, seems to have increased in recent years, although there remain differences between actors. Changes in policy priorities are more likely to occur among large firms, environmental associations and politicians who – thanks to their involvement in international networks – are exposed to the experiences of other countries. Resistance is more likely in the administration, which, especially in the Italian case, tends to tread upon well-known and customary paths.

Although occurring somewhat later and to a lesser degree than in most environmentally advanced countries, the idea of integration has been advanced by two broad paradigms, namely ecological modernization and sustainability. As far as the first is concerned, the idea that the environment represents a resource and an opportunity for economic development capable of generating jobs and profits rather than a burden has made some progress in recent years. This concept, however, had to struggle against well-entrenched ideas. On the one hand, there exists the traditional premise that development is necessarily based on large projects and heavy industrialization, whatever the environmental consequences. On the other hand, there is the prevailing characteristic of Italian political culture that ensures that the production of public goods (such as environmental quality) receives much less support and votes than distributing direct benefits to specific 'clienteles'.

An example of the change that has occurred recently in Italy is represented by public policies aimed at increasing the competitiveness of Italian firms on international markets by promoting their capability to produce environmentally compatible goods and services, as discussed above. Even more interesting is the case of southern Italy's development. The traditional approach has been unable to create widespread economic growth, while disrupting the assets of considerable natural (environmental quality, scenic beauty and cultural heritage) and economic (tourism) value. Interestingly, the governmental document for the development of southern regions for the period of 2000–2006 considers the protection of natural resources as one of its main objectives as a condition required for promoting such development. The document also explicitly refers to the integration of environmental policy with other land management and sectoral policies.[63] Even in industrial policies in southern regions, aspects such as the reduction of emissions and of resource consumption have become parameters used in decisions for granting financial assistance to firms siting new plants in such areas.[64] These are examples in which environmental measures are instrumental to the pursuit of economic aims without losing their environmental objectives (true win–win solutions).

Sustainable development is a concept that strongly implies the integration of economic, social and environmental policies, and thus is closely connected to EPI. After the Earth Summit in Rio, references to sustainability appear with increasing frequency in Italian legislation – for example, in policies concerning urban areas[65] or the development of southern regions for the period of 2000–2006.[66] A National Plan for Sustainable Development enacting Agenda 21 was drafted in 1993 and is today in the process of being updated. In 1996, the Ministry of the Environment created a working group on sustainable cities and, on the basis of its suggestions, supported important initiatives to foster diffusion of the local Agenda 21, such as the Sustainable Cities for Children Prize awarded for the first time in 1998 (Ministero dell'Ambiente, 1998) and the Prize for Sustainable Cities awarded for the first time in 1999.[67] In 1997, the Italian senate passed a formal resolution which bound the Italian government to adopt measures in favour of sustainability in accordance with the commitments made at the United Nations New York 1997 Summit. Act 344/1997, which was approved shortly after, defines provisions for the development and improvement of interventions and employment related to the environment and sustainability. The new Programme for the Protection of the Environment[68] defines interventions relating to six strategic areas, among them instruments for sustainable development. Furthermore, though later than in other Western countries, local Agenda 21 has attracted the interest of a number of municipal, provincial and regional authorities over the last two years (Ramieri et al, 1999). In addition, one of the six departments of the national environmental protection agency (ANPA) has recently been given responsibility for 'integrated strategies'[69] with special reference to sustainable development (ANPA, 1999).

These examples show that the paradigms of ecological modernization and sustainability have begun to put their roots in Italian political and administrative culture and, hence, have created a favourable 'terrain' for environmental integration.

CONCLUSION

One general conclusion that emerges quite clearly from this analysis is that EPI in Italy has made considerable progress during recent years. Although perhaps to a somewhat lesser degree when compared to northern European countries, the *idea* of EPI has become part of today's political culture; this is demonstrated by the increasing frequency with which other policy sectors take account of environmental criteria.

The reasons that account for this shift toward EPI are at least partially related to the political change that occurred in 1996. As part of the centre-left coalition, environmental interests became more willing to promote effective as well as consensual policies in this field, which matched with the need of the coalition as a whole to promote economic growth and employment. In other words, the centre-left government embraced EPI because it was perceived as an approach useful both on the 'internal' front (as a viable answer to the different priorities the partners of the coalition) and on the 'external' one (in tackling both the environmental and the economic growth issues of Italian society). Although the political situation thus seems to have been conducive for EPI to assert itself as a policy approach, several other factors have significantly contributed to creating favourable conditions. This includes the window of opportunity created by a process of administrative and institutional reform and the stimuli represented by international commitments and EU policies. The latter not only imposed real environmental commitments; they also changed the cognitive framework for domestic policy-making, inserting EPI within the 'market of policy ideas'.

Finally, it is important to remember that this conclusion is based only on the policies formulated by the Prodi and D'Alema governments – as expressed by legal provisions passed during this period – and not on their implementation and effectiveness. A careful analysis of these aspects might well bring a different verdict. Some preliminary evaluations have, for example, come to the conclusion that there has been 'difficulty in integrating environmental policies with sectoral policies – energy, industry, transportation, agriculture' (Legambiente, 2000, p159). For instance, eco-taxes can be considered a tool to integrate environmental considerations within everyday business decisions since they may contribute to the internalization of environmental costs. The adoption of a CO_2 tax, furthermore, represents one of the most promising measures in the direction of an integrated approach adopted by the centre-left government. And yet, revenues generated by 'green taxes' (including energy and vehicle taxes) have actually decreased in 1998 compared to 1995, from 11.4 per cent of total tax revenues (and 3 per cent of GNP) down to 9.4 per cent (2.6 per cent of GNP) (Legambiente, 2000, p282). The scarce empirical information available at this stage seems to confirm that the bottlenecks mentioned above might well continue to limit the actual degree of integration to a significant degree.

REFERENCES

Agenzia Nazionale per la Protezione dell'Ambiente (ANPA) (1999) *ANPA per l'ambiente...'98 e '99 in breve*, ANPA, Rome

Aberbach, J, Putnam, R and Rockman, B (1981) *Bureaucrats and Politicians in Western Democracies*, Harvard University Press, Cambridge MA

Amadei, P, Croci, E and Pesaro, G (1998) *Nuovi strumenti di politica ambientale – Gli accordi volontari*, F Angeli, Milan

Cesaretti, C (1995) *La spesa per l'ambiente dello Stato: Aspetti metodologici e primi risultati 1986–93*, dattilo, Ispe, Rome

European Commission (1996) *Implementing Community Environmental Law*, Communication to the Council of the European Union and the European Parliament, Brussels

Frey, M (1993) 'Il governo dell'ambiente e i possibili ruoli di un'agenzia ambientale in Italia', *Quaderni Iefe*, Università Bocconi, June

Gerelli, E (1990) (ed) *Ascesa e declino del business ambientale: Dal disinquinamento alle industrie pulite*, Il Mulino, Bologna

Giuliani, M (1992) *Giochi regolativi: La politica di protezione del paesaggio*, PhD thesis, European University Institute, Florence

Hajer, M (1995) *The Politics of Environmental Discourse*, Clarendon, Oxford

ISTAT (1996) *Statistiche ambientali*, ISTAT, Rome

Jänicke, M (1991) *Institutional and other Framework Conditions for Environmental Policy Success*, FFU Report, no 2, Berlin

Knill, C and Lenschow, A (2000) *Implementing EU Environmental Policy*, Manchester University Press, Manchester

La Spina, A and Sciortino, G (1993) 'Common agenda, southern rules: European integration and environmental change in the Mediterranean states' in D Liefferink, P Lowe and J Mol (eds) *European Integration & Environmental Policy*, Belhaven, London, pp217–236

La Repubblica (1998) 'I burocrati remano contro', 19 June 1998, p26

Legambiente, Istituto di ricerche Ambiente Italia (1996) (ed) *Ambiente Italia 1996: Rapporto sullo stato del paese a confronto con l'Europa*, Edizioni Ambiente, Rome

Legambiente, Istituto di ricerche Ambiente Italia (1997) (ed) *Ambiente Italia 1998: Rapporto sullo stato del paese e analisi della questione infrastrutture*, Edizioni Ambiente, Rome

Legambiente, Istituto di ricerche Ambiente Italia (2000) (ed) *Ambiente Italia 2000: Rappororto sullo stato dell'ambiente*, Edizioni Ambiente, Rome

Lewanski, R (1997) *Governare l'ambiente: Attori e processi della politica ambientale. Interessi in gioco, sfide, nuove strategie*, Il Mulino, Bologna

Malaman, R (1994) 'Dal FIO alla programmazione triennale: gli investimenti per la protezione dell'ambiente in Lombardia' in A Balducci, B Dente, P Fareri, G Gario, G Longhi and R Malaman (eds) *Il nuovo ordinamento della autonomie locali in Lombardia*, F Angeli, Milan, pp35–74

Malaman, R and Ranci, P (1991) 'Italian Environmental Policy', paper delivered at the International Conference on Economy and Environment in the 1990s, Neuchâtel, Germany

Minella, M (2000) 'Largo ai bisonti del mare', *Affari e Finanza*, 22 May 2000, p13

Ministero dell' Ambiente (1992) *Relazione sullo stato dell'ambiente*, Istituto Poligrafico e Zecca dello Stato, Rome

Ministero dell' Ambiente (1997) *Relazione sullo stato dell'ambiente*, Istituto Poligrafico e Zecca dello Stato, Rome

Minsitero dell'Ambiente (1998) *Bilancio 1998. Politiche ambientali in Italia: un anno di attività del Ministero dell'Ambiente*, Rome

Organisation for Economic Co-operation and Development (OECD) (1994) *Environmental Performance Reviews: Italy*, OECD, Paris

Ramieri, E, Wallace-Jones, J and Lewanski, R (1999) *LA21 Implementation in Italy: Converging Pathways between Central and Local Levels of Government?* Paper presented at the SUSCOM Dialogue Conference, Sustainability through Subsidiarity: Implementing Local Agenda 21 in Europe, Barcelona, 18–21 November 1999

Sabatier, P and Jenkins-Smith, H (1993) *Policy Change and Learning: An Advocacy Coalition Approach*, Westview Press, Boulder CO

Salvia, F (1989) *Il Ministero dell' Ambiente*, NIS, Rome

Valentinelli, A (1998) 'Riforme per l'agricoltura', *Legambiente*, Ambiente Italia 1998, Edizioni Ambiente, pp71–74

Zanelli, M (1999) 'Riqualificazione, una definizione al di là degli slogan', *Info Riqualificazione Urbana Metropolitana*, vol 1, July, p3

NOTES

1   All provisions (approximately 650) containing a reference to the environment or to pollution have been analysed.

2   Act 112 of 1998

3   For example, in the case of water pollution all industrial firms can discharge pollutants within prescribed concentration limits into a river, regardless of the cleansing capacity of that specific waterway, the number of industries discharging into it, and the various possible uses of the water (recreation, fishing, drinking water supplies, etc).

4   Ex-post remedies to the disasters caused by floods and landslides cost some 4000 billion lire every year.

5   In 1997, only 11 out the 23 national and interregional authorities had been set up (Ministero dell'Ambiente, 1997, p374).

6   It is interesting to note that the Greens on this occasion were given the Ministry of
     Agriculture, rather than that of environment, which could be seen as an attempt by
     the Green party to integrate environmental concerns in this production sector.
7   Act 152 of 1999
8   The idea, it should be noted, is not new. Already in 1993, Law 537 (Article 1)
     foresaw the creation of one Ministry of Territory competent for both
     environment and infrastructures.
9   Act 300 of 1999
10   Another organizational measure having potentially 'integrative implications' is the
     decision to merge ANPA – the national environmental agency – with the 'national
     technical services' (dams, geological, hydrographic and seas) into one national agency.
11   Act 454 of 23 December 1997 and Decree of 14 October 1998. Act 173 of 30
     April 1998, for example, specifically promotes such modes of transportation for
     agricultural and fishing products.
12   Acts 413 of 1998 and 488 of 1999
13   Both the waterways of the Po Valley and the Italian seaways have been included
     among the major international waterways of the Geneva agreement of 1996,
     ratified by Act 16 of 2000.
14   Act 413 of 1997. The allowed maximum content of benzene in gasoline has been
     lowered to 1 per cent, starting in July 1998. The same provision enacted EU
     Directive 94/63 concerning the control of volatile organic compounds emissions
     during the various phases of transportation and distribution of gasoline.
15   Decree 76 of 1999 introduced such an obligation starting in September 1999 in
     the 25 largest cities, and starting in June 2000 in the rest of the country.
16   Decree of 27 March 1998; the measure is focused on medium- and large-sized
     firms having at least 300 employees.
17   According to Act 53 of 2000, all municipalities with more than 30,000 inhabitants
     are required to draft an ad hoc 'plan' for this purpose and to give a civil servant
     the responsibility for such policy.
18   Article 50, Act 448 of 1998
19   Decree of 22 October 1999
20   Article 22 of Act 266 of 1997
21   Act 30 of 1997
22   Acts 30 and 40, both of 1997
23   Decree 20 of 1997
24   Decree 25 January 2000
25   Old vehicles are to be sent to less developed countries.
26   It should be noted that the Italian economy starts from a favourable position since
     it features very low energy intensity in terms of unit of gross domestic product
     (GDP); per capita intensity shows a tendency to increase since 1985 but is still low
     among OECD countries (OECD, 1994, p141).
27   As agreed by the EU Environment Ministers Council of 17 June 1998.
28   Article 11 of Act 79 of 1999 and Decision of 16 March 2000
29   Act 133 of 1999, Article 10
30   Act 448 of 1998
31   Act 173 of 30 April 1998
32   Act 423 of 1998 and Decree 401 of 1999
33   In 1990 it employed almost 10,000 individuals. Italian industry in this sector was
     about one third the size of industry in Germany and half of industry in France
     (Malaman and Ranci, 1991). In 1995 its proceeds were estimated at 13,000 billion
     lire.

34 Decree 372 of 4 August 1999. Such provision has abandoned the original intention of the Italian government to enact jointly both the IPPC directive and the new EIA Directive 97/11.
35 Act 351 of 1999
36 Decree of 3 March 1999, Article 4.5
37 Act 36 of 1999
38 Article 2, Act 426 of 1998. There are approximately one million illegal constructions, located mainly in southern Italy (Legambiente, 2000, p287).
39 Decree 509 of 1997 and Decree of 14 April 1998
40 See, for example, Decree of 6 October 1999 creating the national park of the Cinque Terre in Liguria. The experience of some of the older parks (as in the case of the Parco Nazionale d'Abruzzi) has demonstrated that they can become a relevant factor of local development.
41 Act 488 of 1999, Article 59. In 1998, biological methods were used in 3.5 per cent of total agricultural land.
42 Act 39 of 2000, for example, aims at protecting the *bergamotto* (a type of citrus fruit), together with the specific environment it grows in.
43 Decrees of 18 November 1997 and 9 April 1999
44 Act 173 of 30 April 1998
45 Act 266 of 1997
46 Decree of 25 May 1998; Decrees of 14 October 1998 and 7 July 1999
47 Approximately 1.5 million old vehicles were substituted (*La Repubblica*, 19 July 1996).
48 Decree of 17 January 2000
49 See, for example, Decree of 29 August 1997
50 Article 6, Decree 67 of 1997
51 Decree 225 of 1 June 1998
52 Decree 460 of December 1997
53 A positive signal, however, is the creation of a service of internal control having among its tasks the analysis of intersectoral programmes; Decree 495 of 1999.
54 Differentiated taxes on airplanes according to their specific noise levels were introduced by the Decree of 3 December 1999.
55 *La Repubblica*, 31 May 2000
56 Act 344 of 1997; Article 22 of Act 266 of 1997; Decree 58 of 1997
57 Decree of 27 March 1998
58 For example, the construction of an average-sized chemical plant requires 14 different authorizations, granted by 9 different agencies, based on 20 distinct pieces of legislation.
59 Decree 112 of 31 March 1998 and subsequent Regulation 447 of the same year
60 Act 403 of 14 October 1999
61 Ratified by Act 175 of May 1999
62 However, one should also be aware that the international context is not always environmentally benign. Liberalization of television and radio stations, on the one hand, and of telephone (and especially mobile phone) services, on the other, has caused considerable concern about the effects of electromagnetic emissions by health authorities. Populations residing near the growing numbers of antennas and transmission lines caused by market competition are also voicing their concern.
63 The new agency, mainly focused on the development of southern regions, Sviluppo Italia, is also entrusted with the task of promoting the 'development of natural and environmental resources' (Prime Minister's Decree of 9 June 1999).
64 Decrees of 20 October 1995 and 21 November 1997

65 Decree of 8 October 1998
66 CIPE Decision of 14 May 1999
67 Ministerial Decree of 3 August 1998
68 Ministerial Decree of 28 May 1998
69 Act 335 of 1997

Part III

EUROPEAN UNION POLICY STUDIES

6

Integrating EU Environmental and Agricultural Policy

Henry Buller

INTRODUCTION

The adoption of environmental prerogatives and objectives within the European Union's (EU) Common Agricultural Policy (CAP) has proved to be one of the more difficult enterprises of environmental policy integration. Even today, although a considerable number of relevant policy instruments and regulatory mechanisms arguably exist at the EU level, genuine policy integration has remained elusive. There are perhaps four basic reasons for this.

Firstly, it has taken a long time for agricultural and environmental policy actors, for the European farming community and, indeed, for European civil society as a whole to come to terms with the fact that agricultural activities, on the one hand, and environmental quality protection and maintenance, on the other, are not intrinsically integrated. The transition from what used to be conceived as an almost symbiotic relationship between farming and rural landscapes to a growing antagonism between the demands for productive farming and the demands for environmental quality marks a shift not only in agricultural techniques (and the means of encouraging and financing investment in these techniques), but also in the nature and conceptualization of the environment and the value placed upon it. Neither the environment nor agriculture is seen today in quite the same light as 30 years ago. In drawing up a framework for agricultural policy, European policy-makers then largely subsumed the environment under the long-standing belief that what was good for farming would necessarily be good for the countryside (in the largest sense of that word).

Secondly, agricultural policy at the EU level is essentially a market policy aimed at encouraging and improving European agricultural productivity and making farming a major export sector. Agriculture is still the largest and one of the oldest interventionist domains of the EU, accounting for around 50 per cent of the total EU budget. Integrating environmental objectives within this well-established mechanism, whose goals are complex, multifarious and slow to change, has proved to be a difficult and largely incremental process that, in most cases, tinkers at the margins rather than addresses the core principles of EU agricultural policy. Indeed, the emergence of an EU agriculture–environment policy agenda, essentially during the 1980s, was arguably driven more by the need to reduce the financial burden of overproduction and surplus management than by concerns for the detrimental effects of agricultural techniques on environmental quality. Even today, some 15 years after the first 'agri-environmental measures' were introduced by EU Regulation 757/85, European Agricultural Guarantee and Guidance Fund (EAGGF) spending on agri-environmental policy amounts to only around 4 per cent of total farm spending within the EU.

Thirdly, not only are the relationships between agriculture, the environment and rural spaces highly complex, but they are also strongly conditioned by varied cultural, historical and territorial influences that, for the most part, operate in a national or sub-national context. Different EU Member States have, understandably, different concerns and preoccupations with respect to these relationships, ranging from the social and territorial implications of farm abandonment in Mediterranean and many upland regions to farm-pollution management in areas of intensive lowland cereal production (Brouwer and Lowe, 1998; Buller et al, 2000). Creating a framework for environmental policy integration that takes into account such variations without, at the same time, provoking greater disparities either in agricultural support or in agricultural production, as well as establishing a commonly applicable policy agenda, have proved difficult as the implementation of the Drinking Water Directive and the Agri-Environmental Regulation (2078/92) have shown (Bodiguel and Buller, 1996; Buller et al, 2000). The necessary division of competencies between the EU and the Member States that this engenders (Jones and Clark, 1998), and the degree of implementation variability that this can create (both intentionally and unintentionally; Jordan, 1998), are key elements in understanding the difficulties of environmental policy integration within the agricultural domain.

Fourthly, and at a more individualistic level, the introduction of an environmental agenda into agricultural policy, particularly after a 30-year period dominated by a policy of agricultural modernization, intensification and productivity, has frequently been seen by farmers as well as by their representatives (who include agricultural trade unions and, in many cases, national governments) as a challenge to their own occupational legitimacy. As a result, environmental goals have been accused of having the effect of 'turning the clock back' on agricultural modernization, and in doing so contesting contemporary farming's very raison d'être (Hervieu, 1996) as well as its historical environmental morality (Lowe et al, 1997). Having been driven into modernity by an often aggressive programme of agricultural intensification and restructuring, many of Europe's farmers view the contemporary shift towards, on the one hand, de-intensification and production ceilings and, on the other hand, environmental protection as the final blow to their increasingly fragile professional identity – as one revolution too far.

This chapter seeks to examine the progressive integration of environmental concerns and objectives into the CAP and to consider how the various hindrances, identified above, have been addressed. The chapter argues that the integration process can be broken down into two basic phases, each responding to a distinct set of demands and concerns. The first, running from the early 1970s to the CAP reforms of 1992, has been led predominantly by agricultural policy considerations and includes, on the one hand, the adoption of a limited 'command-and-control' regulatory style aimed at reducing the impact of those particular agricultural activities deemed responsible for environmental pollution and damage; on the other hand is a far more dominant set of voluntary strategies aimed at encouraging farmers to adopt or maintain environmentally friendly production techniques in the broader public interest. A second, and more recent, stage emerges from a broader cross-sectoral reflection, driven essentially by the EU integration process as a whole and particularly by the Agenda 2000 reforms, but also by emerging consumer concerns for food and environmental safety. This, it is argued here, coincides with a shift towards a greater concern for the territorial component of agricultural and environmental relations, a component that has become a key element in the post Agenda 2000 orientation of EU agricultural and rural development policy.

MITIGATING THE EFFECTS OF THE CAP

> *Agricultural policy-makers are skilled at introducing changes which appear to produce more fundamental reforms than they actually deliver.* (Grant, 1991, p110)

In 1942, the report of the Scott Committee on Land Utilization in Rural Areas, submitted to the British government as part of the groundwork for that country's emerging land-use planning system, maintained that 'the cheapest, indeed the only, way of preserving the countryside in anything like its traditional aspect would be to farm it' (Scott, 1942, quoted in MacEwen and MacEwen, 1982, p10). This dictum, though it has proved time and time again to be essentially false, is rooted in a premise of agricultural stability and in a culture of countryside stewardship peculiar, one might argue, only to post-war Britain. Nonetheless, it remains central to subsequent agricultural and rural environmental policy both within the UK and beyond:

> *Sufficient numbers of farmers must be kept on the land. There is no other way to preserve the natural environment, traditional landscape and a model of agriculture based on the family farm as favoured by society generally.* (CEC, 1991, pp9–10)

Farming and the rural environment are inextricably linked. Indeed, as is often said, the particularity of the European rural environment (since it is often compared to the physical environment in the US, Canada, Australia and much of Southern America) is that it is a farmed and hence essentially constructed environment. Agriculture, as a productive activity, has always been constrained, conditioned and influenced by the physical environment in which it operates and with which it interacts. This is surely one of its defining features (Whitby, 1996a). Thus, at one level, it is almost a paradox to speak of agriculture and environment as distinct policy domains.

Nonetheless, a great deal has happened since 1942 and the publication of the Scott Report. Post-war agricultural modernization both under the CAP and under national agricultural development programmes has been largely predicated upon farming's greater or lesser disassociation from environmental constraints through economic (price supports and subsidies which encourage farmers to intensify production) and technological means. The result has been that farming or, rather, certain types of farming, from being 'the only way of preserving the countryside', have become perhaps the single greatest threat to the rural environment (Baldock and Lowe, 1996). Brouwer and Lowe (1998) remind us that many other changes have occurred in rural Europe since the 1950s and to place all the blame for rural environmental degradation at the CAP's door is naive, particularly since one of the more positive effects of the CAP has been to maintain agricultural activities in areas of high landscape value. However, it is significant that the CAP, and its various amendments and reforms, remains the principal vehicle and indeed target of environmental policy integration within the agricultural and rural sectors.

For the first 20 years (1962–1982) of its history, the CAP remained almost completely divorced from environmental considerations. In part, this was due to the fact that the Treaty of Rome itself largely ignored the environment as a policy domain for the European Community. In part also, however, it reflects the importance given to the productivist agenda, which was, at that time, wholly dominant in agricultural policy. Within individual Member States, protected zones, whether national parks, natural parks, nature reserves or heritage areas, tended to be designated in areas of low intensity agriculture, often upland or mountain regions. This exacerbated a growing territorial polarization between agriculture and environmental protection that persisted well into the 1990s and has largely defined subsequent European protected area policy.

The need for a greater degree of integration of environmental policy into agricultural policy gradually became increasingly evident in the late 1970s and early 1980s. The reasons for this have been well documented elsewhere (Buller, 1992; Lowe, 1992; Whitby and Lowe, 1994) and are still, for the most part, with us today (for example, Stanners and Bourdeau, 1995; Brouwer and Van Berkum, 1996; CEC, 1999a). This chapter offers merely a brief summary of the principal explanations:

- a growing awareness among policy-makers, the scientific community and civil society of the increasing level of environmental damage caused by agricultural intensification within parts of Europe;
- increasing recognition of the role of the CAP in encouraging that intensification;

- the manifest failure of the CAP to support and sustain those more 'traditional' modes of agricultural production considered to be more environmentally friendly;
- the expanding financial cost of the CAP that became difficult to justify in the face of tangible environmental disbenefits;
- the emergence of a growing environmental policy agenda within the EC which, while not necessarily targeting directly agricultural activities, had an increasingly important impact upon them.

The gradual build-up of these various internal and external, Community and domestic, pressures on European agricultural policy eventually led to an initially slight, but later more profound, shift in the direction of CAP development. The principal components of this shift are outlined in Table 6.1, which identifies both CAP measures and environmental policy measures having a direct input into agricultural practices and management.

Table 6.1 *Agricultural and Environmental Policy Developments*

Agricultural policy developments	Environmental policy developments directly affecting agriculture
1975 Directive 268/75 – Less Favoured Areas	
	1979 Directive 409/79 – Birds Directive
	1980 Directive 778/80 – Drinking Water Directive
	1980 Directive 68/80 – groundwater protection
	1983 Third Environmental Action Programme
1985 Regulation 797/85 – Article 19 offering Member States the possibility of creating environmentally sensitive areas	
1987 Regulation 1760/87 – co-funding for ESA schemes	1987 Single European Act
	1987 Reform of the structural funds and introduction of 5b zones
1990 Regulation 866/90 – grants for organic farming	
1991 Regulation 2328/91 – compensatory allowances for Less Favoured Areas	1991 Directive 676/91 – Nitrates Directive
1991 Regulation 2092/91 – labelling and marketing of organic products	
1992 Regulation 2078/92 – agri-environmental schemes	1992 Directive 43/92 – Habitats Directive
1992 Regulation 2080/92 – aid scheme for forestry measures in agriculture	1992 Fifth Environmental Action Programme
1996 Regulation 746/96 – concerning the implementation of the agri-environment regulation	

Source: adapted from various sources including CEC (1997a); Baldock and Lowe (1998)

Without providing a detailed examination and assessment of each of these components, this section traces the growth and development of an environmental input into Community agricultural policy through three stages: the less favoured areas stage, the environmentally sensitive area (ESA) stage and the agri-environmental policy stage. What is crucial here is that these stages can be seen as responses to an essentially agriculture-led agenda rather than a specific environmental agenda. Agricultural pollution, whether in the form of nitrates, pesticide residues or other chemical traces in water, air or food, was – and to some extent continues to be, while definitely not a side issue – largely excluded from the central thrust of agri-environmental policy.

The Less Favoured Areas (LFA) Stage

If the expanding environmental policy sector has influenced agricultural policy evolution during the 1980s and 1990s, one particular component of agricultural policy nonetheless predates the emergence of an explicit environmental agenda.

Structural policy has always been a component of the CAP even though it has long been the poor cousin of agricultural market policy. The 1975 Directive (268/75) on less favoured areas (LFA), whose principal objective was to maintain agricultural activities in those regions marked by structural handicaps, may be viewed as a precursor for later more specific agri-environmental policy. In a number of European regions, notably central France and the mountain areas of Germany, the UK, France and Italy, LFA policy was seen as a means of maintaining agricultural activities in zones otherwise menaced by agricultural land abandonment and rural community decline. Such largely social concerns, which became translated into environmental concerns in the sense that they relate to the maintenance and preservation of particular agricultural landscapes, are of paramount importance in countries such as France. Today, France still retains a large number of small upland family farms engaged essentially in extensive low-revenue farming activities. In other countries, however, notably the UK, the payment of grants to farmers under LFA schemes according to the number of animals held on a farm has been a major factor in the intensification of livestock densities in some upland areas with resultant habitat loss. This, coupled with the 'indirect' environmental effects of LFA policy (grants have not generally been made available for specific undertakings delivering environmental quality improvements), has been at the heart of much criticism of the environmental component of LFA policy.

To a certain extent, the reform of the structural funds in 1988 sought to address these issues by making countryside protection a necessary condition for the receipt of EAGGF Guidance money within Objective 1 and 5B regions and under Objective 5a (Regulations 2081/93). Nonetheless, LFA policy leaves a powerful legacy within subsequent agri-environmental policy in the considerable emphasis that continues to be placed upon maintaining traditional farming systems as a means of protecting the rural environment (IEEP, 1998; Buller et al, 2000). For the most part, such traditional systems are found in those regions where intensification has been handicapped by structural (including physical) factors, yet where high landscape natural value is largely dependent upon the maintenance of extensive forms of grazing (Baldock and Beaufoy, 1993). Whether this emphasis is justifiable today is discussed at the end of this chapter.

The Environmentally Sensitive Area (ESA) Stage

If the 1992 Agri-Environment Regulation (2078/92) marks the start of a more integrated, albeit limited, marriage of environmental and agricultural policy, Article 19 of Regulation 797/85 marks the official beginning of a hesitant courtship. Under this Agricultural Structures Regulation, Member States were, for the first time, permitted to grant subsidies to those farmers wishing to retain traditional cultivation and husbandry practices with a view to protecting environment and landscape quality otherwise threatened by the potential intensification of agricultural activities. Without going into the details of this regulation and subsequent legislation (notably Regulation 1760/87, which permitted EU co-funding of up to 50 per cent for such subsidies), a number of observations can be made concerning both its genesis and its implementation (for further reading, see Whitby, 1996b; Potter, 1998).

Article 19 and the establishment of environmentally sensitive areas (ESAs) that followed was very much a northern European, and specifically British-led, agenda. The UK played a key role in negotiating the policy within Brussels and was indeed the first Member State to implement the policy (Baldock et al, 1990; Buller, 1998a; Hart and Wilson, 1998). Concerned both by the high costs and the inadequacies of the implementation procedures associated with their own Wildlife and Countryside Act of 1981 (Lowe et al, 1986), the British government, including the ministries of agriculture and the environment, sought to initiate a voluntary system based upon tiered payments to farmers within broad landscape areas. Drawing upon a tradition of rural custodianship and stewardship, the scheme proved a success with the agricultural community, who appreciated its voluntary nature, and the Ministry of Agriculture, which saw it as a means of countering environmentalist critics (Whitby and Lowe, 1994). Other northern European Member States, notably Germany, the Netherlands and Denmark, were also quick to take up the possibilities offered by the regulation, mindful of their increasingly vocal environmental lobbies. Italy too ultimately became a significant force in Article 19 policy implementation, though largely as a result of the blanket designation of upland and mountain regions as ESAs (Povellato, 1996).

Furthermore, early northern Europe-led agri-environmental policy, emerging at a time when many southern states were in the processes of aligning their agricultural sectors to the CAP, was often seen by these states as a potential impediment to their own agricultural modernization and intensification (Potter, 1998). As Table 6.2 shows, the application of Regulation 797/85, with the notable exception of Italy, demonstrates a strong bias in favour of the northern Member States.

However, in terms of integrating environmental and agricultural policy under a single approach, ESA policy fell a long way short of the mark. Three reasons for this may be identified. Firstly, ESA policy, both in its original conception and in its subsequent application, has tended to focus upon the

Table 6.2 *Land Designated under Article 19 of EU Regulation 797/85 (1990)*

Country	Area designated (hectares)	Area under contract (hectares)	Number of participants
Denmark	127,970	28,060	3459
France	114,620	36,620	nd
Germany	2,560,000	291,646	40,780
Greece	0	0	0
Ireland	1140	nd	nd
Italy	944,430	229,259	6038
Luxembourg	2800	610	4
The Netherlands	75,800	26,815	5013
Portugal	0	0	0
Spain	0	0	0
UK	740,930	282,351	4997
TOTAL	4,567,690	895,461	60,291

Note: nd = no data available.
Source: adapted from Potter (1998)

maintenance of existing environmentally friendly farming practices within tightly defined areas. In this, it has not only set the model for virtually all subsequent agri-environmental policy but has proved to be relatively user-friendly, particularly in those Member States or regions where there is less peer group disapproval associated with a farmer's decision not to intensify. As such, ESA policy has been criticized by the seeming lack, in many cases, of any broad-based environmental quality gain or additionality, though part of this criticism has been directed at the evaluation methodologies adopted (see, for example, Whitby, 1994). At a time of mounting public criticism over the environmental effects of modern farming, maintaining the status quo in a few, often extensively farmed, zones could not be construed as a major shift in agricultural policy evolution.

Secondly, and again anticipating criticisms later made of wider agri-environmental policy, ESAs rapidly became recognized as an additional form of income support, particularly in the more marginal agricultural regions of the EU. This was very much how Italy (Povellato, 1996) and, to a lesser extent, France (Boisson and Buller, 1996) saw the early development of the policy in the late 1980s. While the European Commission to some extent endorsed this interpretation (CEC, 1987) – and, indeed, there is no reason why environmentally friendly management should not be financially rewarding – the very absence of tangible environmental gain and the growing sense that farmers, in certain zones, were effectively being paid not to pollute merely increased the distance between ESA policy and genuine agriculture–environment policy integration.

Finally, the ESA phase in agriculture–environment policy evolution ultimately did not go far enough. It remained limited to those Member States or regions with a strong tradition of environmental stewardship and manifestly failed to address the increasingly central issues of combating agricultural pollution control and providing genuinely sustainable forms of agricultural development. The ESA phase ultimately failed to bridge the gap between, on the one hand, the long-standing European assumption that farming – and hence the maintenance of agricultural communities – was the best way to protect the rural environment and, on the other hand, the increasingly apparent need for a more holistic notion, not only of what the rural environment actually consisted of, but of what the role of European farming in that environment might be.

Regulation 2078 and the Agri-Environmental Policy Stage

The CAP reforms of 1992, driven initially by the need to reduce costs and to modify the systems of market support and later, under the influence of the General Agreement on Tariffs and Trade (GATT) negotiations, by the need to directly reduce subsidies (notably those relating to the exportation of agricultural produce), gave rise to a major shift in the objectives and the funding of agri-environmental policy. A number of economic, administrative and environmental reasons for such a shift can be identified, among them the need to:

- reduce agricultural overproduction and cut production levels within the Community and therefore promote more extensive forms of agricultural activity;
- provide new methods of subsidy to farmers as an alternative to the pre-existing price support mechanisms that were seen to encourage agricultural intensification and overproduction;
- address the issues raised by growing concern over the environmental consequences of agricultural intensification, notably with respect to water pollution, biodiversity loss and landscape change;
- comply with the Maastricht Treaty (in force from 1993 onwards), which required that EU environmental policy be integrated within all EU policies;
- comply with the fifth Environmental Action Programme (EAP) of the EU;
- produce a voluntary 'agricultural policy' response to the issue of agricultural pollution and therefore avoid the imposition of a mandatory and more regulatory agenda.

The internal debates within the EU Commission over these various considerations have been analysed, among others, by Groenendijk (1993) and, more recently, by Jones and Clark (1998). Both demonstrate that the division of competencies between the EU and the individual Member States (the partial 'renationalization' of the CAP) became a central issue during the negotiations over CAP reform, particularly with respect to the proposed agri-environmental regulation. Major differences in the strength and importance of pre-existing national agri-environmental agendas therefore made their incorporation into a broad and coherent framework that would guard against possible trade distortions all the more important.

Regulation 2078/92, which emerged as one of the three 'accompanying measures' to the CAP reforms, had two principal objectives (CEC, 1997a): to combine beneficial effects on the environment with a reduction of agricultural

Table 6.3 *Scheme Objectives Eligible for Aid under Article 2 of Regulation 2078/92*

	Fundable objective
a	• reduce substantially the use of fertilizers and/or plant protection products, or • maintain the reductions already made, or • introduce or continue with organic farming
b	• change, by means other than those referred to in (a), to more extensive forms of crop, including forage production, or • maintain extensive production methods introduced in the past, or • convert arable land into extensive grassland
c	• reduce the number of sheep and cattle per forage area
d	• use other farming practices compatible with the requirements of protection of the environment and natural resources, as well as maintenance of the countryside and landscape, or • rear animals or local breeds in danger of extinction
e	• ensure the upkeep of abandoned farmland or woodlands
f	• set aside farmland for at least 20 years with a view to using it for purposes connected with the environment, in particular for the establishment of biotope reserves of natural parks or for the protection of hydrological systems
g	• manage land for public access and leisure activities

Source: EU Council Regulation 2078/92 of 30 June 1992

production and to contribute to agricultural income diversification and rural development. Under the terms of the regulation, Member States were required to submit national agri-environmental programmes comprised of any number of national, regional or local schemes. Although states could draw up their own agri-environmental strategies, all programmes submitted to the Commission for co-funding (up to 50 per cent or 75 per cent in Objective 1 regions) had to respond to the seven basic objectives specified in the text (see Table 6.3).

Regulation 2078/92, unlike its predecessor, Regulation 797/85, was mandatory upon all Member States, though farmer adhesion to individual schemes remained voluntary. Between its launch and the first comprehensive assessment of its uptake and impact (CEC, 1997b; CEC, 1998a), all Member States had submitted and implemented national and, where appropriate, regional or sub-national agri-environmental programmes. All of these include large numbers of individual measures either independently operated or falling within broader frameworks, such as the Austrian *Ökologische Evaluierung des Umweltprogrammes* (OPUL) or Finnish General Agri-Environmental Protection Scheme (GAEPS) (Buller, 2000a; Brouwer and Lowe, 1998).

The measures and schemes adopted by the different Member States cover a far wider range of agricultural activities and strategies of agricultural development than previous attempts to reconcile agriculture and environment through voluntary mechanisms have done. Some schemes exist to encourage the adoption of environmentally beneficial productive methods: organic farming, non-organic farming with environmental improvements and the maintenance of existing low-intensity systems. Others advocate the management of non-productive farmland. Collectively, the various schemes address agricultural pollution, biodiversity loss and management, and landscape protection and management, as well as the maintenance of traditional practices.

Assessments of the impact of Regulation 2078/92 have multiplied over the last few years[1] and include the national monitoring reports produced following EU Regulation 746/96. Agri-environmental schemes concern some 17 per cent of EU farms and around 20 per cent of the total utilized agricultural area (UAA) of the EU (CEC, 1998a), though these averages reveal considerable variation in levels of take-up between individual Member States (see Table 6.4) (for an analysis of these geographical variations, see Buller, 2000a). Countries also differ with respect to the organization and targeting of agri-environmental schemes. Although most have adopted targeted or zonal measures on the ESA model (for example, the UK and Danish ESA or the French *Opérations locales*), others have employed 'wide and shallow' or horizontal schemes, which – within certain eligibility criteria – operate over the whole national or regional territory (for example, the French *Prime à l'herbe*, the Austrian OPUL programme or the *Marktentlastungs- und Kulturlandschaftsausgleich* (MEKA) programme in Baden-Württemberg in Germany). Furthermore, Member States are by no means equal in the importance they give to each of the 'objectives' laid down in the original regulation (Buller, 2000b). While Austria, Belgium and Sweden accord a large proportion of the 2078 budget to supporting organic farming, expenditure in this category in the UK is virtually non-existent and in France is minimal. Similarly, schemes aimed at reducing agricultural pollution represent a significant part of the Danish and German strategies but remain underrepresented in the UK, France, Spain and Italy. By way of contrast, the maintenance of traditional and extensive practices dominates 2078 policy in these latter states (Buller et al, 2000).

The Commission's own assessment of the environmental impact of agri-environmental policy, based upon the national monitoring reports, states that '[t]he evidence presented from the programmes is on the whole positive and shows that substantial environmental benefits accrue from agri-environmental programmes' (CEC, 1998a, p123), a viewpoint confirmed by independent research (see, for example, IEEP, 1998; Schramek et al, 1999). This chapter's interest, however, lies not so much in the impact of agri-environmental schemes (be it on the environment, farmers' incomes or upon farm development strategies), but rather on the extent to which the implementation of Regulation 2078/92 represents a significant step forward in integrating environmental policy within agricultural policy.

Certainly, the mandatory nature of Regulation 2078/92 upon Member States represents a significant step forward in policy integration. In terms of its impact, the fact that approximately 17 per cent of European farmers (far more in certain countries) are actively engaged in providing public environmental goods and are being paid to do so (in some cases, such payments amounting to as much as 20 per cent of total farm income; Schramek et al, 1999) suggests an important shift both in the nature of farm support and in farmers' awareness of their role in environmental management. Yet, it is also clear that despite unequivocal successes at the local territorial level, Regulation 2078/92 and agri-environmental policy are far from being a major driving force within the CAP as

Table 6.4 *Participants in Aid Schemes under Regulation 2078/92 (mid 1998)*

State	Total number of 2078 contracts (x 1000)	Total area under contract (x 1000 hectares)	Proportion of total utilized agricultural area under contract (per cent)
Austria	173.4	2429.0	67.8
Belgium	2.0	22.7	1.7
Denmark	8.0	107.30	3.9
Finland	77.8	1877.5	86.9
France	171.0	6901.4	22.9
Germany	*	6741.0	38.9
Greece	2.4	34.8	0.6
Italy	176.3	2291.3	13.6
Ireland	32.2	1089.6	24.1
Luxembourg	1.9	96.6	75.9
The Netherlands	6.7	34.5	1.9
Portugal	137.9	664.2	16.8
Spain	33.9	871.1	2.9
Sweden	56.6	1642.2	51.6
UK	25.4	2322.9	14.6
TOTAL	EU 14: 905.4	27,126.0	19.5

Note: * Impossible to determine with any accuracy since many farms hold multiple contracts.
Source: CEC (1998a, p21)

a whole. In terms of its implementation, agri-environmental policy has proved most effective in maintaining extensive and environmentally friendly farming systems and practices. It has proved notably less effective in bringing about any major de-intensification of agriculture in the most sensitive areas in terms of environmental pollution, either because of poor take-up rates or because schemes have not been targeted in such zones (in anticipation of poor take-up rates or because the payments necessary to attract farmers into schemes would be too costly). Furthermore, the generally poor levels of environmental impact monitoring that have accompanied scheme implementation have not, as yet, permitted a clear picture of the medium- and long-term effects of individual actions and schemes. In financial terms, agri-environmental policy during the 1993–1999 period accounted for a very minor part of total CAP expenditure. For farmers, compensatory payments and other production-related aids continue to be far superior to those gained from adopting environmentally sensitive farming practices or from providing positive environmental goods in the form of landscape quality, biodiversity, public access and so on. Some of these limitations are surely not failures of policy integration. They reflect, above all, the limitations of voluntary schemes which, to be successful, must be attractive to farmers. It comes as no surprise, therefore, that the greatest levels of take-up are recorded in those schemes or tiers of schemes where the constraints placed upon farmers are minimal.

Although the European Commission might confidently assert that 'despite the different nature of the competence, the very existence of a common agricultural policy may facilitate integration of environmental requirements all over the EU' (CEC, 1997a, p12), this integration has been difficult and partial. Nonetheless, the mere development of an EU environmental policy, irrespective of the various specific modalities of policy integration that it has induced, has undoubtedly had an effect upon contemporary agricultural policy evolution. One of the most immediate effects has been to force agricultural policy to address issues other than those linked wholly to agricultural production. A series of Commission documents published in the 1980s (CEC, 1985; 1988a; 1988b) made a point of emphasizing the role of agriculture in protecting and maintaining rural environments and natural resources.

While some might interpret this as a reluctant and essentially rear-guard attempt to seize some of the initiative, it nevertheless marks an implicit recognition of agricultural policy's failure, up to that point, to appropriately address the environmental consequences of agricultural modernization. A second impact has been to oblige the agricultural policy community to deal, and negotiate, with actors and institutions that hitherto lay beyond the immediate agricultural policy community. By opening up the agricultural policy agenda to include environmental considerations, agricultural policy becomes de facto a more pluralist domain. Within the European Commission, this has become evident in the increasing number of contacts, joint statements and collaborations between the Agriculture Directorate-General (DG VI) and the Environment Directorate-General (DG XI). Beyond the Commission, organized groups representing environmental interests have begun to demand a far greater input into the agricultural policy agenda-setting. However, as Grant (1993, p40) warns: 'one must be aware of the limits of this process. Farmers remain a well-entrenched interest in the Community, not least because of their influence on political parties in government'.

In their 1997 review of the relationship between agricultural and environmental policy, the European Commission describes the period between the creation of the CAP and the implementation of agri-environmental policy as being a passage from 'indifference to integration' (CEC, 1997a, p9). Yet, ultimately what stands out from this period, particularly from the later years, is less the establishment of a common and integrated agenda for European farming and its role in protecting and maintaining environmental quality, than the adoption of a series of measures designed largely to redress the environmental consequences of agricultural policy itself. Regulation 2078/92, for all its potency as an icon of policy integration, remains an 'accompanying measure' to a CAP reform driven essentially by concern for the costs of commodity management.

FROM ENVIRONMENTAL PROTECTION TO SUSTAINABILITY

Agricultural policy must contribute to our environment's objectives and not undermine them… Integration of environmental considerations into the CAP must never be confined to paper alone. It must be reflected in reality – in real and genuine changes in the way production and financial support is organised.
(Bjerregaard, 1999)

Emerging concerns

The 1992 EU Agri-Environmental Regulation represented, to a large degree, an extension of the approach adopted throughout the 1980s: namely, of encouraging farmers to adopt environmentally friendly practices as a means of de-intensifying their production (and hence reducing surplus costs within the CAP); of protecting the rural environment (and hence responding to critics of the CAP); and, for certain farming systems, of maintaining rural economic and social cohesion (and thereby redressing the polarizing effects of the CAP). It also marked a transition towards a somewhat different agriculture–environment agenda whose objectives ultimately stretch beyond the single agricultural policy sector. The components of that new agenda might be summarized as follows.

The persistence of wide-scale instances of agricultural pollution point to a failure both in the implementation of classic command-and-control measures, such as those designed to maintain water quality, and in the use of purely voluntary measures, such as the schemes designed to reduce entrants. The fact that many of the farmers concerned should continue to receive financial allowances, either directly or indirectly, through compensatory and other payments suggests the need to combine (under a more unitary framework) compliance to environmental rules and objectives and farm support mechanisms. Although assessments of the environmental impacts of CAP regimes under the 1992 reform show a general tendency towards reductions in livestock densities and the use of agrochemicals (Brouwer and Lowe, 1998, 2000), these are often the result of commodity price reductions rather than environmental policy integration. Investigations into the operation of Regulation 2078/92 (see, for example, Schramek et al, 1999) have similarly revealed a number of inconsistencies between the goals and mechanisms of agri-environmental policy and the more traditional forms of commodity support, such as (most typically) compensatory payments for forage maize. These inconsistencies suggest an only limited degree of genuine environmental policy integration within the CAP. Moving away from a conception of the environment as an 'accompaniment' or as an alternative form of farm support to becoming an integral part of the European agricultural policy therefore becomes a central feature of this new agenda.

A second component derives from the shifting notion of what constitutes European rural areas and the emergence of the idea of a 'European model of agriculture' (Fischler, 1998). If, as shown above, the CAP was born at a time when a productive agriculture was considered the sine qua non of an economically and socially healthy countryside, not only are the rural areas of Europe today considered less dependent solely upon an agricultural economy, but agriculture too has become multifunctional. It is seen as providing a growing combination of market and non-market goods within a broader rural framework (CEC, 1996; Buckwell, 1997). The process of environmental policy integration therefore needs to extend beyond the purely agricultural policy domain to take on board a broader and more holistic notion of sustainable rural and territorial development, within which farming is an, albeit central, element. This reflection has been at the centre of EU thinking during much of the late 1990s (for example, CEC 1995; 1999a; 1999b) and has since emerged as a key element of the Agenda 2000 measures. Nevertheless, much of the responsibility for achieving that integration has been handed to individual Member States through the rural development plans.

The recent emphasis on the greater integration of agricultural and environmental policy has also been driven by new legal and political requirements at the EU level, formulated to address what has been widely seen as failure in the broad objectives of environmental policy integration and implementation as a whole (Jordan, 1998). Following the so-called Cardiff process, named after the Cardiff European Council meeting of June 1998, the European Commission and European Council were asked to develop strategies for greater integration of environmental dimensions within sectoral policies (Cardiff European Council, 1998), an objective originally laid down in Article 6 of the Amsterdam Treaty, which came into force on 1 May 1999. For agricultural policy, the Commission's own assessment (1999b), as well its review of the fifth EAP (CEC, 1999c), identified considerable scope for further action with respect to particular farming systems (notably intensive production systems) and to the overall architecture of EU agricultural policy. Responding to the Cardiff process and to the subsequent Vienna Council meeting in December 1998, the Agriculture Council in its 'strategy' (Agriculture Council, 1999) noted, among other factors, the significance of a series of environmental directives for agriculture, the need for the CAP to 'take note of international commitments on biodiversity, climate change, the Desertification Convention, the Pan-European Biological and Landscape Diversity Strategy and the planned UN–ECE protocol against acidification and eutrophication', and the role of agriculture in the stewardship of rural landscapes, the protection of the environment and the viability of rural areas.

Undoubtedly a final element in the emerging agenda has been the development of a more refined understanding of the process of environmental policy integration. Ten years ago, ESAs were heralded as examples of a 'significant departure for agricultural policy' (Baldock et al, 1990). More recently, and using the European Environmental Agency's (EEA's) checklist for assessing the integration of environmental actions within sectoral policies (EEA, 1998, p284), which includes criteria such as whether or not 'environmentally damaging subsidies are being withdrawn' and 'external costs are internalised into market prices', the Dutch Centre for Agriculture and Environment (CLM) concludes that the rate of environmental integration in agriculture is 'very limited' (CLM, 1999, p9). This new concern for the identification of targets and for the assessment of integration performance has led to increasing focus on the elaboration of monitoring procedures and the development of suitable indicators (Brouwer and Crabtree, 1999; OECD, 1997). The evaluation of agri-environmental policy, in particular, is fraught with a number of difficulties, such as the absence of clear targets at the outset, the confusion of policy objectives and the considerable diversity of implementation strategies. Nonetheless, monitoring and assessments have undoubtedly multiplied in recent years (CEC, 1998a) even if the conclusions drawn are not always clear (Buller, 2000b). Furthermore, they are likely to multiply further as, increasingly, monitoring is forwarded as the panacea for greater integration (CEC, 1999b; 1999d; Cardiff European Council, 1998).

Coupled to monitoring and assessment is an often implicit rather than explicit recognition that it is increasingly up to Member States now, and that monitoring is a means of achieving the harmonization of Member State responses. In this final section, the future mechanisms of integration are examined and a new set of instruments as well as a new subsidiarity (associated with deployment and implementation) are noted.

Green-boxing the CAP

The various concerns identified above, coupled with traditional preoccupations – such as the continued high costs of the CAP, the problems associated with EU enlargement (including the application of CAP mechanisms to new, particularly eastern European, states) and agricultural trade liberalization – gave rise, in the closing months of the 20th century, to the eventual emergence of a new framework both for agricultural policy and for its integration with environmental policy. The Agenda 2000 proposals (CEC, 1998b), adopted in a slightly watered-down form by the European heads of government in March 1999, and the subsequent Rural Development Regulation (1257/99) have been put forward as 'the most radical and wide-ranging reform of the CAP in its history', ensuring that 'farmers are rewarded not only for what they produce but also for their general contribution to society' (DG VI, 1999, p2). Although there are different ways of categorizing the contents of the final Agenda 2000 package, it is possible to identify seven distinct features (see Table 6.5). Perhaps the single most important innovation of the Agenda 2000 package lies, however, in its overall architecture (Lowe and Ward, 1998). The CAP is hitherto composed of two 'pillars'. The first is commodity support, the traditional domain of CAP intervention. The second is the Rural Development Regulation, an attempt to bring together under one roof, on the one hand, existing agri-environmental schemes, farm structural supports, less favoured area policy and certain structural measures such as the former Objective 5b areas and, on the other hand, a series of rural development measures (the so-called Article 31 measures) which include, among others, the marketing of quality products, the improvement of rural living conditions, water resource management and environmental conservation and management. Of the measures identified in Table 6.5, three in particular address the issue of integrating environmental goals within the CAP: the agri-environmental schemes, the codes of good agricultural practice and cross-compliance. Modulation serves additionally as a potential means of channelling money away from commodity support towards environmental objectives.

Clearly, it is far too early to assess the degree to which the Agenda 2000 package will genuinely facilitate environmental policy integration, though a number of recent studies have explored its potential impact (see, for example, CLM, 1999; Lowe et al, 1999, Lowe and Brouwer, 2000). A number of points might, however, be drawn even at this early stage. To some extent, the Agenda 2000 reforms change little. The principal mechanisms for environmental policy

Table 6.5 *Measures for Integrating Environmental Objectives within Agricultural Policy under the Rural Development Regulation*

	Measure	Criteria
1	Good agricultural practice	All farmers should respect basic environmental standards, defined by Member States in Codes of Good Agricultural Practice, which include relevant legal requirements, without receiving payments for doing so
2	Optional cross-compliance	Member States have the option to introduce mandatory environmental conditions (above the basic standards) to agricultural support payments
3	Monitoring	Member States are charged with monitoring the impact of environmental measures in agriculture
4	Agri-environmental measures	As under Regulation 2078/92, Member States must draw up agri-environmental schemes under which farmers receive payments for maintaining or improving environmental quality
5	Modulation	Member States can redistribute a part of farmers' direct payments under CAP commodity regimes towards schemes designed to improve or maintain environmental quality
6	Zoning	The territorial coverage of rural development and environmental measures is extended in that certain measures that were formerly only applicable in selected areas (Objective 5b areas, for example), are now available over much wider areas
7	Programming	All Member States are required to produce seven-year rural development plans that provide the framework for rural development and agri-environmental policy

integration remain the agri-environmental measures introduced in 1992 and the improved implementation and enforcement of broad and essentially pre-existing environmental legislation, such as that relating to water and habitats. Critically, the more innovative and radical mechanisms – cross-compliance and the respect of baseline environmental standards (some of which come under existing environmental legislation) – remain optional. The European Commission initially saw these as central to the reform (CEC, 1998b). Even the Agriculture Council has recently maintained: 'integration of the environment into the CAP starts by recognising that a reference level of good agricultural practices, which is dependent on local conditions, should be respected in all agricultural areas of the EU' (Agriculture Council, 1999). Yet, the original proposals were substantially watered down during the ultimate process of interstate negotiation. Furthermore, as the European Parliament notes (1997, p22), '[m]ost Member States have not yet shown any great enthusiasm for the concept of cross-compliance'.

For those states who wish to adopt such measures, the reforms undoubtedly offer the basis for potentially substantial advances in controlling the negative environmental effects of certain contemporary agricultural practices, even though the implementation of such mechanisms may well prove delicate, as the UK agriculture ministry (MAFF) acknowledges (MAFF, 1999, p5). For others, there is no obligation and commodity-related payments may be made irrespective of whether environmental conditions are being met (see, for example, Bel et al, 1999). According to the CLM study, this is one of the 'most important weaknesses' of the reforms (CLM, 1999, p34). Again, the farming sector would appear to escape from the universal application of obligatory command-and-control environmental legislation that is applied in other sectors, such as transport and industry.

The Agenda 2000 reforms therefore maintain and, to some extent, exacerbate the different and distinct policy-making competencies of the EU and individual Member States who have characterized agricultural and environmental policy relations until now. While the reforms lay out a framework, there is, in reality, a considerable degree of freedom and discretion available to Member States with regard to implementation, as the Commission acknowledges (CEC, 1999d). Indeed, as the range of available mechanisms increases, so too might the distance between Member State responses. Already, there are substantial variations in the way national governments have addressed environmental policy integration in their draft rural development programmes (Lowe et al, 2001). The emphasis placed in some states on rural development and farm diversification in the Rural Development Regulation may ultimately mark a weakening of the specifically environmental preoccupations addressed by the original 1992 agri-environmental regulation (2078/92). Nevertheless, this can be compensated for by applying cross-compliance and the mandatory respect of baseline standards where, and if, these measures are implemented.

The extent to which Agenda 2000 represents a real 'decentralization' of the CAP has been the subject of much commentary and debate before and after its adoption. The principle of modulation has provoked the ire of farmers' representatives throughout Europe, partly because it is designed to reduce the payments allocated to the richer and more vocal farmers, partly too because it is seen as penalizing successful farm enterprise. For environmental policy integration, there is a balance to be achieved between, on the one hand, the mandatory and universal respect of EU-wide environmental legislation – which would provide, according to the Commission, 'tangible evidence of a commitment to integration' (CEC, 1999d, p10) and which would require a considerable strengthening of the monitoring and enforcement capacity and functions of the relevant authorities – and, on the other hand, national, sub-national or local voluntary policy mechanisms that are capable of responding to local concerns and local agricultural and territorial conditions.

As a mechanism for environmental policy integration, therefore, the Agenda 2000 reforms herald few, if any, major advances. The CAP remains the principal delivery mechanism for environmental actions within the agricultural domain, while EU environmental legislation remains characterized by seemingly poor levels of implementation. The budget for rural development and agri-environmental action remains largely unchanged, at least in the short term, with the bulk of CAP expenditure going to commodity support. The emphasis placed upon environmental monitoring and policy assessment marks a tangible concern that has emerged throughout the 1990s. It also represents a necessary response to the growing freedom of Member States in selecting policy instruments.

CONCLUSIONS

The integration of environmental concerns within the CAP has been shown a lengthy and complicated process that is far from being fully achieved. Indeed, for some commentators, including members of the European Commission, the Agenda 2000 reforms mark, to some extent, a step backwards both from what was originally anticipated at the crucial Cork Conference in 1996 and from what was originally proposed in the early Agenda 2000 documents. Three concerns remain:

1   The implementation and respect of EU environmental legislation within the agricultural sector.
2   The optional nature of cross-compliance and base-line environmental standards.
3   The relationship of commodity support mechanisms to rural development and environmental protection measures.

All three relate to the current and future operation of the CAP. Yet, the integration of environmental considerations within the agricultural policy sector can also take place outside of the structure and workings of the CAP. The introduction of eco-taxes, independent national or sub-national measures and the growth of private market initiatives are but three examples. The first of these has, for the moment, only a limited application within Europe (for example, nitrate and/or pesticide taxes in Denmark and Sweden). The recent proposal by the minister of the environment to introduce a similar measure in France (the *taxe générale sur les activités polluantes* or TGAP) initially led to the sacking of her Paris office by angry farmers in January 1999. However, for the minister, such a tax constitutes a necessary step forward, not only in the application of the polluter pays principle but also in making sustainable activities more economically attractive (Voynet, 1999). More readily accepted by the French agricultural community have been the plethora of independent measures, such as Fertimieux, Pyto-mieux and the Forum de l'Agriculture Raisonnée Respectueuse de l'Environnement (FARRE) (Sebillotte, 1999; Bel et al; 1999), which operate outside the CAP itself yet seek voluntary reductions in the use of inorganic fertilizers and other potentially environmentally damaging inputs. One of the notable advantages of such measures is that they address environmental issues in areas of intensive cereal production, something that agri-environmental schemes have notably failed to achieve (Buller and Brives, 2000; Buller, 2000b). Finally, the development of private market initiatives, often responding to consumer demands and driven by the retail sector and, in particular, by the larger supermarket chains and/or specialist networks (such as those associated with organic farming), is rapidly becoming a significant force in de facto agriculture–environment integration, albeit operating largely outside of the individual agricultural and environmental policy communities (Anderson and Primdahl, 2000; van de Grijp and den Hond, 1999).

Ultimately, however, policy integration needs to take place at a series of different levels in order to be effective – from that of policy formulation at the European level and policy implementation at the national and sub-national level, down to the actions and attitudes of farmers and farming communities. While research on farmer responses to agri-environmental schemes has been mitigated in terms of revealing any comprehensive shift towards genuine and long-term environmental commitment (Schramek et al, 1999; Wilson, 1996; Lobley and Potter, 1998; Buller, 1999b; Pech and Ruas, 1999; Billaud et al, 1996), this is arguably due to the dominant orientation of the general operating framework, the CAP (as well as the institutions and actors associated with it and the economic and scientific values they advocate), within which such schemes are propagated. Nevertheless, these studies are virtually unanimous in their identification of an increasing readiness on the part of farmers to adapt their practices to environmental prerogatives, both in recognition of the possible financial advantages to be gained from doing so (and the financial penalties or costs to be avoided) and in response to growing consumer and indeed social demand for greater environmental responsibility. Although one might claim that the implementation of agri-environmental policy under Regulation 2078/92 has largely focused upon maintaining existing environmentally friendly practices, rather than de-intensifying potentially damaging agricultural activities (IEEP, 1998, Schramek et al, 1999; Buller et al, 2000), this nonetheless represents a legitimate recognition for the farmers whose economic activities have long been included within the epithets of marginality, structural disadvantage and poor economic returns.

One undeniable trend in the evolution of agricultural and environmental policy integration has been the gradual movement of the policy-making and policy implementation focus away from Brussels and the instances of the EU towards the Member States and their own sub-national administrative and governing structures. This should not be seen wholly as an active process of EU policy renationalization (or decentralization). As shown in this chapter, European agricultural policy did not, until comparatively recently, possess an environmental dimension. Rather, this represents the emergence of new EU-defined competencies and choices at the national and sub-national level, operating within a broad juridical, regulatory and financial policy framework of the EU. In part, this trend has been in response to financial and administrative concerns within the Commission (Jones and Clark, 1998). Yet, it also recognizes the fact that the relationship between agricultural activities and environmental protection is fundamentally conditioned by multifarious cultural and territorial influences that operate at the national and sub-national scale. Environmental policy implementation, if it is to be effective, must occur here and in a way that not only ensures comparable environmental standards but also maintains agri-environmental diversity.

REFERENCES

Agriculture Council (1999) *Strategy on Environmental Integration and Sustainable Development in the Common Agricultural Policy*, Agricultural Council, Brussels

Anderson, E and Primdahl, J (2000) 'Denmark' in H Buller, G Wilson and A Holl (eds) *Agri-Environmental Policy in Europe*, Ashgate, Basingstoke, pp31–50

Baldock, D and Beaufoy, G (1993) *Nature Conservation and New Directions in the EC Common Agricultural Policy*, Institute for European Environmental Policy, London

Baldock, D and Lowe, P (1996) 'The Development of European Agri-Environmental policy' in M Whitby (ed) *The European Environment and CAP Reform*, CAB International, Wallingford, pp8–25

Baldock D, Cox, G, Lowe, P and Winter, M (1990) 'Environmentally Sensitive Areas: Incrementalism or Reform', *Journal of Rural Studies*, vol 6, no 2, pp143–162

Bel, F, Lacroix, A, Mollard, A and Regairaz, E (1999) 'Reduire la pollution azotée: les choix préalables d'une politique publique' in *Courrier de l'Environnement de l'INRA*, vol 36, pp5–24

Billaud, J-P, Bruckmeier, K, Patricio, T, Pinton, F, Riegert, C and Valadas de Lima, A (1996) *Sociological Enquiry into the Conditions Required for the Success of the Supporting Environmental Measures within the Reform of the CAP: Final Report*, Report to the DG XII of the European Commission (EV5V-CT94-0372)

Bjerregaard, R (1999) quoted in European Commission, Press Release IP/99/48 of 27 January

Bodiguel, M and Buller, H (eds) (1997) *La qualité des eaux dans l'Union Européenne*, L'Harmattan, Paris

Body, R (1983) *Agriculture: the Triumph and the Shame*, Temple Smith, London

Boisson, J-M and Buller, H (1996) 'Agri-Environmental Policy in France', in M Whitby (ed) *The European Environment and CAP Reform*, CAB International, Wallingford, pp105–130

Brouwer, F and Crabtree, B (eds) (1999) *Environmental Indicators and Agricultural Policy*, CABI International, Wallingford, the Netherlands

Brouwer, F and Lowe, P (eds) (1998) *CAP and the Rural Environment in Transition*, Wageningen University Press, Wageningen

Brouwer, F and Lowe, P (1998) 'CAP Reform and the Environment' in F Brouwer and P Lowe (eds) *CAP and the Rural Environment in Transition*, Wageningen University Press, Wageningen, pp13–38

Brouwer, F and Lowe, P (2000) *CAP Regimes and the European Countryside*, CABI International, Wallingford

Brouwer, F and van Berkum, S (1997) *CAP and Environment in the European Union: Analysis of the Effects of the CAP on the Environment and Assessment of Existing Environmental Conditions in Policy*, Wageningen Pers, Wageningen

Buckwell, A (1997) *Towards a Common Agricultural and Rural Policy for Europe*, Office for Official Publications of the European Communities, Luxembourg

Buller, H (1992) 'Agricultural Change and the Environment in Western Europe' in K Hoggart (ed) *Agricultural Change, Environment and Economy*, Mansell, London, pp68–88

Buller, H (1999a) 'Les mesures agri-environnementales en Grande Bretagne: enjeu national, politique communautaire', *Economie Rurale*, no 248, pp55–61

Buller, H (1999b) 'Evaluating Participation in Agri-Environmental Schemes' in J Schramek, D Biehl, H Buller and G Wilson (eds) *The Implementation and Effectiveness of Agri-Environmental Policy after Regulation 2078/92*, Final Consolidated Report to

DG VI of the European Commission, Contract FAIR CT95 274, DGVI (Agriculture) of the Commission of European Communities, Brussels, pp99–120

Buller, H (2000a) 'Regulation 2078: Patterns of Implementation' in H Buller, G Wilson and A Holl (eds) *Agri-Environmental Policy in Europe*, Ashgate, Basingstoke

Buller, H (2000b) 'The Agri-Environmental Measures' in F Brouwer and P Lowe (eds) *CAP Regimes and the European Countryside*, CABI International, Wallingford, pp195–215

Buller, H and Brives, H (2000) 'From Rural Production to Rural Product: Agri-Environmental Measures in France' in H Buller, G Wilson and A Holl (eds) *Agri-Environmental Policy in Europe*, Ashgate, London, pp9–30

Buller, H, Wilson, G and Holl, A (eds) (2000) *Agri-Environmental Policy in Europe*, Ashgate, Basingstoke

Cardiff European Council (1998) *Presidency Conclusions*, SN 150/98, European Council, Brussels

Commission of the European Communities (CEC) (1985) *Perspectives for the Common Agricultural Policy*, CEC, Brussels

CEC (1987) *Agriculture and the Environment: Management Agreements in Four Countries of the EC*, CEC, Brussels

CEC (1988a) *Environment and Agriculture*, COM (88) 338, Office for Official Publication of the European Community, Luxembourg

CEC (1988b) *The Future of Rural Society*, COM (88) 371, Report of the Commission to the Parliament, Brussels

CEC (1991) *The Development and Future of the CAP*, COM (91) 100, Report of the Commission, Brussels

CEC (1995) *Agricultural Strategy Paper*, COM (95) 607, CEC, Brussels

CEC (1996) *European Conference on Rural Development: Rural Europe*, CEC, Cork

CEC (1997a) *Agriculture and the Environment*, CAP Working Notes, Office for the Official Publications of the European Communities, Luxembourg

CEC (1997b) *Report from the Commission to the Council and the Parliament on the Application of Regulation 2078/92*, COM (97) 620, Brussels

CEC (1998a) *Evaluation of Agri-Environment Programmes*, DG VI Working Document 7655/98, Brussels

CEC (1998b) *Agenda 2000: Commission Proposals*, COM (98) 158 Final, Brussels

CEC (1999a) *Agriculture, Environment, Rural Development*, DG VI Working Document, Brussels

CEC (1999b) *Directions Towards Sustainable Agriculture*, Communication from the Commission to the Council, COM (99) 22 Final, CEC, Brussels

CEC (1999c) *Europe's Environment: What Directions for the Future?* Communication from the Commission, COM (99) 543 Final, CEC, Brussels

CEC (1999d) *From Cardiff to Helsinki and Beyond: Report to the European Council on Integrating Environmental Concerns and Sustainable Development into Community Policies*, SES (99) 1941 Final, CEC, Brussels

CLM (1999) *EU Agricultural Policy after 2000: Has the Environment Been Integrated?* Report to the European Environmental Bureau, CLM, Utrecht

DG VI (1999) *The CAP Reform – A Policy for the Future*, Factsheet, Direction General of Agriculture, CEC, Brussels

European Parliament (1997) *Environment and Agriculture*, Briefing No 1, PE 167.298, the European Parliament, Strasbourg

European Environmental Agency (EEA) (1998) *Europe's Environment: The Second Assessment*, Elsevier, Oxford, and Office for Official Publications of the European Communities, Luxembourg

Fischler, F (1998) *A Strong Agriculture in a Strong Europe: the European Model*, Speech of the European Commissioner for Agriculture to the European Agriculture Congress, 1 October, Ljubljana, Slovenia

Grant, W (1991) *The Dairy Industry: an International Comparison*, Dartmouth, Aldershot

Grant, W (1993) 'Pressure Groups and the European Community: an Overview' in S Mazey and J Richardson (eds) *Lobbying in the European Community*, Oxford University Press, Oxford, pp27–46

Groenendijk, J G (1993) 'A New Direction for the CAPO? Decision-Making on CAP Reform between the Rationalities of Technical Potential and Politics' in E Bolsius, G Clark and J G Groeninindjk (eds) *The Retreat; Rural Land-Use and European Agriculture*, Netherlands Geographical Studies, no 172, the Netherlands, pp52–65

Hart, K and Wilson, G A (1998) 'UK Implementation of Agri-Environment Regulation 2078/92/EEC: Enthusiastic Supporter or Reluctant Participant?', *Landscape Research*, vol 23, pp255–272

Hervieu, B (1998) *Les Agriculteurs*, Presses Universitaires de France, Paris

Institute for European Environmental Policy (IEEP) (1998) *Assessment of the Environmental Impact of Certain Agri-Environmental Measures*, IEEP, London

Jones, A and Clark, J (1998) 'The Agri-Environment Regulation EU 2078/92: the Role of the European Commission in Policy Shaping and Setting', *Environment and Planning C*, no 16, pp51–68

Jordan, A (1998) 'The Implementation of EU Environmental Policy: a Policy Problem without a Political Solution?', *Environment and Planning C*, no 17, pp69–90

Lobley, M and Potter, C (1998) 'Environmental Stewardship in UK Agriculture: a Comparison of the Environmentally Sensitive Area Programme and the Countryside Stewardship Scheme in South East England', *Geoforum*, vol 29, no 4, pp413–432

Lowe, P (1992) 'Industrial Agriculture and Environmental Regulation', *Sociologia Ruralis*, vol 32, no 1, pp1–188

Lowe, P, Buller, H, and Ward, N (2001) *Setting the Next Agenda? British and French Approaches to the Second Pillar of the Common Agricultural Policy*, CRE Working Paper 53, Centre for Rural Economy, University of Newcastle, Newcastle upon Tyne

Lowe, P and Brouwer, F (2000) 'Agenda 2000, a Wasted Opportunity?' in F Brouwer and P Lowe (eds) *CAP Regimes and the European Countryside*, CABI, Wallingford, pp321–334

Lowe, P, Cox, G, MacEwen, M, O'Riordan, T and Winter, M (1986) *Countryside Conflicts*, Gower, Aldershot

Lowe, P, Clark, J, Seymour, S and Ward, N (1997) *Moralizing the Environment: Countryside Change, Farming and Pollution*, University College London Press, London

Lowe, P, Falconer, K, Hodge, I, Moxey, A, Ward, N and Whitby, M (1999) *Integrating the Environment into CAP Reform*, Final Report to the Countryside Commission et al, Centre for Rural Economy, Newcastle-upon-Tyne

Lowe, P and Ward, N (1998) *A 'Second Pillar' for the CAP ? The European Rural Development Regulation and Its Implications for the UK*, CRE Working Paper No 36, Centre for Rural Economy, University of Newcastle, Newcastle-upon-Tyne

Ministry of Agriculture, Fisheries and Food (MAFF) (1999) *A New Direction for Agriculture*, MAFF, London

MacEwen, A and MacEwen, M (1982) *National Parks: Conservations or Cosmetics?*, Allen and Unwin, London

Organisation for Economic Co-operation and Development (OECD) (1997) *Environmental Indicators for Agriculture*, OECD, Paris

Pech, M and Ruas, J-F (1999) 'Agri-Environnement: le Comportement des Agriculteurs', *Courrier de l'Environnement de l'INRA*, no 36, pp77–80

Potter, C (1998) *Against the Grain*, CAB International, Wallingford

Povellato, A (1996) 'Italy' in M Whitby (ed) *The European Environment and CAP Reform*, CAB International, Wallingford, pp131–154

Schramek, J, Beihl, D, Buller, H and Wilson, G (eds) (1999) *The Implementation and Effectiveness of Agri-Environmental Policy after Regulation 2078/92*, Final Consolidated Report to DG VI (Agriculture) of the European Commission, Contract FAIR CT95 274, Brussels

Sebillote, M (1999) 'Agriculture et risques de pollution diffuse par les produits phtyosanitaires', *Courrier de l'Environnement de l'INRA*, no 37, pp11–22

Scott, Lord Justice (1942) *Report of the Committee on Land Utilisation in Rural Areas*, Cmnd 6378, Her Majesty's Stationery Office, London

Stanners, D and Bourdeau, P (1995) *Europe's Environment: The Dobris Assessment*, European Environmental Agency, Copenhagen

Van der Gijp, N and den Hond, D (1999) *Green Supply Chain Initiatives in the European Food and Retailing Industry*, Vrije Universiteit, Amsterdam

Whitby, M (1994) 'What Future for ESAs?' in M Whitby (ed) *Incentives for Countryside Management: the Case of Environmentally Sensitive Areas*, CAB International, Wallingford, pp253–280

Whitby, M and Lowe, P (1994) 'The Political and Economic Roots of Environmental Policy in Agriculture' in M Whitby (ed) *Incentives for Countryside Management: the Case of Environmentally Sensitive Areas,* CAB International, Wallingford, pp1–24

Whitby, M (1996a) 'The Prospects for Agri-Environmental Policy within a Reformed CAP' in M Whitby (ed) *The European Environment and CAP Reform*, CAB International, Wallingford, pp227–240

Whitby, M (ed) (1996b) *The European Environment and CAP Reform*, CAB International, Wallingford.

Wilson, G A (1996) 'Farmer Environmental Attitudes and ESA Participation', *Geoforum*, vol 27, no 2, pp115–131

NOTE

1   IEEP, 1998; Buller et al, 2000; Schramek et al, 1999; CEC, 1997b, 1998a; see also Annex 2 of CEC, 1998a, which provides a list of EU commissioned research on agri-environmental policy.

7

Why Does Environmental Policy Integration Fail? The Case of Environmental Taxation for Heavy Goods Vehicles

Christian Hey

INTRODUCTION

Environmental policy integration (EPI) within other sectors is part and parcel of an efficient and preventive environmental policy approach. It addresses environmental damage caused by sector decision-making. Environmental policy integration is seldom well defined (Jahns-Böhm and Breyer, 1991 and 1992; Rengeling, 1993). In this context it will be defined as early coordination between sector and environmental objectives, in order to find synergies between the two or to set priorities for the environment, where necessary (cf Task Force, 1993; OECD, 1996). Environmental policy integration therefore requires environmental objectives and quantifiable targets, effective coordination mechanisms and policy instruments that 'green' public (infrastructure) expenditure and sector market orders (EURES, 1996; Hey and Röder, 1998).

The importance of EPI has already been acknowledged in the early environmental programmes of the 1970s. Nevertheless, the idea was only revitalized after the paradigmatic environmental policy shift towards sustainable development emerged during the late 1980s (cf Weale, 1992; OECD, 1992). The European Commission has made considerable efforts on this principle since the fifth Environmental Action Programme (EAP) (see Chapter 1 in this book). However, most activities that are declared to represent environmental policy integration are mainly additive and purely technical (see, for example, European Commission, 1997). So far, the fundamental sector policy objectives and dynamics have rarely been challenged by environmental policy.

This chapter analyses the institutional and political reasons for this failure. The insights are based upon a comparative research project on environmental policy integration in six European countries and the EU (EURES, 1996; Hey, 1998). Here, the case study on the history of cost internalization for the freight transport sector is presented.

A THEORETICAL FRAMEWORK TO ANALYSE EPI

EPI is a relatively new field for policy analysis. Little literature is available that tries to understand the institutional and political conditions for integration processes (cf Lenschow, 1997; Müller, 1986; Hey, 1998). Environmental economists who focus on the right choice and efficient mix of policy instruments dominate the field. EPI is considered to be synonymous with the application of economic instruments to other sectors. Fiscal instruments, such as an ecological tax reform or a critical review of subsidies, environmental cost–benefit analysis, environmental indicators or tradeable permits are frequently discussed as potential instruments (cf OECD, 1996). However, economists largely fail to explain why policy-makers have not implemented their recommendations. There is much advice, especially in the transport area, but little actual change.

In contrast to the economists' perspective, this analysis is inspired by actor-centred institutionalism (Mayntz and Scharpf, 1995). In short, actor-centred institutionalism assumes that political institutions (as a set of rules and principles) influence both the preferences of actors and the outcome of the political process without fully determining them. This approach has been developed to assess successful sector regulation and needs to be modified for cross-sectoral coordination between environmental and other policies.

On the basis of empirical work and theoretical analysis (see, for example, Prittwitz, 1990; Weidner, 1996; Jänicke, 1996) two institutional characteristics seem to be essential for successful environmental policy integration: a certain regulatory capacity of public authorities and at least a balance of power and resources between environmental and sector stakeholders and authorities in the sector decision-making process. Influence depends upon the capacity to mobilize and to form broad coalitions, the access of those coalitions to the policy-making system of the sector and its responsiveness. Regulatory capacity depends upon the resources available to achieve change in the sector. The degree of centralization, finances, legal competencies, legitimization, support by the sector target groups and information on the sector influence regulatory capacity. The problem starts when just one of the two conditions is met. In many cases, there is a trade-off between these two variables. Open and responsive political institutions often lack regulatory capacity and vice versa. The consequences can be illustrated by Figure 7.1.

If the sector regulatory capacity is strong but the influence of environmental stakeholders is weak, a sector growth strategy may be the outcome that ignores environmental objectives and hence has negative impacts on the environment (the right of Figure 7.1). If the opposite is the case – weak regulatory capacity and strong environmental stakeholders – some kind of symbolic policy might be

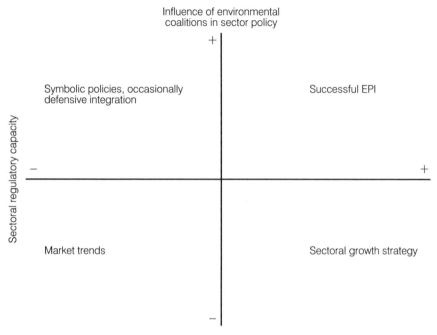

Source: Hey (1998)

Figure 7.1 *Theoretical Framework to Analyse EPI*

the output. Statements on principles, far-reaching objectives or action plans accommodate environmental demands, but implementation will be weak due to a lack of regulatory resources. Sometimes environmental stakeholders are sufficiently strong to block damaging plans. This might be the case if infrastructure measures have to be postponed due to financial constraints and public pressure. If both, the 'regulatory state' and environmental stakeholders are weak (the left of Figure 7.1), trends within historically grown market orders will prevail. Those market orders often combine elements of market and government failure (Button, 1992). The resulting trends are neither economically efficient nor environmentally benign.

This general typology will serve as a background for the case study presented here. The general argument developed in the following sections is that the institutional system of European taxation policy is characterized by opposite opportunity structures in the agenda-setting and the decision-making phases. The influence of environmental coalitions can be observed in the agenda-setting phase, but they are widely excluded from decision-making. The result is that the two political streams – the more intellectual, foresighted discourse on the need to correct market failure in the transport sector and the more short-sighted, decision-making processes, defending vested interests – do not come together. Agenda-setting and decision-making tend to be decoupled from each other. Cost internalization remains a symbolic policy in the classic sense (Edelman, 1976).

THE INSTITUTIONAL OPPORTUNITY STRUCTURE FOR GREEN TAXATION IN THE EU

A special characteristic of the institutional system of European taxation policies is the nearly opposite opportunity structure of environmental policy integration in the agenda-setting and the decision-making phases. The agenda-setting arena is supra-national, strategic and frequently responsive to environmental arguments – decision-making is sectoral and conservative.

Responsive Agenda-Setting

The EU often has been characterized as an agenda-setting paradise (Peters, 1994). Political innovation may have many sources. They may come from Member States, from the Commission, the European Parliament, from epistemic communities or from international organizations. Due to this variety of potential sources of legitimate policy ideas, the agenda-setting phase is not strongly determined (Petersen, 1995).

There is one key player in the agenda-setting process – the European Commission. The Commission is not a traditional administration with basic executive functions. Its central roles are to initiate policies and take over legislative functions. One of the formal privileges of the Commission is its monopoly to initiate policies (Ludlow, 1991). This singular role of the Commission is both an opportunity and a constraint for EPI.

Not least due to its relative autonomy from party politics (Arp, 1995), the Commission has a *technocratic identity* (Jachtenfuchs, 1996) oriented towards producing more economic efficiency and welfare (Scharpf, 1996). Hence, it is responsive to sound economic reasoning but reluctant to go for conflict-intensive proposals with redistributive effects. Also, the Commission is structurally dependent upon external expert input (Wallace, 1996), which may give environmental epistemic communities access that would be foreclosed in a less technocratic context.

The EU multilevel structure produces dynamics that can create progressive policy results. In order to be effective, the Commission has to analyse and to consider the different positions of the Member States. This does not necessarily imply the adoption of a minimalist proposal. On the contrary, national interest constellations in new policy areas may be so diffuse and complex that they leave some scope to find *winning coalitions* (Tsebelis 1994; cf Jachtenfuchs, 1996) by introducing innovative proposals.

Also in this context, the informal ways of agenda-setting for Member States are important. Countries tend to safeguard or even export their domestic policies to the international level, either to avoid disadvantages or to promote new markets for their national industries. The Commission is the first place that Member States lobby. There is a 'first mover' advantage for the country, which can convince the Commission to initiate a policy on the basis of its own model. Héritier et al (1994) identify such *regulatory competition* as a special feature of European environmental policies.

Because of the different mechanisms that may be at work (technocracy, competition, coalition-building), the Commission can be generally characterized as a 'marketplace' for innovative approaches. Because of the heterogeneity of 15 national backgrounds, the arguments and ideas represent a broad spectrum of opinions and positions (Mazey and Richardson, 1993, p22). There are always a number of legitimate alternatives from Member States. Writing before the last enlargement, Peters observed (1994, p19):

> *The presence of twelve different systemic agendas in the twelve different member countries presents policy entrepreneurs within the EC itself with the opportunity to select issues that have already been legitimated in one or more national contexts.*

However, the Commission also suffers from constraints:

- The low level of control over the decision-making process and, hence, the limited control over the outcome of its proposals cause the Commission to anticipate decision-making constraints and to be rather cautious.
- As the 'watchdog of the Treaty' (Ludlow, 1991, p121), the Commission has to take care that all proposals are compatible with the internal market programme, which may limit the adoption of market regulations in the context of environmental policy.

Generally, the agenda-setting phase will not necessarily create environmentally friendly proposals; but it offers opportunities, if some conditions are given, especially if environmental arguments find strong support on the basis of economic efficiency considerations or if there is strong pressure from national levels. Environmental taxation therefore was an attractive instrument for the Commission. It addresses market failures and hence inefficiencies of the transport systems. It is compatible with the internal market objective and may serve economic and environmental objectives at the same time. In short, its potential to increase overall efficiency seemed to make it worthwhile to test the instrument despite institutional hurdles to implement it (see proceeding section).

Conservative and Sectoral Decision-Making in the Field of Taxation

Taxation policy is generally framed by unanimity voting in the Council of Ministers and the exclusion of the European Parliament. This has changed partially with the Amsterdam Treaty, which entered into force in April 1999. The case studied here falls into a period of change of the decision-making regime, which came too late to affect the process.

The unanimity rule
The unanimity rule gives a veto power to all governments, regardless of their size (and weighed votes in the council). This, it has been argued, has two main effects: status quo-oriented decision-making resulting in, at most, incremental change;

and high barriers to decide redistributive measures. According to Scharpf (1985) the EU multilevel structures produce 'joint policy-making traps', strengthening the position of 'status quo-oriented' parties, which can defend their interests effectively by a veto. Redistributive policies are particularly prone to being 'trapped' since they produce clearly visible costs for some actors with veto power. In regulatory policy, unanimity voting is perceived as leading to incrementalism (Scharpf, 1991, p60; Jarras and Neumann, 1994, p81ff). The dilemma for taxation policy lies in its frequently redistributive nature, implying a high level of conflict and a probable blockade by the financial losers of such policy.

This criticism of the unanimity rule, however, may be qualified by the argument that veto powers also protect minorities with environmental preferences that are supported by the status quo (cf Holzinger, 1994; Pellegrom, 1997). The concerns of transit countries such as Austria, which have a special interest in greening traffic taxation, may therefore be better respected (but see Chapter 8). Furthermore, unanimity creates pressures to find efficient welfare-increasing solutions that either do not create losers or compensate them (Scharpf 1996). In the transit example above, this may lead to derogations for Austria rather than to generally greening transport taxation in the EU.

A number of scholars of EU policy-making argue that, in comparison to international regimes, the EU has developed a number of institutional incentives and informal rules which help to ease cooperation even under the constraints of the unanimity rule (see Liefferink, 1995; Liefferink et al, 1993; Gehring, 1994; Héritier, 1995; Arp, 1995). The initiation and process power of the Commission helps to overcome the first mover dilemma[1] and eases cooperation, since the Commission has a vital interest to find a consensus on its proposals (Gehring, 1994, p229). Compared to an international regime, the decision-making rules and procedures must not be negotiated separately, but they have been defined and modified during the different phases of institution-building and reforms of the EU (ibid, p213). Furthermore, package deals and issue linkages may offer opportunities to move beyond the Pareto frontier, making the EU 'a unique forum for international co-operation' (Liefferink et al, 1993, p3).

Yet, good conditions for cooperation do not amount to sufficient capacities for EPI. If certain interests are not represented, than even cooperation-easing institutions may create externalities on the non-respected interests. Marginalized and diffuse interests may not be helped by the informal mechanisms to overcome the hurdles of the unanimity requirement. This is exactly what happened in the case of taxation policies. There is little or no participation of the Environment Council or any other environmentally oriented player (such as, potentially, the European Parliament) in decision-making. Also at national level, environmental authorities are not systematically involved in preparing national negotiation positions on transport taxation (EURES, 1996). The decision-making process remains sectoral and exclusive, forcing only the sector players to formulate a mutually acceptable policy package.

In sum, while the unanimity voting rule may reduce the sectoral regulatory capacity less than expected, it does not produce a framework capable of forming coalitions in support of policy reform. In addition, the informal mechanisms to overcome the hurdles of the unanimity rule tend to limit the participation of environmental interests. As a result, the confirmation of market trends is more likely than EPI. For the full picture, one of the excluded players in the sectoral taxation decision-making process merits further analysis: the European Parliament (EP).

The exclusion of the European Parliament

Decision-making on tax issues (old Article 99) and on transport issues before 1999 (old Article 175) did not require more than the consultation of the EP. Hence, the parliament was excluded from transport taxation decision-making. This has changed slightly since the Amsterdam Treaty came into force in 1999. Now the cooperation procedure applies to transport policy issues (but not to taxation).

The EP is a potentially progressive force in EPI. There are two major arguments: its 'integrationist' identity and minority friendly procedures and culture. The EP is often characterized as 'integrationist' (Tsebelis, 1994). It favours political solutions that require a stronger European role and hence solutions, which require a stronger participation of the parliament itself. To the extent that EPI requires stronger supranational solutions, the EP is likely to be supportive. The parliament is often characterized as a player in the EU which takes environmentally friendly positions (Holzinger, 1994, p111; Arp, 1995, p336; Eichener, 1996, p273). There are several reasons why this is not merely accidental:

- Since the EP is elected directly, minorities are much better represented in the European Parliament than in the Council of Ministers (Holzinger, 1994). Even though environmentalists will still be a minority compared to the older social movements (Hey and Brendle, 1994), their interests have a better chance for articulation through direct legitimization, rather than through indirect legitimization (Hey, 1994, p55). Furthermore, due to different electoral systems and voting behaviours, the presence of green parties in the EP is higher than in most national parliaments.
- In the EP there is no stable ruling majority; neither the Social Democrats nor the Christian Democrats can build stable majoritarian alliances – even if they regularly coordinate their activities – but they depend upon smaller parties (Arp, 1992; Boyce, 1995, p148). This constellation transfers considerable influence to smaller parties such as the Greens and it furthers a consensual culture.
- The minority friendly structure is reflected in the system of committee reports, which have a strong impact on parliament decisions (Arp, 1992). Frequently, members of the European Parliament (MEPs), sympathizing with environmental arguments, have the opportunity to become rapporteurs for certain issues (Arp, 1992, p36ff).[2]

All of these arguments suggest that the exclusion of the EP from decision-making in the field of taxation is detrimental to environmental interests. It would be wrong, however, to expect the co-decision procedures to ensure EPI. The negotiating position of the EP depends upon many contingencies and is not uniformly pro-environmental.

Contradictory Opportunity Structure and Decoupled Policy Cycles

In conclusion, the contrasting opportunity structures in the agenda-setting and the decision-making cycles point to a decoupled treatment of key issues in both arenas. Taxation policy oscillates between an open responsive agenda-setting arena and a sectoral decision-making phase with limited regulatory capacity. Depending upon the use of the Commission's initiation monopoly and the position taken by the EP, green taxation policies are likely to reflect either symbolic policy or the market trend. The following case study offers empirical evidence for this argument.

FREIGHT TRANSPORT TAXATION AND THE ENVIRONMENT

Freight transport taxation plays a key role both for completing the internal market for freight transport and for the environment. Different levels of national taxation may distort competition, especially if national taxes hit national freight companies' harder then foreign competitors (the case of vehicle taxation). Some Member States therefore insisted on the harmonization of taxation prior to freight transport liberalization. Freight transport liberalization by itself will lead to transport cost reduction and hence to higher transport demand. Due to the higher levels of intra-Community trade as a result of the internal market programme, international freight transport was growing faster than gross domestic product (GDP) during the late 1980s and 1990s (see Chapter 8). The transport sector meanwhile has been identified as the fastest growing source of carbon dioxide (CO_2) emissions in Europe.

Several studies (see proceeding section) show that technical measures alone will not be sufficient to mitigate pollution from freight transport growth. Green taxation can be used potentially to mitigate transport growth, to create incentives in favour of environmentally friendlier transport modes or to reduce the specific emissions of the road transport sector. It may also offset the environmentally negative side effects of transport market liberalization. Green taxation or the internalization of external costs is therefore one essential instrument for EPI in the transport sector.

The following case study shows how cost internalization appeared on the EU agenda, how it was conceptualized by the Commission and how the Commission tried to keep it on the agenda despite several failures to find support in the Transport Council. The case reveals how the negative opportunity structure in the decision-making phase initiates learning processes within the Commission without letting the Commission drop its idea completely. Despite such learning processes, green taxation is still a rather symbolic activity, widely decoupled from decision-making. Here, two policy cycles will be analysed:

1   The two agenda-setting cycles between 1989–1996 and 1998–2002, which attempted to get the idea of cost internalization accepted for freight transport;

2   The two decision-making cycles on freight transport taxation between 1987–1993 and 1997–1999, which excluded the issue from the agenda.

The analysis is not presented in chronological order but treats the agenda-setting cycles and the decision-making cycles as parallel, interdependent but separate political streams (cf Huber, 1997). This non-chronological presentation underlines the argument that the policy cycles analysed here are widely decoupled and are not sequential due to the specific political opportunity structure in the EU.

THE AGENDA-SETTING CYCLES

The following analysis shows that open and pluralistic policy networks played a crucial role in taking the environmental dimension on board during the two agenda-setting cycles. It also shows the critical role of the Commission as doorkeeper, pushing and selecting certain policy options and rejecting others.

Pluralistic Policy Networks in Environmental Taxation for Transport

During the 1990s, a pluralistic actors' network working on environmental taxation emerged at EU level. Next to the traditional players, such as the road lobby, the vehicle manufacturers and industry federations, railways and environmental organizations emerged as important players (cf Hey, 1998 and 2000). As a consequence of the liberalization of the railway sector, railways ceased to be state bureaucracies and gradually developed an independent lobbying capacity. Environmental organizations had founded a specialized federation in 1990, Transport & Environment (T&E), working on transport issues. The early focus of this organization was on a campaign for 'Getting the Prices Right' (Kageson, 1993).

All interest groups tried to influence the debate by providing scientific reports on the level of external costs and the right way to internalize them (cf Aberle, 1993, for the International Road Union (IRU); Kageson, 1993, for T&E; INFRAS/IWW, 1994, for the European Railways). Furthermore, a substantial amount of scientific work on transport economics and external costs was produced at Organisation for Economic Co-operation and Development (OECD) and European Conference of Ministers of Transport (ECMT) levels (ECMT, 1994). Experts from all interest groups were intensively involved in discussions and the Commission's proposal on transport and environment. In this context, T&E could form alliances with environmental economists and the railways. With its widely acknowledged study on 'Getting the Prices Right', it could play the role of an influential agenda-setter, despite being a newcomer with little staff capacity. The Commission was responsive to the ideas promoted by environmental organizations – however, as explained in the proceeding section, it did not adopt them in the end.

Gloomy Prognosis and Problem Perception by the Commission: 1989–1992

Between 1989 and 1994, different Commission services financed a number of reports on the problems of transport growth and the policy options to mitigate them. Taxation was one of the instruments that was evaluated from the beginning.

Several reports commissioned by the Environment Directorate-General (DG XI) concluded that 'green taxation' is necessary in order to control the emissions from the transport sector (Samaras, 1994; Tanja et al; 1992, Task Force, 1993). The reports began with an environmental balance sheet for different modes of transport, which listed the specific and total emissions from different modes of transport and then calculated probable growth rates of emissions for the next 20 years. The growth of road transport was identified as a major challenge. Despite considerable progress in reducing specific emissions by emission norms, transport growth would negate much of this. Some pollutants, especially CO_2 emissions, would continue to grow considerably; meanwhile, other reduction-oriented targets would be difficult to achieve by technical standards alone. Tanja (1992, p127) concludes: 'price related measures and transport market regulation measures [are] most effective to reduce CO_2 emissions'. The 1988 established task force group, headed by Commission officials but mainly gathering environmental economists, adopted a wider perspective and assessed the environmental impacts of the internal market programme. It concluded that both the internal market and freight transport liberalization would induce additional road transport growth and argued in favour of a tax policy compensating for the environmentally damaging price decreases (1993, p100ff).

Studies that were less closely associated with DG XI also confirmed the general thrust of these reports. Notable is the internal report by the Forward Studies Unit (1990), which is a strategic advisory unit that directly assists the president of the Commission, as well as the report for the Energy and Transport Directorate-General (DG VII) from the Group Transport 2000, which was composed of high-level politicians and scientists from Member States. The latter concluded (Group Transport 2000 Plus, 1990, pp20, 29):

> ... *if users will be unaware of external transport-related costs, these will be ignored when calculating the real cost of transport... To realize this, there will have to be a total change in transport mode preferences away from unlimited private car and road haulage growth towards public and multi-modal freight transport. This will not happen automatically and a 'push–pull' approach is needed including financial incentives (these need to be economically justifiable in the long term).*

The Group Transport 2000 estimated the social costs for transport as 0.10 ECU per vehicle kilometre.

The Commission (following the lead of DG VII) reacted to this 'gloomy prognosis' (O'Riordan, 1991) with the Green Paper on Transport and the Environment (European Commission, 1992a) and the White Paper on the

Future of Common Transport Policies (European Commission, 1992b). The Commission's synthesis was more cautious in its assessment of the trade-off between the internal market and the environment, but it endorsed the idea of environmental taxation. The White Paper states: 'as prices do not reflect the full social cost of transport, demand has been artificially high' (European Commission, 1992b, p31). This has several negative consequences, such as the threat of congestion and limited road infrastructure capacities, underused rail and shipping capacities, as well as road transport growth. 'The constant relative reductions in road costs charged to users stimulated this process' (European Commission, 1992b, p39).

In sum, the Commission soon identified environmental taxes as an effective tool to correct the risks of a one-sided modernization process in the framework of the prevailing neo-liberal, market-oriented philosophy. In the next phase, this initial assessment of the problem led to concrete policy commitments and the preparation of legislative proposals.

The Commission's Action: 1987–1996

The activities of the Commission itself can be separated into two phases:

1 the phase of symbolic policies and commitments during 1989–1994;
2 the preparatory phase for technically elaborated proposals during 1994–1996.

During the early phase, some protagonists of cost internalization in the Commission tried to find support for the principle, whereas the more technical preparatory work was neglected. The principle of cost internalization was mentioned in numerous strategy papers and even in Commission proposals.[3] Since the beginning of the 1990s, the Economic and Financial Affairs Directorate-General (DG II) and DG XI led the discussion on the use of fiscal instruments for transport. Staff from DG II initiated theoretical reflections on the right choice of instruments for internalization and impact modelling for market-oriented instruments (Koopman, 1995). DG XI commissioned the scenarios already described. Both were successful in establishing commitments in principle; however, their work was met with cautious reservation from DG VII.

DG VII invested few resources during the period of 1990–1994 to build up its own knowledge base. This low level of activity is in sharp contrast to the high profile of commitments on environmental taxation issued during this period, as expressed in the Green and White papers, and to the potential need to justify such a controversial instrument with strong arguments. Several factors can explain this apparent reservation to engage in operational policy:

• The Commission did not want to overload the ongoing decision-making process on the allocation of infrastructure costs by including additional complicated issues. The parallel discussion on vehicle taxation (see below) was so contentious that the Commission did not believe the elaboration of a strong concept on environmental taxes would be successful.

- The difficulty in finding support for the energy–CO_2 tax proposal in May 1992 contributed to the reluctance to initiate a second proposal for an economic environmental policy instrument. There was little hope that an initiative for environmental taxes in the transport sector would find support in the Council for Economic and Financial Affairs (ECOFIN Council).
- From the reactions to the Green Paper on Transport and the Environment, the Commission knew that road lobbyists would oppose environmental taxes.
- The studies indicated problems in calculating external costs exactly and highlighted the need for further investigation and research. As a result, the data supporting the proposals for green taxation remained vulnerable to criticism.
- The staff capacities and resources within DG VII were too limited to prepare a concept that would stand up against scientific interest groups and national criticism. This was a result of the political priorities of the commissioner (such as the completion of the internal market or the promotion of the Trans-European Networks), which did not include environmental taxation. The resources of other DGs, such as DG II and DG XI, to develop a concept were also limited. A high-profiled action of these two DGs would have interfered with the competencies of DG VII.

In short, despite support in principle, the Commission services perceived little chance for a successful initiative until 1994. Considering the anticipated resistance in the ECOFIN and Transport Councils and among powerful interest groups, the Commission services, and especially DG VII, acted very cautiously and did little else but look for support for the principle. Effective work only started in 1994 and was speeded up by Transport Commissioner Kinnock and his cabinet in 1995.

The Green Paper on Fair and Efficient Pricing

Under the leadership of the new commissioner and his cabinet, the Commission adopted a Green Paper on Fair and Efficient Pricing in Transport in 1995 (European Commission, 1995). The Commission developed an approach that joins mainstream economists. As a result, it did not join the arguments of the road lobby, nor did it fully adopt those of the environmentalists. Emphasis was placed on efficiency and potential positive-sum solutions, whereas potential conflicts between transport growth and the environment, and especially the CO_2 problem, were rather neglected.

The analysis of the Green Paper contained a clear hierarchy of 'externalities'. Road congestion received the strongest attention (European Commission, 1995, p12ff). The external costs of congestion were estimated at 120 billion ECU, or 2 per cent of GDP, and congestion pricing was considered the only alternative to traffic bans or the present inefficient allocation of road space. As a second priority, the Commission listed the cost of accidents, which should be reduced by a reform of the insurance system (European Commission, 1995, p25). Air pollution only received third priority, not least because costs were estimated to be relatively low, excluding cost estimates for greenhouse gases for transport (European Commission, 1995, p27). The Commission conceded that this choice may 'underestimate the costs of air pollution by several orders of magnitude' (European Commission, 1995, p27).

As to the internalization strategy, the Commission opted for a differentiated and decentralized approach. Congestion pricing, for instance, 'must be differentiated in time and space' to reduce temporal peaks on specific corridors (European Commission, 1995, p14). This implied the decentralization of the competencies to define the appropriate tax level within a Community framework that avoids discrimination or distortion. Furthermore, the Commission wanted to investigate an 'electronic kilometre charge for heavy vehicles', which also may be differentiated according to regional or environmental criteria. With regard to the appropriation of tax revenues, the Commission preferred to earmark tax-income to the road sector (European Commission, 1995, p15). This 'would also bolster the efficient provision of infrastructure', since it would improve the cost-benefit ratio of new infrastructures (European Commission, 1995, p15). Generally, the internalization approach on air pollution was focused on the traditional pollutants. A general fuel price increase was rejected because 'increased fuel prices do not trigger a number of highly effective response options' (European Commission, 1995, p30). Therefore, economic instruments should 'complement the existing regulatory approach' to protect the environment, rather than influence transport demand or modal choice (European Commission, 1995, p31). The environmental policy choice of the Green Paper therefore had a low depth of intervention. Tax differentiation to influence fuel and vehicle choice received highest priority (European Commission, 1995, p31). It should be 'non-discriminatory across modes' (European Commission, 1995, p39). Incentives for a change of modal split or even for rationalizing transport demand dropped from the Commission's agenda.

With its Green Paper, the Commission made a clear choice for 'efficient' pricing. This choice offers win–win solutions to different groups. Private transport users may avoid expensive time losses or even traffic bans on sensitive corridors. Infrastructure planners may receive an improved calculation basis for 'efficient infrastructure planning'.[4] The decentralized and differentiated approach may offer the regions and national governments an opportunity to maintain or introduce taxes in accordance with their preferences. Governments, industry and especially health insurance systems may benefit from reduced costs or at least improved cost coverage of uncovered accident costs. Even environmentalists supported the Green Paper,[5] because it confirmed many of their arguments and because the suggested road-pricing technology offered opportunities to consider the environmental dimension in the long run.

By seeking win–win proposals and avoiding conflict-intensive ideas with a strong redistributive effect, the Commission opted to drop climate change from the agenda. In environmental terms, the strategic choice was to improve vehicle technology rather than to manage transport growth or to create incentives for modal choices. Many problems of the transport sector may be managed by this approach – but not the greenhouse problem. The Commission hence opts for a strongly mitigated EPI strategy. The potential of 'green taxation' to modify market trends is not really exploited. Taxation is not considered as a tool to strengthen railways or to promote the efficient use of transport as such; it is only targeted at efficiency improvements within the road sector.

The general efficiency orientation of the tax proposal is strongly linked to the limited authority of the Commission to push conflict intensive proposals against the resistance of powerful interest groups and Member States. The Commission follows a network approach to policy-making rather than a hierarchical form of governing. This reflects the fact that, institutionally, the Commission is a central player in a pluralistic network rather than an executive administration with strong enforcement powers. The limited institutional conflict capacity of the Commission constitutes a strong filter for the choice of policy options.

Despite the concessions implied in this Green Paper, the Commission failed in its subsequent proposals. The Transport Council rejected most ideas related to cost internalization (see proceeding section). Nevertheless, the Commission tried to keep the idea on the agenda. In 1998 a new agenda-setting cycle was initiated, despite the defeat of the previous phase.

A New Agenda-Setting Cycle Since 1998

During late 1997, after the informal request of the environmental commissioner, several Member States initiated a high-level political process in order to specify the upgraded integration requirement of the Amsterdam Treaty (see Chapter 1). In the framework of this so-called Helsinki Process, the Commission was asked to formulate a strategy to 'mainstream environmental policy integration'. One essential pillar of this strategy was to get sector councils to promote integration strategies. As early as 1998, the UK presidency identified the transport sector as a priority area for integration and organized an informal and a formal joint Environmental and Transport Council.

As an input to the joint informal meeting, the Commission adopted a *Communication on Transport and CO_2* in March 1998 (European Commission, 1998a). It addresses the need to reduce the expected 40 per cent growth of CO_2 emissions from transport by 2010 in light of the Kyoto commitments (see Chapter 9). It lists potential CO_2 reduction measures and their potential. In contrast to the above analysis, the Commission expected a significant contribution to CO_2 reduction from the implementation of the Green Paper on Fair and Efficient Prices. It argued that 'inefficient provision of transport infrastructure ... impede CO_2 reduction in transport' (European Commission, 1998a). Considerable reduction was also expected by differentiated electronic road-pricing systems. By extrapolating the results of two case studies of road pricing in London and Brussels to the EU, the Commission expected a reduction of the trend of CO_2 emissions by 11.5 per cent. Such arguments may not stand critical analysis. It is, however, important that the Commission concluded: 'the most important reductions ... would come from the internalisation of external costs' (European Commission, 1998a).

The Commission also published a White Paper on Infrastructure Pricing in July 1998 (European Commission, 1998b), which would become an essential pillar of the Transport Council strategy to integrate the environment (cf Council, 1999). This paper mainly relied upon a high-level expert group report that had been published only a month before, in June 1998. The focus of the paper is the development of an efficient infrastructure charging system that allocates fixed and variable infrastructure costs to the respective users.

One of the central objectives is to optimize the use of existing infrastructure corridors. Earmarking infrastructure charges for new investments will ease the construction of new infrastructure and provide a basis for a stronger involvement of the private sector in infrastructure development, especially for the highly utilized and more profitable road links. With this proposal, the Commission further develops ideas first aired in the Green Paper, which amount to a radical change in most Member States.

It also suggests 'marginal social cost' as general pricing principle. This concept includes all running costs, the investment costs for new infrastructures and the external costs, but it does not cover the costs of the already existing infrastructure capital stock. The Commission suggests a phased programme to implement its ideas. Member States may be allowed to introduce tax schemes taking into account the external costs in earlier phases; but the Commission suggests a European approach for those external costs, which have a transboundary dimension at a later stage. This reform package is challenging, because it requires a fundamental change in many national transport taxation systems. Many countries use transport-related taxation as a source of general fiscal income and focus on public expenditure for infrastructure investments. The suggestion to link tax levels methodologically to internal and external infrastructure cost means that the Commission is moving towards earmarking taxation. This would constrain national discretion both on the income and expenditure side. Considerable political conflicts may be anticipated.

Environmentally, the balance of the new approach is not evident. It is uncertain whether writing off the existing capital stock would reduce transport costs on some corridors more than would be compensated for by including external costs. Furthermore, the new pricing system may be used for the expansion of infrastructure capacities in congested areas; it is uncertain whether cost-internalization will counterbalance the negative environmental impacts of the expected capacity extension in the long run. The Commission also excludes private passenger transport from the scope of the paper, making the whole approach less consistent. Finally, it is doubtful if the concept of external costs will survive the political conflicts surrounding changes in the national transport taxation systems. Compared to the Green Paper, the White Paper has a lower environmental profile, focuses on a fundamental reform of taxation principles for all transport modes, but paradoxically neglects road passenger transport.

Both initiatives, the transport and CO_2 communication and the White Paper, were embedded in a wider framework with very different policy objectives. The first was about climate protection, the second about a fundamental change of national transport infrastructure pricing systems. Compared to the previous Green Paper on Fair and Efficient Prices, the policy status of green taxation has been considerably reduced, now linking and subordinating the idea to the wider issues of climate protection and public–private partnership on infrastructure policies. Nevertheless, the controversial idea was kept on the agenda and was promoted in an incrementalist way (Hey, 1998). In both cases, the environmental benefits of the Commission strategy are not evident. The Commission's proposals make clear concessions to the unfavourable opportunity structure in the decision-making cycle. The following section will illustrate why cost internalization could only survive on the Commission's agenda within a new framework and with a lower profile.

THE DECISION-MAKING CYCLES

Two decision-making cycles can be observed over the last decade:

1   the negotiations on freight transport taxation between 1987–1993;
2   the revision of the Eurovignette Directive after 1996.

The First Cycle: 1987–1993

The harmonization of freight road taxation was part of a wider policy package to liberalize transport markets. The issue of external costs was a marginal aspect of a difficult political task to overcome antagonistic interests. The Commission had included the reference to 'external costs' in its proposal mainly as a means of tactical support to some high-tax countries. But this environmental element did not play a role in the negotiations of the Transport Council. In order to harmonize tax levels, the interests of export countries to gain cheap access to the markets of other countries had to be reconciled with the fiscal interests of transit countries to increase the revenue from foreign hauliers. Making things even more difficult, this distribution conflict had to be resolved under the unanimity rule.

The negotiations between 1987 and 1993 included a whole package of tax policies. This included a harmonized level of vehicle taxation, the possibility to introduce a time-dependent charge for the use of motorways (the Eurovignette) and, informally linked to this process, the harmonization of diesel taxation. What is most apparent is that the parallel discussion on the environmental consequences of transport and on the Green Paper on Transport and the Environment had no visible effect on the council negotiations.

The first cycle cannot be presented here in its chronological order. The six years of negotiations were conflict intensive and included several far-reaching modifications of the Commission's proposals (cf Hey, 1998). A political interpretation of the 1993 compromise is presented in brief.

The final package of 1993, the so-called Eurovignette Directive, contained elements that respected the interests of nearly every country in the EU:[6]

- Countries with a low level of vehicle taxation (France, Germany, Spain and Ireland) received a transitional period until the end of 1997 during which they could charge less than the minimum vehicle tax.
- The minimum vehicle tax was set at a low level so that it was acceptable for most countries.

- Member States were permitted to introduce a user charge on motorways – the Eurovignette. Unlike road tolls, the user charge buys the right to use a motorway for a certain limited time, such as one year. Two or more Member States can introduce a common user-charge system applicable to their combined territory. Five countries (Benelux, Denmark and Germany) have already decided to introduce this system. The maximum level was set at 1250 ECU, which was much less than Germany had originally suggested but more than the opposing countries of the Netherlands and Denmark had been willing to accept initially.
- The low minimum levels for vehicle taxation gave the Netherlands and Denmark an opportunity to compensate their national hauliers for the introduction of the Eurovignette.
- There was an implicit German–Dutch agreement to increase diesel taxation. Considering the already high taxation rates in both countries (compared to harmonized EU levels) and the decline of world oil prices, neither country perceived this as a problem for their hauliers.
- The directive invited the Commission to present a report by the end of 1997 and – if necessary – new proposals to improve infrastructure cost coverage. With this revision clause the directive assumed a dynamic character, offering opportunities for tax increases in the future.
- The Transport Council decided to develop a harmonized approach for road pricing systems that would allow for the full application of the territoriality principle without the need of border controls.
- External costs were no longer mentioned in the final decision. However, an implicit option remained open in the framework of the review process and the development of road pricing systems.

As a result, a compromise was found that especially reduced competitive distortions implicit in different levels of taxation. The way towards the completion of the internal market for the transport sector was opened. However, a reference to the environment had been dropped from the Transport Council agenda. The package implied only marginal indirect positive and negative environmental side effects within different countries. The process shows that under very specific historical circumstances, the interests of high tax countries may be protected. This is relevant for EPI since individual countries may be able to opt for green transport taxation at national level. EPI as a general principle seems much more difficult to apply.

It seems more surprising that the compromise contained an element of redistribution and that it, nevertheless, satisfied every participant. There are five points that might explain this 'paradox' in the unanimity procedure:

1 The preferences of former antagonists of Germany had changed due to environmental and fiscal reasons, so that higher taxation levels for their national hauliers were more acceptable than at the beginning of the negotiations.

2 The compromise package offered sufficient flexibility for every country to adapt its tax structure to the national preferences. In the end, actual tax

levels where above the harmonized, low common denominator levels. Differences of tax levels may be acceptable to national transport industries within certain margins.

3   The core of the conflict was a zero-sum game on the distribution of taxes. The act of solving this distribution conflict had an external helper: OPEC. Since oil prices fell during the period in question, finance ministries could increase taxation on oil products without imposing additional costs to the transport sector. This allowed for the informal Dutch–German realignment because it guaranteed cheap transport for the Dutch and high government revenue from transport for the Germans. Therefore, the higher diesel prices must not be interpreted as an indicator of the incorporation of the environmental dimension but of fiscal rationality.

4   The issue is related to other policies, and the strong pressure to find an agreement should not be underestimated. Solving the tax issue was a precondition for the liberalization of freight transport in the EU. This was an accepted policy objective by all partners. Therefore, the pressure to find a compromise was strong – particularly on the Danish presidency in the first half of 1993.

5   Finally, the aggressive foreign policy approach of Germany was not without impact. Its threat of a 'national solution' on the vehicle tax issue was credible. Furthermore, it could establish a link to the road liberalization discussion and threaten to prevent free cabotage of foreign hauliers in Germany. For the antagonists, a compromise with the Eurovignette was a 'lesser evil' than the threatened 'exit option'.

In total, the strong informal pressure to find a consensus for the sake of the internal market was sufficiently strong for Member States to make certain concessions – within strict limits. The compromise had some characteristics of a Pareto-optimal solution and, in this sense, is in line with game-theoretical assumptions on the impact of unanimity voting rules.

However, the solution had a victim. 'External costs' were used as a tactical element in the negotiation process, but the decision-makers never took them seriously. Clearly, the issue did not belong to the core interests of the closed transport network. The European Parliament (EP) was excluded from the difficult negotiations and with it a supporter of the environmental dimension. Environmental considerations had little influence in national transport politics. They slightly softened the Dutch and Danish positions; but in total national environmental ministries were marginalized as players in the sectoral decision-making process.

The compromise of the Transport Council created a political and judicial aftermath. The EP raised a complaint since it had not been consulted on the second reading of the Eurovignette Directive. In 1995, the European Court of Justice confirmed the EP's accusations and decided that the directive had to be renegotiated. This opened the door to future negotiations.

The Second Decision-Making Cycle: 1996–1999

The European Commission used the need to revise the 1993 Eurovignette Directive as an opportunity to push forward the ideas of the Green Paper on Fair and Efficient Prices. It even used its initiation power to include, and to specify, the ideas of the Green Paper before a wider consultation process on this discussion paper was finalized. Informally in February and formally in November 1996, the Commission presented its first proposal, which contained green taxation elements for freight transport:[7]

- The Eurovignette should be increased from 1250 to 2000 ECU per year and differentiated according to the level of pollution from heavy vehicles. Most modern vehicles will receive a considerable rebate from the 2000 ECU.
- The concept of 'sensitive corridors' was introduced. On ecologically vulnerable corridors, Member States are allowed to charge a maximum of 0.5 ECU per kilometre in addition to the infrastructure charges.
- Member states can charge a maximum of 0.03 ECU per kilometre for the external costs of transport.
- Vehicle taxation was reduced by about 50 per cent and could be differentiated according to the pollution of the vehicles.

The strategic idea behind this attempt to green freight transport taxation was to establish a link between the internal revision process and the external negotiations with Switzerland on a bilateral agreement on land transport (Hey, 2000; see Chapter 8 in this book). This linkage improved the prospect of a successful green taxation. Alpine transit was a controversial issue between the EU and the two alpine countries of Austria and Switzerland.

After the Swiss population had refused accession to the European Economic Area in 1992 and voted for a modal shift of all alpine freight transport from road to rail by 2004, the bilateral links between Switzerland and the EU were complicated. To keep the door open for the accession of Switzerland to the EU in the long run, both agreed to negotiate the outstanding issues within seven bilateral treaties, which where perceived as a policy package. One of them concerned the alpine transit problem. In early 1996, Switzerland offered the concession to substitute its 28-tonne weight limit for foreign transit lorries through a levy that would tax the productivity gains of a 40-tonne lorry compared to a 28-tonne one. The suggested tax level reached 355 ECU per alpine transit and would make alpine rail transit competitive. Austria (by now an EU member) was concerned about the possibility of unequal treatment and asked for an equivalent tax for the Brenner axis, to be accepted by the EU. As discussed by Lauber in Chapter 8, the Brenner problem resulted in conflict within Austria as well as between Austria and the EU.

The Commission hoped to accommodate the concerns of the alpine countries through the concept of 'sensitive corridors'. This concept would safeguard equal treatment of Austria and Switzerland. Furthermore, it would link the bilateral negotiations with Switzerland and the internal negotiations on the Eurovignette and create an opportunity to get green taxation accepted.

During the first transport councils in late 1996 and early 1997, the Commission persuaded the Transport Council on the advantages of the issue linkage. However, in the course of 1997 conflicts escalated. Switzerland was not strongly committed to a compromise on tax levels and a strong coalition of low tax countries was formed in the council during the Dutch presidency. Even Germany changed its general position towards lower tax levels to avoid any opposition from hauliers before the German elections in 1998. As a result, the concept of 'sensitive corridors' was rejected by the council and substituted with a special solution for the Brenner corridor. This, however, did not satisfy Austria. After Austria vetoed the solution in autumn 1997, the internal negotiations came to a standstill.

The negotiations between the Commission and Switzerland were also officially stopped in May 1997 and only continued informally. In January 1998, the chief negotiators for Switzerland and the EU found an agreement that came close to the original offer of the EU. However, this compromise was not acceptable for Germany. The negotiation process was frozen from spring to autumn of 1998 in order to wait for the German elections. A compromise with Switzerland and a Common Transport Council position on the revised Eurovignette Directive was reached in December 1998, after the change of government in Germany. Directive 1999/62 was formally adopted in June 1999 (Wolf, 2000). The bilateral result amounts to a defeat for Switzerland. It had to agree to an average tax level of 180 ECU, which was considerably below its original demands. After a transition period, the tax could be raised to 200 ECU by 2005. The partners also agreed to generous transit rights for a specified number of lorries during a transition phase and a safeguard mechanism to prevent an unanticipated decline of the Swiss railway market. This solution will reorient North–South lorry transit from the much longer Brenner route (in Austria) towards the Swiss routes.

With regard to the revised Eurovignette Directive, the council agreed to reduce vehicle taxation rates and slightly increased and differentiated the Eurovignette. Smaller lorries would only pay half of the price for large lorries. Lorries that meet the existing standards for new vehicles would also be able to reduce their Eurovignette fees. Four countries obtained further extensive derogation for lower taxes. Only Austria received a derogation to maintain parts of its previous user-fee increases on the Brenner highway. Despite the use of a singular policy window for getting a broader concept of external costs accepted by the Transport Council, the Commission's second attempt failed. The only green element will be tax differentiation to promote greener lorries. The Transport Council rejected the use of taxes as incentives for a modal shift along environmentally sensitive or congested corridors. A revision clause and the reference to the German plans for electronic road pricing, however, offer some prospects for the future.[8]

In total, the second decision-making cycle confirmed the conservative orientation of the first one (Wolf, 2000). Transport ministers rejected effective steps towards EPI. In spite of ten years of strategic reflection on EPI and green taxation in the transport sector, the sectoral transport ministers' network simply decided to ignore this discussion. The institutional system of the EU allowed them to do so.

CONCLUSIONS AND RECOMMENDATIONS

The case of environmental taxation in European freight transport spans ten years of ambitious reflection with little political impact. This can be generally explained by the nearly opposing circumstances for environmental policy integration in the agenda-setting and decision-making arenas. Agenda-setting of environmental taxation took place in open, scientifically oriented policy networks that included economists from different DGs, environmental groups and universities. Interest groups (environmental organizations, railways, and road hauliers) applied scientific evidence and counter-evidence to influence the Commission services. The case of taxation is a positive example of a pluralistic agenda-setting arena with open access to all who have the capacities to present scientifically underlined arguments. In the end, an informal network within the Commission sympathized with arguments presented by environmental economists.

The positions finally adopted by the Commission were independent from any lobby. The Commission anticipated the strong political and economic hurdles of a tax initiative in the council. Its Green Paper may not have been 'opportunistic' but it was 'success oriented' by concentrating on issues where everybody can win. Efficiency became the normative principle of the Commission's discussion paper on green taxation in the transport sector. CO_2 was excluded as a policy issue for environmental taxation since it would have carried a high conflict potential and would not have been manageable for the Commission. This process offers an insight into the limited capacities of the EU to engage in 'active integration' in the transport sector (and beyond).

The decision-making arena was not conducive to achieving change, even with regard to the Commission's cautious proposals. Environmental interests were not represented; the European Parliament was not a relevant player in the 1990s; the unanimity hurdle generally favours conservative decisions; and national finance ministries consider taxation policies as core policies of national sovereignty. Furthermore, any tax reform has redistributive consequences, creating winners and losers. The last point may explain the high conflict intensity of the negotiation process on tax harmonization.

An agreement on taxation between the divergent national interests was found thanks to external help (falling oil prices) and external pressure (internal market), but it was not beneficial for the environment. It ignored the concerns of those not sitting at the negotiation table. With regard to environmental taxation, the EU is still in the 'joint decision-making trap' (Scharpf, 1985). On the one hand, national action is restricted, though not fully impeded, by the constraints of the internal market and the taxation compromises during 1993 and 1999 (Wolf, 2000). On the other hand, progressive EU action is blocked by the unanimity rule.

In summary, the institutional system of European transport taxation is characterized by a combination of responsiveness to environmental interests (during agenda-setting) and low or moderate regulatory capacity. It therefore tends to produce symbolic policies and trend-enhancing policy decisions.

In order to achieve EPI, institutional reform is necessary. The first and most important step is qualified majority voting with the co-decision power of the European Parliament. Secondly, institutional reform has to address the sectoral structure of the (non-)decision-making system, which tends to exclude controversial issues to protect core interests. Environmental issues continue to belong to such excluded issues.

If these institutional reforms are not achieved, the solution must be sought on the national level. As long as the rational top-down approach of the Commission fails due to its inability to implement an integrated approach, Member States must be given high autonomy in pursuing EPI solutions. In transport taxation, this implies the full application of the territoriality principle. According to the territoriality principle, taxation is linked to infrastructure use on a certain territory and not to the nationality of the holder of the enterprise. This gives Member States the freedom to decide upon their tax levels, without discriminating between national and foreign hauliers. In the field of transport and taxation, EPI requires such autonomy in order to allow bottom-up pressure in some environmentally aware countries to change the national context. This might, at a later stage, also create a new momentum at EU level.

REFERENCES

Aberle, G (1993) *Der volkswirtschaftliche Nutzen des Straßengüterfernverkehrs*, Justus-Liebig Universität, Giessen

Andersen, M S and Liefferink, D (1997) (eds) *The Innovation of EU Environmental Policy*, Scandinavian University Press, Copenhagen

Arp, H A (1992) *The European Parliament in European Community Environmental Policy*, EUI Working Paper, European University Institute, Florence

Arp, H A (1995) *Multiple Actors and Arenas: European Community Regulation in a Polycentric System. A Case Study on Car Emission Policy*, PhD thesis, Department of Political and Social Sciences, European University Institute, Florence

Boyce, B (1995) 'The June 1994. Elections and the Politics of the European Parliament', *Parliamentary Affairs*, no 1, pp141–156

Button, K (1992): *Market and Government Failures in Environmental Management: The Case of Transport*, OECD, Paris

Council (1999) *Council Strategy on the Integration of Environment and Sustainable Development into the Transport Policy*, submitted by the Transport Council to the European Council of Helsinki, Luxembourg, 6 October 1999

Delbeke, J (1991) 'The Prospects for the Use of Economic Instruments in EC Environmental Policy', paper presented at ECPS business policy seminar on 'Setting New Priorities in EC Environmental Legislation', Brussels, 11 April 1991

Edelmann, M (1976) *Politik als Ritual. Die symbolische Funktion staatlicher Institutionen und politischen Handelns*, Campus, Frankfurt

Eichener, V (1996) 'Die Rückwirkungen der europäischen Integration auf nationale Politikmuster' in M Jachtenfuchs and B Kohler-Koch (eds) *Europäische Integration,* Leske+Budrich, Opladen, pp249–280

European Commission (1992a) *Green Paper on the Impact of Transport on the Environment: a Community Strategy for 'Sustainable Mobility'*, COM(92) 46, Brussels

European Commission (1992b) *Die künftige Entwicklung der gemeinsamen Verkehrspolitik. Globalkonzept einer Gemeinschaftsstrategie für eine auf Dauer tragbare Mobilität,* KOM(92)494 endg., Brussels

European Commission (1995) *Towards Fair and Efficient Pricing in Transport: Policy Options for Internalising the External Cost of Transport in the European Union,* Green Paper, Brussels

European Commission (1997) *Communication on the Integration of Environmental Considerations in Policy-Making and Management,* 11 July 1997

European Commission (1998a) *Communication on Transport and CO_2,* COM(98) 204, 31 March, 1998

European Commission (1998b) *Fair Payment for Infrastructure Use: a Phased Approach to a Common Transport Infrastructure Charging Framework in the EU,* July 1998, Brussels

European Conference of Ministers of Transport (ECMT) (1994) *Internalising the Social Costs of Transport,* Paris

EURES/CE/INFRAS/SRS/IEEP/AKF (1996) *The Incorporation of the Environmental Dimension into Freight Transport Policies,* EURES–Institute for Regional Studies in Europe, Freiburg im Breisgau

Forward Studies Unit (1990) *Transport and the Environment: a Global and Long-Term Policy Response by the Community,* Brussels

Group Transport 2000 Plus (1990) *Transport in a Fast Changing Europe,* European Commission, DG Transport, Brussels

Gehring, T (1994) 'Der Beitrag von Institutionen zur Förderung der internationalen Zusammenarbeit. Lehren aus der institutionellen Struktur der EG', *Zeitschrift für internationale Beziehungen,* no 2, pp211–242

Héritier, A (1995) *Die Koordination von Interessenvielfalt im europäischen Entscheidungsprozeß und deren Ergebnis: Regulative Politik als, Patchwork',* MPIFG Discussion Papers, Max-Planck Institut für Gesellschaftsforschung, Köln

Héritier, A, Mingers, S, Knill, C. and Becka, M (1994) *Die Veränderung von Staatlichkeit in Europa. Ein regulativer Wettbewerb: Deutschland, Großbritannien, Frankreich,* Leske + Budrich, Opladen

Hey, C (1994*) Umweltpolitik in Europa. Fehler, Risiken, Chancen. Ein Greenpeace-Buch.* C H Beck, München

Hey, C (1998) *Nachhaltige Mobilität in Europa. Akteure, Institutionen und politische Prozesse,* Westdeutscher Verlag, Opladen

Hey, C (2000) 'Die Revision des Steuerkompromisses von 1993 – auf dem Weg zu "fairen und effizienten Preisen im Verkehr"' in S Kux (ed) *Institutionen, Prozesse und Strategien der europäischen Verkehrspolitik und deren Wechselwirkungen mit der Schweiz,* Forschungsbericht, NFP 41, Zürich

Hey, C and Brendle, U (1994) *Umweltverbände und EG: Strategien, Politische Kulturen und Organisationsformen,* Westdeutscher Verlag, Opladen

Hey, C and Röder, R (1998) 'Güterverkehrs – und Umweltpolitik in Europa – Ein internationaler Vergleich', *Zeitschrift für Angewandte Umweltforschung,* vol 11, no 1, pp115–124

Holzinger, K (1994) *Politik des kleinsten gemeinsamen Nenners. Umweltpolitische Entscheidungsprozesse in der EG am Beispiel der Einführung des Katalysatorautos,* Edition Sigma, Berlin

Huber, M (1997) 'Leadership in the EU Climate Policy: Innovative Policy Making in Policy Networks' in M S Andersen and D J Liefferink (eds) *The Innovation of EU Environmental Policy*, Scandinavian University Press, Copenhagen, pp133–155

INFRAS/IWW (1994) 'External Effects of Transport: Project for UIC', Final Report, Karlsruhe/Zürich

Jachtenfuchs, M (1996) 'Regieren durch Überzeugen: Die europäische Union und der Treibhauseffekt' in M Jachtenfuchs and B Kohler-Koch (eds) *Europäische Integration*, Leske+Budrich, Opladen, pp429–454

Jänicke, M (ed) (1996) *Umweltpolitik der Industrieländer. Entwicklung – Bilanz – Erfolgsbedingungen*, Edition Sigma, Berlin

Jahns-Böhm, J and Breier, S (1991) 'Güterkraftverkehrspolitik und Umweltschutz nach dem EWG-Vertrag: Überrollt der Straßengüterverkehr die Umweltschutzerfordernisse der Europäischen Gemeinschaft?', *EuZW*, no 17, pp523–530

Jahns-Böhm, J and Breier, S (1992) 'Die umweltrechtliche Querschnittsklausel des Art. 130r II EWGV: Eine Untersuchung am Beispiel der Güterkraftverkehrspolitik der Europäischen Gemeinschaft', *EuZW*, no 2, pp49–55

Jarass, H D and Neumann, L F (1994) *Umweltschutz und Europäische Gemeinschaften: Rechts- und sozialwissenschaftliche Probleme der umweltpolitischen Integration*, Reihe Studien zum Umweltstaat, Economica Verlag, Bonn

Kageson, P (1993) *Getting the Prices Right: A European Scheme for Making Transport Pay Its True Costs*, Transport & Environment, Stockholm and Brussels

Koopman, G J (1995) 'Policies to Reduce CO_2 Emissions from Cars in Europe: A Partial Equilibrium Analysis', *Journal of Transport Economics and Policy*, January, pp53–70

Lenschow, A (1997) 'Variation in EC Environmental Policy Integration: Agency Push within Complex Institutional Structures', *Journal of European Public Policy*, no 4, pp109–127

Liefferink, J D, Lowe, P D and Mol, A P J (eds) (1993) *European Integration and Environmental Policy*, Belhaven Press, London and New York

Ludlow, P (1991) 'The European Commission' in R Keohane and S Hoffmann (eds) *The New European Community. Decisionmaking and Institutional Change*, Westview Press, Boulder, San Francisco, Oxford, pp85–132

Mayntz, R and Scharpf, F W (1995) 'Der Ansatz des Akteurszentrierten Institutionalismus' in R Mayntz and F W Scharpf (eds) *Gesellschaftliche Selbstregulierung und politische Steuerung*, Campus, Frankfurt a.M., pp39–72

Mazey, S and Richardson, J (1993) 'Introduction: Transference of Power, Decision Rules, and Rules of the Game' in S Mazey and J Richardson (eds) *Lobbying in the European Community*, Oxford University Press, Cambridge, pp3–26

Müller, E (1986) *Innenwelt der Umweltpolitik: sozial–liberale Umweltpolitik – (Ohn)macht durch Organisation?* Westdeutscher Verlag, Opladen

O'Riordan, T (1991) 'Environmental Government', *The Political Quarterly*, no 2, pp167–185

Organisation for Economic Co-operation and Development (OECD) (1992) *Science Responses to Environmental Threats: Country Studies*, OECD, Paris

OECD (1996) *Integrating Environment and Economy: Progress in the 1990s*, OECD, Paris

Pellegrom, S (1997) 'The Constraints of Daily Work in Brussels: How Relevant Is the Input from National Capitals' in M S Andersen and D J Liefferink (eds) *The Innovation of EU Environmental Policy*, Scandinavian University Press, Copenhagen, pp38–58

Peters, B G (1994) 'Agenda Setting in the European Community', *Journal of European Public Policy*, vol 1, no 1, pp9–26

Peterson, J (1995) 'Decision-Making in the European Union: Towards a Framework for Analysis', *Journal of European Public Policy*, no 2, pp69–93

Prittwitz, V (1990) *Das Katastrophenparadox: Elemente einer Theorie der Umweltpolitik*, Leske+Budrich, Opladen

Rengeling, H-W (ed) (1993) *Umweltschutz und andere Politiken der Europäischen Gemeinschaft*, Erste Osnabrücker Gespräche zum deutschen und europäischen Umweltrecht am 26–27 November 1992, Referate und Diskussionsberichte, Carl Heymanns (Schriften zum deutschen und europäischen Umweltrecht, Bd 1), Köln, Berlin, Bonn, München

Samaras, Z (1994) *Road Transport and Greenhouse Gas Emissions in the European Community*, European Conference of Ministers of Transport, Brussels

Scharpf, F W (1985) 'Die Politikverflechtungs-Falle. Oder: Was ist generalisierbar an den Problemen des deutschen Föderalismus und der europäischen Integration?', *Politische Vierteljahresschrift*, no 4, pp323–356

Scharpf, F W (1991) 'Political Institutions, Decision Styles and Policy Choices' in R Czada and A Héritier (eds) *Political Choice. Institutions, Rules and the Limits of Rationality*, Campus, Frankfurt, pp53–86

Scharpf, F W (1996) 'Politische Optionen im vollendeten Binnenmarkt' in M Jachtenfuchs and B Kohler-Koch (eds) *Europäische Integration*, Leske+Budrich, Opladen, pp109–140

Tanja, P T, Clerx, W C G, Ham, J van, Ligt, T J and Rijkeboer, R C (1992) 'Possible Community Measures Aiming at Limiting CO_2 Emissions in the Transport Sector', Final Report, Delft

Task Force (1993) *La Dimension Environnementale de '1992'*, Rapport de la Task Force L'Environnement et le Marché Interieur, Economica Verlag, Bonn

Tsebelis, G (1994) 'The Power of the European Parliament as a Conditional Agenda Setter', *American Political Science Review*, vol 88, no 1, pp128–142

Wallace, H (1996) 'Die Dynamik des EU-Institutionengefüges' in M Jachtenfuchs and B Kohler-Koch (eds) *Europäische Integration*, Leske+Budrich, Opladen, pp141–164

Weale, A (1992) *The New Politics of Pollution*, Manchester University Press, Manchester

Weidner, H (1996) *Basiselemente erfolgreicher Umweltpolitik. Eine Analyse und Valuation der Instrumente der japanischen Umweltpolitik*, Edition Sigma, Berlin

Wolf, R (2000) 'Rechtsprobleme einer Schwerverkehrsabgabe', *Zeitschrift für Umweltrecht*, vol 2, pp123–128

NOTES

1 In an anarchic environment, the first mover who reveals his interest in a solution may be cheated by those who try to exploit this problem orientation for their own benefits (cf Gehring, 1994, p229; Huber, 1997). This is a disincentive for the first mover to reveal his preferences.

2 The Dutch Green MEP Neill van Deijk was rapporteur on the Green Paper on Transport and Environment; the Belgian Green MEP P Lannoye was rapporteur on the revised Environmental Impact Assessment Directive; a number of German Social Democrats (Topman, Piecyck) with pro-environment positions were rapporteurs on different transport questions.

3 See, for instance, the Commission proposals on the harmonization of vehicle taxation (Com (87) 716 fin, in OJ C 79/9 from 26 March 1988 and Com (90) 540).

See also the proposal on diesel tax harmonization (cf Delbeke, 1991, p13). A commitment on principles at the council level was reached in the Dublin Declaration of the European Council in June 1990 and the Environmental Council in October 1990 (cf Delbeke, 1991). Further commitments by the Commission and the council were formulated in the White Paper on the Common Transport Policy and the Fifth Environmental Action Program in 1992.

4   ECIS already has understood the new opportunities for private financing that the paper offers ('Kinnock releases pricing paper', ECIS newsletter, January 1996).

5   'T&E welcomes Kinnock's Green Papers on Fair Transport Prices and Citizen's Networks', in T&E bulletin, February 1996

6   Directive 93/89, OJ L 279/32 from 12 November 1993; minutes of the 1668th Council Meeting from 19 June 1993

7   OJ 59/06 from 26 February 1997

8   'Results of Transport Council' (Internal Memo, DG VII); Presse communiqué of the 4142nd Transport Minister Council

The Sustainability of Freight Transport Across the Alps: European Union Policy in Controversies on Transit Traffic

Volkmar Lauber

Transport and Sustainability in the European Community: The Programmatic Level

Sustainable mobility is a declared goal of the European Commission at least since 1992, with the publication of two documents on the subject (European Commission, 1992a; 1992b) that were the first instalments of a continuous flow of publications and proposals on the subject (EEA, 1999, p64). But sustainable transport proved an evasive goal, and today the EC seems further removed from it than it was nearly a decade ago. A 1999 report by the OECD states that transportation is unsustainable on three counts: firstly, because of its excessive use of a non-renewable resource for which no renewable alternatives are developed at a commensurate rate; secondly, because of emissions that exceed the assimilative capacity of the environment; and thirdly, because its impacts 'damage the health of humans and other organisms and affect the integrity of ecosystems' (OECD, 1999, p11).

The European Commission itself shared this view in its progress report of 24 November 1999 (EWWE, 26 November 1999, p2). Between 1985 and 1996, carbon dioxide (CO_2) emissions increased by 40 per cent in the EC (European Commission, 1999, figure 7.5); there was no improvement in energy efficiency during this time (EEA, 1999, p63). In its 1999 assessment of the environment in the EC, the European Environment Agency (EEA) reviewed environmental policy integration in a variety of sectors. While it found progress in agriculture, energy and industry, damage was still growing in the transport and household sectors (EEA, 1999, p398). 'Transport is the fastest growing sector relevant to the environment' (EEA, 1999, p416). Apart from air transport, which is less important because of its limited volume, this applies with particular force to road freight, which is expected to increase by 50 per cent between 1994 and 2010 (EEA, 1999, p66).

For this reason, the European Commission has proposed a variety of measures to promote a shift of goods transport from road to rail. The question is whether these proposals will be adopted and if they are bold enough to significantly affect the trend of the last decades. During this time, road freight in most EC countries gained market shares from rail transport, which until 1996 declined not only in relative but also in absolute terms – that is, in tonne-kilometres (European Commission, 1999, figures 4.4 and 4.7). So far, the Transport Council has shown little ambition to integrate environmental concerns. A first joint meeting of transport and environment ministers in 1998 produced few results, with the Transport Council having 'the interests of the road haulage industry uppermost in mind' (EWWE, 19 June 1998, p15). The increase of ritual calls for stepped-up integration in recent years need not reflect a decisive shift.

TRANSPORT AND SUSTAINABILITY: COMMUNITY DECISIONS CONCERNING ALP-CROSSING FREIGHT TRAFFIC

After a brief glance at the programmatic level, this chapter now examines actual decisions which had to be taken by the EC in the case of Alp-crossing freight traffic. In the alpine region, resistance against heavy goods traffic became particularly intense because of the latter's concentration on very few routes, its greater environmental impact due to a highly sensitive milieu and because of the general scarcity of inhabitable terrain (narrow valleys). In addition, there is a perception in those regions that this traffic is not home grown. It is transit traffic in the sense that it serves only other areas, not the regions in which it is most concentrated.

The European Community's policy clearly compounded this problem. While it made little progress in transport policy until the mid 1980s, the subsequent years saw a series of measures opening the field of cross-border road freight for competition and lifting quantitative restrictions. Hardly any progress was made regarding railroads, where resistance against reform was stronger. This improved the competitive position of road freight at a time when, due to Common Market integration, transportation volume was already soaring. Between 1984 and 1989, cross-border road freight in the Community increased by 84.4 per cent, compared to a growth of 50 per cent in domestic freight in the various Member States (Bernhard, 1995, p7). This increase was concentrated in the Alps on the very small number of routes. Both Austria and Switzerland opposed the surge of road traffic in the name of its ecological and social impact. They developed positions on sustainable freight transport that invoked goals and principles also accepted by the EC (for example, in the context of the Alpine Convention; see subsequent section on p157) but which clashed with EC practices. From this resulted a process of interaction that has more weight than mere policy statements.

The following questions are relevant to this chapter:

- How did the alpine countries and regions define sustainable transport and how did the stand of the EU develop when confronted with these demands?
- Did the EU infuse its own concepts of sustainable transportation with life and try to promote them?
- Did the EU at least agree to sustainable approaches, or did it do its best to inhibit them?

Answers to these questions should emerge in the following 'country' sections.

SWITZERLAND

Switzerland has a long tradition of restricting truck traffic because of its social and environmental costs. Since 1933, there has been a ban on night-time (and Sunday) driving for heavy goods vehicles. When, after World War II, weight and size limits for trucks were increased in most European states, Switzerland did not follow suit. In 1972, it increased maximum permissible weight to only 28 tonnes and did not modify this limit until the 1998 agreement with the EU (Stampfli, 1993, pp189–190). A toll charge for trucks was introduced in 1984. Confronted with the steady increase of motorized traffic, the Swiss population voted for an expensive modernization programme for public transport in 1987 (Hirter et al, 1994, p158). In fact, Swiss railroads are economically among the most successful in Europe. They handle a larger share of freight than any EC Member State. This applies particularly to freight in transit, which is still overwhelmingly going by rail, despite a decline in the share of rail since the opening of the Gotthard motorway in 1980. During that year, the road took only about 7.5 per cent of total freight crossing the Swiss Alps. In 1994, this share had risen to 25 per cent. The increase was particularly pronounced for transiting trucks whose freight volume increased by approximately 850 per cent during this time (Eidgenössisches Verkehrs und Energiewirtschaftsdepartement, 1996, p32). These figures should be kept in mind when considering the reactions that came from Swiss politics and, in particular, from Swiss citizens in the course of the 1990s.

There is another element to this picture. Due to its geography, Switzerland is ideally placed for much of the North–South traffic – road and rail – across the Alps. Due in part to its restrictive policy on trucking, it handled 'only' 31 per cent of that traffic in 1994 (Eidgenössisches Verkehrs und Energiewirtschafts-departement, 1996, p19). This led to irritation among neighbouring countries when road traffic became a problem with the public in the 1980s. While freighters pointed to the high cost of bypassing Switzerland, governments objected to the additional 'detour traffic', which they claimed to be quite significant. Things came to a head with the dramatic increases in freight transport in the 1980s and the perspective of the imminent completion of the internal market. The Swiss government wanted the country to join the European Economic Area (EEA). The Community, in turn, viewed a transit treaty with Switzerland as a precondition for such membership. It was during this period that negotiations on transit were conducted, even if, in the end, the Swiss population voted against joining.

The Transit Agreement of 1992

In the negotiations preceding this treaty, the EC wanted to obtain a significant liberalization of truck transit, in particular a corridor for 40- or even 42-tonne trucks. On the other hand, it had little interest at first in combined traffic (Hummer, 1993b, p5). By contrast, Switzerland wanted to maintain the 28-tonne limit and the clear preference given to freight transport by rail, if necessary by expanding combined traffic – that is, rail shipment of containers or of entire trucks.

The Transit Agreement (valid from January 1993 to January 2005) resulted in the following compromise. Switzerland maintained its 28-tonne limit but committed itself to important railroad investments that would allow increased and accelerated transport of freight containers and whole trucks over the coming 10 to 15 years. This was to be achieved in several steps: at first by upgrading existing tracks, later by building two North–South axes, with long tunnels under the Gotthard and Lötschberg mountains. This project came to be discussed as the NEAT (Neue Eisenbahn–Alpentransversale) (see Figure 8.1).

If no combined traffic facilities were available, a limited number of 40-tonne trucks (100 per day at the most) were, under certain conditions, permitted to transit across Swiss territory with special permits. In fact, this clause acquired

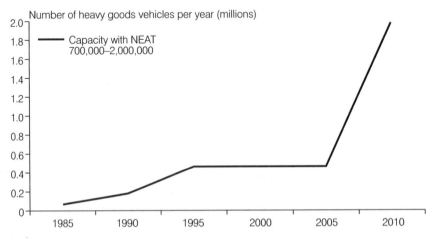

Source: adapted from Stampfli in Hummer (1993, p198)

Figure 8.1 *Projected Capacity of Swiss Railroads for Combined Traffic across the Alps, 1985–2010*

little importance; during the first two years, only six such permits were issued (Hirter et al, 1994, p151).

The handling of such a large volume of combined traffic by rail requires an appropriate infrastructure (terminals, enlarged tunnels) also outside Switzerland. Since the EC at that time did not yet dispose of the necessary powers (infrastructure came to be included only later on with the TransEuropean Networks), a trilateral agreement providing for significant investments in this area was signed parallel to the transit agreement by Switzerland, Germany and Italy. It was supplemented by an agreement between the different railroad administrations concerned (Hummer, 1993c, pp361–371).

With regard to financing, the enormous railroad investments – which included tunnels of record length (57 kilometres for the Gotthard tunnel) – were guaranteed by the Swiss government. Fees were supposed to repay those investments within 60 years and would be calculated accordingly. This fits in quite well with the already dominant Swiss notion that over the long term each kind of traffic should cover the full costs it occasioned; fees would therefore depend upon real costs and include external costs as well. This was in contrast to the EC, who at that time discussed similar concepts but did little to implement them in the near future (Maibach et al, 1999).

The fact remains that the NEAT railroad project represented a considerable financial risk. About half of an annual budget of the Swiss Federation was to be invested in rail infrastructure without guarantee that this would ever be paid back – for example, in case the EC was able to impose the road passage of heavy trucks after the expiration of the Transit Treaty (or even earlier). It also represented an environmental nuisance by multiplying rail freight traffic many times over. For this reason, Swiss environmental groups, joined paradoxically by the automobile association and the automobile party which feared that the railroad would drain funds from road construction, moved to gather the 50,000 votes necessary to initiate a popular referendum to oppose NEAT. In September 1992, however, a clear majority – 63.6 per cent of the voters – pronounced themselves in favour of NEAT. Two months later, the voters rejected EEA membership.

The Alpen Initiative

The Transit Agreement of 1992 placed no limit on transiting trucks below 28 tonnes, whose numbers grew steadily. Besides, there was reason to assume that the protection it offered against heavy goods vehicles might be transitory (Arnold, 1993, A3–A7). While it could be expected to slow down the further deterioration of the environment near the major transit roads, it was unlikely to bring about a net improvement by actually reducing traffic, one of the central demands of anti-transit movements and one of the goals of the Alpine Convention (signed by Switzerland, the EC and all alpine states in 1991). This convention contains the goal of 'reducing burdens and risks of inner-alpine and crossing traffic to a measure that can be supported by humans, animals and plants, in particular by an increased shift of traffic, especially freight traffic, to rail' (Article 2 of the Alpine Convention; Arnold, 1993, C5).

Confronted with this situation, in 1989 a small group of people launched a project that was considerably more radical than the approach taken by the Swiss government. The Alpen Initiative – as it called itself – proposed a referendum on a constitutional amendment requiring quite simply that within ten years from its adoption, all Alp-crossing transit traffic had to be by rail. It also prohibited all capacity increases of Alp-crossing transit roads, except for local bypasses.

The Swiss government – legislative and executive alike – strongly rejected this initiative in 1992 and 1993. Transport Minister Ogi argued that it represented a provocation of the EC, since it discriminated between transit traffic and other (export, import or domestic) Alp-crossing traffic. Indeed, the EC reacted adversely to this initiative once it was adopted. But even earlier, it put pressure on Switzerland to modify the traffic regime of the Transit Treaty (Arnold, 1993, C3; Hirter, 1993, pp152–154). Indeed, the Swiss government seemed inclined to make concessions on the question of weight limits and also prepared important infrastructure investments to handle increased road transit (Arnold, 1993, A7). The Alpen Initiative countered these conciliatory developments and argued that their move represented an ideal supplement to NEAT since it would make the shift from road to rail more effective and thus help to amortize a project that might otherwise turn out to be financially ruinous. It also pointed out that the initiative did not prescribe a positive prohibition of truck transit but could be achieved by economic incentives – that is, a transit fee high enough to effectively discourage trucks from passing through Switzerland.

The initiative was put to a popular vote in February 1994. In the end, 51.9 per cent of the voters – and 16 out of 23 cantons – voted in its favour, an outcome 'particularly impressive in light of the rarity with which Swiss voters approve popular initiatives', the Alpen Initiative being 'only the sixth initiative to win a double majority in the entire post-war era' (Kobach, 1997, p196). In order to contain irritation on the part of the EC, the Swiss transport minister declared that not only transit traffic but all Alp-crossing traffic (including import, export and domestic traffic) would be required to go by rail. Despite this declaration, the EC at first suspended the planned traffic negotiation with Switzerland in protest, arguing that the Alpen Initiative was incompatible with the Transit Agreement (Hirter, 1995, p149). In fact, the two instruments could barely overlap in time.

By September 1994, the Swiss government announced the principles for implementing the Alpen Initiative. The ban on Alp-crossing truck traffic would be achieved in a non-discriminatory and non-compulsory way by a system of road pricing for all trucks (LSVA or *Leistungsabhängige Schwerverkehrsabgabe*: a fee based on actual road use of all roads, not just motorways, by heavy goods vehicles), supplemented by a fee for alpine roads and tunnels. This would be combined with subsidies to combined traffic (Urstöger, 1997, p129).

EC–Swiss Negotiations Subsequent to the Alpen Initiative

Although the Alpen Initiative was now part of the Swiss constitution (Eidgenössisches Verkehrs und Energiewirtschaftsdepartement, 1996, p23), the

EC tried to have it repealed (Hirter, 1995, p150) and later worked to undercut its provisions. To begin with, there was the problem of 'detour traffic' of trucks via Austria and France. The Austrian and French governments wanted to make sure that Swiss fees would not be so high as to perpetuate bypass traffic through their own territories, especially since the Swiss government proposed to calculate full costs, including external costs for LSVA. Germany and Italy opposed high fees as a discouragement of trade and as an obstacle to the internal market. The EC thus pressed Switzerland for low traffic fees (rather than one oriented on 'true' or full costs) and for abandoning the 28-tonne limit for trucks in favour of a 40-tonne limit by the year 2005 (*Neue Zürcher Zeitung*, 7/8 December 1996, p9).

Switzerland was also confronted with another major problem – that of financing the necessary rail infrastructure for NEAT. Given the state of the federal budget, this project came to look prohibitively expensive, and no one appeared to have a ready solution. Under these circumstances the admission of heavy trucks, as demanded by the EC, offered one significant advantage: it could help pay for the NEAT project.

After several years of negotiations, a first agreement was reached on 23 January 1998 between Transport Commissioner Kinnock and Swiss Transportation Minister Leuenberger. This draft (the Kloten agreement) contained the following elements. Switzerland would give up its 28-tonne limit and admit 40-tonne trucks without quantitative restrictions by 2005. In the same year, Switzerland would introduce a system of road pricing applicable to all trucks (Swiss as well as EC), graduated according to emissions and which, on average, must not surpass 200 euro for one 300 kilometre-crossing from Basel to Chiasso. The 200 euro average LSVA fee was also calculated to include external costs in addition to financing the necessary road infrastructure (*VCÖ Zeitung*, no 7, October/November 1998; *T&E Bulletin*, no 74, December 1998). In the period from 1999–2005, Switzerland would admit increasing quotas of 40-tonne trucks, beginning with 120,000 in 1999 (*Euro Echo*, 2/1998, pp1, 4).

This package was put to the Transport Council on 17 March 17 1998 for approval. The council, however, rejected it, with the most strenuous opposition to the draft coming from Germany, which vetoed the proposal. German (CDU) Transport Minister Wissmann questioned the Swiss calculations for the LSVA and made it clear that Germany would only approve a substantially lower price tag (*Standard*, 18 March 1999). Italy was reported to ask for a reduction from 200 to about 170 euro (*Salzburger Nachrichten*, 18 April 1999). Several other countries – including Austria and France – were also reported to oppose the deal (EWWE, 2 October 1998, p10). Germany's vocal opposition was generally traced to the upcoming Bundestag elections; many observers assumed that no decision could be expected before that date (the end of September).

On 27 September 1998, the Swiss voted in a referendum to accept LSVA, with a majority of 57.2 per cent (*Standard*, 2 October 1998), thus replacing existing taxes on trucks that were substantially lower (during that time, one transit across Switzerland still cost only about 25 euro). Another referendum on the transit issue took place on 29 November 1998 and related to the financing of NEAT and other rail projects, scheduled to cost about 19 billion euro over the next 20 years. While NEAT had already been accepted in 1992, the assumption then was that it could be financed mostly by government loans. The new financing mode provided that taxes should produce about three-quarters of the necessary amount (*Standard*, 30 November 1998). After several last-minute concessions by Switzerland, the Council of Transport Ministers accepted the agreement with Switzerland unanimously in early December 1998. The concessions meant a delay in the application of the full fee (to be collected only in 2007), and more rapidly increasing quotas of 40-tonne trucks beginning in the year 2000 (*CIPRA Info*, 53/1999, p6; Wicki, 1999, pp89–90).

No one anticipates that this agreement will be able to stabilize Alp-crossing truck traffic. From an estimated 1.1 million in 1998, the number of trucks is expected to rise to 1.5–2 million by the year 2005 (*CIPRA Info*, 53/1999, p6). On the other hand, LSVA is expected to bring in a substantial amount of revenue. By the year 2005, this might be in the range of 0.9–1 billion euro, paid to the ratio of one third by transit trucks, the other two-thirds being furnished by domestic traffic. Two-thirds of these revenues will be devoted to railroad construction and noise protection rather than to road infrastructure maintenance (EWWE, 2 October 1998, p10; *VCÖ Zeitung*, no 7, October/November 1998; *Acid News*, December 1998).

At first, environmental groups were strongly critical of the agreement achieved in December 1998 and announced that they would try to repeal it by referendum (*Europa-Info*, October/November 1999, p11). However, in October 1999, the Swiss parliament voted to commit 1.8 billion euro to make railroad transport of freight more attractive, to aim for a 50 per cent reduction of the Alp-crossing trucks by 2009 and to take additional measures in case that goal should not be reached. After this vote, environmental groups supported the agreement (*T&E Bulletin*, 83 (41), November 1999, pp1, 3), which received its final approval by referendum on 21 May 2000.

AUSTRIA

A high level of development of both motorways and railroads marks Austrian transport infrastructure. In grand coalition years (during 1947–1966 and during 1987 to early 2000, Austria was governed by a coalition of Social Democrats and Conservatives), the transport ministry that is in charge of the railroads was controlled by Social Democrats. By contrast, the economics ministry – in charge of federal roads and motorways – is traditionally dominated by business interests and was held by the Conservative or People's party. The individual provinces in the Austrian federal system also have considerable influence on road construction.

For freight traffic, rail was, and still is, quite important. In 1997, its share was 250 per cent of EC average while road freight was about half of EC average (European Commission, 1999, figure 4.4). This used to apply even more strongly to North–South transit traffic, with the Alps representing a natural obstacle to heavy trucks on steep and curvy roads. However, the completion of the motorway across the Brenner in the early 1970s, linking Germany and Italy, soon reversed this pattern. The driving force behind this project on the political level was Tyrol's dominant People's party and its long-time governor who planned additional North–South motorways for the province. For some time the Austrian government actually tried, without success, to secure a financial contribution from the European Community for North–South motorways on the grounds that they served primarily EC needs (Ogrinz, 1993, p143). This position was abandoned only in 1985 when large-scale motorway construction was stopped in the course of the country's budget consolidation.

After the completion of the Brenner motorway in 1972, truck traffic on this route increased steeply, while the growth of rail freight almost came to a halt. Within less than a decade, the public mood shifted: plans for additional motorways across Tyrol had to be shelved in the face of local and regional resistance. The fact that such motorways are still continuing to 'creep up' towards the Austrian border in Italy and Germany led to considerable conflict in the context of the Alpine Convention in the 1990s.

First Conflicts over Truck Traffic in Tyrol

An important turning point for Austrian infrastructure politics came in 1985. The minister of transport declared that the Austrian road system had reached the limits of its growth and that any further capacity increases for freight transport would have to come from the rail system. During 1980 to 1998, Austria had the largest growth of rail freight of any EC Member State in absolute terms (tonne-kilometre) (European Commission, 1999, figure 4.7).

The year 1985 also marked an important turning point for Austrian environmental politics. For the next half-decade at least there was strong environmental activism and considerable government willingness to make concessions to the environmental movement (Lauber, 1997).

In Tyrol, local and regional resistance to truck traffic began to enjoy increasingly strong popular support. By this time, truck transit on the Brenner had grown by more than 400 per cent since 1970, about twice as fast as EC traffic in general (Molitor, 1996, p20). The issue was defined as concerning transit traffic, which had particularly high rates of growth, and was concentrated almost exclusively on an alpine valley with a high population density and vulnerability to noise and fumes. The Conservative governor and his party, backed by a two-thirds majority in the provincial diet, remained largely unresponsive at first. However, local initiatives, usually based on all-party support, spread throughout the province. In 1986, the governor showed first signs of responding to public pressure by submitting – or rather, resubmitting – the idea of a North–South tunnel that would cross Tyrol largely underground. After a provincial election in 1989 in which they lost a quarter of their support, the Tyrolean Conservatives reluctantly joined the other parties in demanding restrictive federal legislation for trucks (Bertsch, 1991, pp170–172).

The Transit Agreement of 1991 and the Accession Treaty of 1994

As in the case of Switzerland, the perspective of a single European market led the Austrian government to proclaim membership in the European Economic Area as a new foreign policy goal; by 1989 it went a step further and deposited a formal request for European Community membership (Kramer, 1996, pp171–177). For the issue of truck traffic, this meant the need to come to terms with the European Community. A transit agreement was negotiated between December 1987 and October 1991. During this time citizen initiatives organized and weighed in with demands to follow the Swiss example on the 28-tonne weight limit, reduce the number of trucks on the Brenner by about 80 per cent, and exclude the building of any additional infrastructure for truck transit. In addition, they proposed to charge full costs, including external costs of traffic, and to ban certain types of transit altogether, such as night-time driving or low-value goods (Sickinger and Husserl, 1993). To some extent, these positions were endorsed by the Tyrolean provincial diet in May 1991.

Broadly speaking, the goals of the Austrian government were similar to those of Switzerland – to put a stop to the further growth of road transit and to shift freight traffic from road to rail. Nevertheless, the Austrian government did not make common cause with Switzerland and, in fact, attacked that country for maintaining the 28-tonne limit which, it claimed, produced 'detour transit'. This transit was estimated to comprise 40 per cent of the Brenner transit volume. By contrast, the Transport Council of the EC wanted liberalized road traffic, free transit, free choice of the mode of transport and the removal of all technical and administrative obstacles. The council was unimpressed by the European Parliament's position, formulated in 1986 and particularly in 1988, that the EC should promote combined traffic and participate in Alp-crossing rail infrastructures (Topmann, 1993, pp178–182; Ogrinz, 1993, p145).

In 1989, negotiations began in earnest. The Austrian delegation – which by this time included a representative of the Tyrolean government – argued that in view of the general increase in freight volume, the problems experienced in Austria were just a foretaste of things to come in other regions of Europe as well, even though the Alps were particularly sensitive. It appears that this led to a shift in the attitude of the EC delegation. For the medium and long term, the delegation came to accept the necessity of a shift from road to rail and the reduction of the burden on the local population (Ogrinz, 1993, pp146–147).

Austria's first concrete proposals in 1990 aimed at reducing the qualitative and quantitative impact of traffic. This included an upper limit for transiting trucks on all transit routes, not just the Brenner (to avoid shifting the problem around). From this upper limit, to be reached in 1993, numbers were to decline by one third to one half. Of this figure, detour traffic shifted back to Switzerland and traffic shifted to rail would be deducted. In addition, truck exhaust would be reduced according to a predetermined schedule. Finally, Austria wanted a durable agreement, partly because the necessary infrastructure investments for the shift from road to rail required long-term amortization (up to 80 years in the case of tunnels), and partly because it wanted a settlement that would survive Austrian accession to full EC membership.

The EC at first was not prepared to accept a lid on total transit volume, much less to reduce this volume. With regard to reducing truck emissions, it argued that such reductions must flow from EC legislation (Ogrinz, 1993, pp148–151; Pösel, 1991, pp189–193). The EC also insisted that any agreement would have to be limited in time to a maximum of ten years, and made clear that Austrian reluctance to accede to EC demands would represent an insurmountable obstacle to Austrian accession. This point was also urged by several EC Member States which threatened to veto Austrian EEA accession if the Transit Agreement was too restrictive.

A compromise was finally reached in 1991. Its central provision related to the limitation of truck emissions on all transit routes according to a system of eco-points proposed by the Austrian negotiators. A fixed and thereafter declining number of eco-points is issued by Austria to the EC, which distributes them to member countries free of charge. Each eco-point corresponds to a certain volume of nitrogen oxide (NOx) emissions considered representative of other pollutants. Within 12 years, NOx emissions caused by transiting trucks over 7.5 tonnes must decline by 60 per cent; this means that 20 million eco-points issued in the first year should decline to 8 million by 2003. As transit trucks become cleaner, they need fewer eco-points for each passage, so the system has built-in flexibility. As an additional safeguard, the agreement provided that the number of transit trucks must not exceed 108 per cent of the level of 1991, set later on at 1,264,000 crossings of EC registered trucks (Hummer, 1993c, pp349–150). Should this happen anyhow, then the number of eco-points will be reduced accordingly by a committee composed equally of Austrian and EC representatives (Hummer, 1993c, p356).

With regard to rail, the agreement provided for investments in combined traffic in Austria and in certain EC countries (such as the enlargement of tunnels, the construction of rail terminals in Germany, the Netherlands and Italy and the improvement of tracks). The Austrian railroad pledged to increase the number of trains for combined traffic from 24 in 1991 to about 12–20 times that number by 2010. The completion of the Brenner tunnel, with additional capacities, is envisioned by 2010 (Hummer, 1993c, pp341–156). The agreement also stated that the contracting parties might subsidize combined traffic.

In addition, a special article provided that the parties intend to introduce charges for road traffic ('agreed as far as possible'), which in a first phase will cover only road costs, but in a second phase will also include external costs, in particular environmental costs. These charges will be based on the territoriality principle as far as possible and take into account the special costs of the alpine region (Agreement 1992, Article 14).

When the Transit Agreement entered into force in 1993, there was one big surprise: freighters needed only about 70 per cent of the eco-points issued for that year. This meant that the baseline figures had been 'overestimated' by about 40 per cent or more (*VCÖ Zeitung*, February 1995, p1; *Standard*, 30 November 1995). It is difficult to imagine that such an error was possible without cooperative behaviour on the part of both EC and Austrian authorities. In any case, this 'error' postponed the potentially restrictive effects of the agreement for seven years and led to considerable irritation with the anti-transit movement.

For Austria's accession to the European Community, the European Commission insisted that the Transit Agreement was incompatible with the *acquis* and therefore must be renegotiated. Negotiations on this issue were extremely difficult and were concluded only during the last top-level meetings in March 1994. The duration of the Transit Agreement was reduced by one year. The eco-point system and the upper limit on truck crossings were maintained, but were now scheduled to expire by the end of 2000 unless the stated goals were not reached, in which case expiration would come in 2003. The chief effect of the renegotiation was that Austria had to comply with Vignette Directive 93/89/EEC and gradually give up quotas for bilateral traffic with EC countries, reduce its road-usage fees for heavy trucks by about 75 per cent, abolish border stops, and calculate tolls according to the criteria of the Vignette Directive. All this made rail transport even less competitive.

As to rail, Austria and certain EC member countries committed themselves to a series of infrastructure investments, and Austria pledged to develop additional rail capacities beyond the volume already provided for in the Transit Agreement. The projected rail tunnel under the Brenner was listed as one of the top 11 Trans-European Networks, which in Austria raised hopes of financial support by the EC for this project. With the Brenner tunnel included, new rail capacities amounted to about twice the volume to be created by the Swiss NEAT, although generally at a lesser expense (except for the Brenner tunnel).

The Transit Agreement of 1991 contained a clause, which stated that during the second half of its validity, external costs – especially environmental costs – could be charged for road infrastructure use. This clause was now replaced by a declaration appended to the Accession Treaty in which the EC Council asked the Commission to develop a durable ecological framework for the European transport system. This framework would include specific measures for internalizing external costs, developing rail and combined traffic and providing technical standards for vehicles (such as exhaust and noise). Although this provision was only a political commitment and lacked legal value, it was celebrated by the Austrian delegation as a major success (*VCÖ Zeitung*, July 1994, p3). Among the leading political figures, only the Tyrolean governor seemed to hesitate in his support for the transport provisions of the treaty; but he was soon disciplined by his own party, which as a member of a grand coalition government had been directly involved in the negotiations.

The Brenner Toll Controversy and the Weakening of Austria's Position

After accession in 1995, there was a substantial increase of transit road freight, whereas combined traffic on rail went down (*Standard*, 27 November 1995; *VCÖ Zeitung*, 1996, p21). Austria reacted to the new situation by two toll increases on the Brenner motorway. In July 1995, this toll was nearly doubled to about 75 euro, drawing mild protest from the EC. This was followed in February 1996 by a second increase: 'clean' trucks according to the 1996 standards (Euro II class) paid about 83.5 euro, other trucks 109 euro. Between 10.00 pm and 5.00 am, all trucks paid 167 euro. The toll increase did not apply to local traffic (to trucks that did not travel the whole length of the Brenner motorway). The new increase drew strong protests from European freighters and some governments, as well as an angry condemnation by the European Parliament. Within a few weeks, the Commission made clear that Austria must take back the increase or expect legal proceedings before the European Court of Justice for violation of Directive 93/89/EEC. At the same time, the Commission announced that a proposal to replace this directive was under preparation and might be submitted soon (*Standard*, 6 February 1996). This draft contained a provision for a possible surcharge applying to sensitive areas (*Standard*, 21 February 1996).

It is obvious that the European Commission hesitated to take Austria to court for approximately two years; clearly, some form of consensus with Austria was sought. The Austrian government hoped that the new directive would come in time to make a court decision irrelevant, and to negotiate a favourable solution. This hope was, in part, prompted by the ongoing EC negotiations with Switzerland. If Switzerland was allowed to set tolls in range of 200 euro, transit trucks would arguably shift to Austria or France unless comparable fees could be charged in those countries as well. In fact, the new Brenner toll was less than half the amount discussed for Switzerland. However, Austria failed to present a coherent position over time and thus damaged its own prospects.

In early 1998, Austrian Transport Minister Einem (a Social Democrat) made several proposals to settle the conflict. He suggested that Austria should pay part of the Brenner toll – which he hoped to increase substantially – into a European fund for rail infrastructure, at least until Germany started road pricing on its motorways (*Standard*, 23 January 1998). Later on, he added the proposal that the Brenner toll be 'stretched'– in other words, charged not just for the 34 kilometres from Innsbruck to the Italian border but also for the northern section of the Brenner axis leading to the German border at Kufstein, which is about twice as long. But his position was immediately undercut by Tyrolean political leaders who refused this extension of the toll road to the north of Innsbruck, proposing instead to use 'excess' tolls on the Brenner route for financing railroad construction (*Standard*, 11 and 13 March 1998). Transport Minister Einem still worked to achieve a compromise with the EC. This included the acceptance, by the Community, of the current average toll level of 84 euro as long as the toll road was extended northwards ('stretched'); of night-time tolls at about double the day-time rate; and of a safeguard clause in case detour traffic did not shift back to Switzerland as expected as a result of the EC–Swiss agreement (*Standard*, 18 March 1998).

Nevertheless, due to the German veto, the Transport Council of March 1998 rejected the compromises negotiated by the Commission with both Switzerland and Austria. However, Commissioner Kinnock reaffirmed his interest to avoid a lawsuit and to arrive at a negotiated settlement with Austria, keeping in mind the perspective of the new Road Cost Directive that was on the way. Kinnock stated though that he could not wait eternally for Austria's 'stretching' of the Brenner toll road.

From then on, the Austrian People's party consistently undercut an agreement with the EC. Minister of the Economy Farnleitner, who was in charge of roads, agreed to toll-road stretching for 2001 at the earliest. In reaction to this, the European Commission handed in the complaint against Austria on 29 May 1998, accompanied by a statement that proceedings could be frozen if a satisfactory agreement was achieved. The complaint argued that Austria, by its toll increases of 1995 and 1996 (which predominantly affected trucks from other member countries), had violated Article 7b of Directive 93/89/EEC. It also violated Article 7h by collecting higher toll fees than necessary to cover construction, operation and further expansion of the Brenner motorway. Farnleitner reacted with new proposals that were hardly designed to be taken seriously. Indeed, Kinnock rejected them out of hand.

At the Transport Council in December 1998, Switzerland concluded its agreement on transit. A compromise was also reached with Austria that provided for only a slight reduction of the average toll on the Brenner and was made conditional on Austria's collecting 30 to 40 per cent of the Brenner toll on the stretch between Innsbruck and the German border. The event was greeted domestically as 'the biggest success of the Austrian EC presidency' (*Standard*, 2 December 1998).

While the anti-transit movement and the Tyrolean Greens and Social Democrats welcomed this compromise, Minister of the Economy Farnleitner made alternative proposals, including some already rejected by Kinnock (*Salzburger Nachrichten*, 2 and 10 December 1998). This was in line with top-level business organizations and the Tyrolean People's and Freedom parties, who solidly refused toll stretching as a 'disaster'. The Tyrolean governor threatened (and later ordered) administrative delays for the construction of toll booths on the northern stretch unless they were part of a common Austrian system of road pricing discussed for some years. After new provincial elections in 1999, this position was also adopted by the Tyrolean Social Democrats, junior partners of the People's party in the new provincial government (*Standard*, 31 March 1999). The fees of the road pricing system (applicable throughout Austria) were planned to be considerably lower than for the Brenner axis. It became clear that Tyrol wanted high toll fees only for transiting 'foreign' trucks, as if to confirm the European Commission's argument that the Brenner toll was indeed discriminatory.

In yet another respect, the Austrian government undermined measures to limit transit traffic, on which it had insisted for many years. In the context of the International Alpine Convention, Austria had long argued that no major new transit roads must be built across the Alps for ecological reasons. At the very least, new projects must first secure the consent of all states concerned. This had led to conflict with Germany and Italy; but Austria had not yielded and held up all other protocols under the convention since 1993. In June 1998 – upon Tyrolean insistence – the Austrian Ministry of the Economy shifted its position and opposed the consent requirement for new projects for the first time (*Standard*, 6 June 1998). After the alpine tunnel disasters in France (Mont Blanc) and Austria (Tauern) during the first half of 1999, Austrian business, Conservative governors and Minister Farnleitner made use of this opportunity by asking for the doubling of three Alp-crossing motorway tunnels, a proposal promptly accepted by the government (*Standard*, 1 and 2 June 1999). However, by early 2000, the prohibition of new Alp-crossing motorways or similar roads seemed to be accepted by all signatories of the Alpine Convention (*Standard*, 31 March 2000; CIPRA Österreich, 2000).

When, in February 2000, the governing grand coalition was replaced by one between the People's party and Haider's Freedom party, road and rail policies were for the first time concentrated in the hands of a single infrastructure minister from the Freedom party. Although, in February 2000, the advocate general of the European Court of Justice argued that Austria, by its toll increases of 1995 and 1996, had discriminated against foreign hauliers and overcharged them with tolls unjustified by appropriate infrastructure expenditures, the new minister was not prepared to adjust the Austrian position. Tyrol asked the federal government to impose a total ban on night-time trucking on the motorway in case of a negative decision by the European court. Other than this, there was no new initiative on the part of the Austrian government. Remarkably enough, no steps were taken to seek to exploit whatever opportunities were offered by the new directive on the charging of heavy goods vehicles for the use of certain infrastructures (the new Eurovignette Directive 1999/62/EC) that had entered into force in July 1999, replacing the old Vignette Directive 93/89/EEC. Article 9 of the new directive provides that Member States may set aside a percentage of the tolls or user fees and devote them to environmental protection, or the balanced expansion of the transportation network under consideration. (The old Vignette Directive had not only ignored environmental costs; under its Article 7h, tolls and user charges could only be used for the construction, operation or expansion of the relevant *road* network.)

As a result, in early 2000, major questions regarding the future of transit across Austria were still unsettled. The Transit Agreement as modified in 1994, with its restrictive system of eco-points and its upper limit on the number of truck crossings, was set to expire in 2003. According to decrees signed in February 2000, Austria will introduce road pricing in mid 2002 (*Standard*, 18 February 2000). However, rates will amount to only one fifth of those to be practised in Switzerland: about 0.15 euro per kilometre for heavy trucks. This could mean that in Austria, after the fall of the last quantitative restrictions for trucks and a likely reduction of the Brenner toll, the new rail capacities – which represent enormous investments – may not be fully used, at least as long as motorways are not so congested as to deter all further freight traffic.

This situation could be further aggravated by EC enlargement towards eastern Europe. Anticipating a further increase of transit traffic from such a development, former Transport Minister Einem, at the opening of the enlargement negotiations in late 1999, proposed to extend the eco-point system beyond 2003, hinting that Austrian consent would depend upon a satisfactory solution of this problem. This could include the construction of modern rail terminals in eastern Europe, road pricing and other measures (*Standard*, 3, 6 and 13–14 November 1999). There are no indications that the new infrastructure minister (of the Freedom party) has responded to the problem so far.

SOUTH TYROL (ALTO ADIGE)/TRENTINO

Another region strongly affected by road freight traffic – and, in particular, transit traffic – due to its mountainous characteristics, is Trentino/Alto Adige, crossed by the *autostrada del Brennero*, the Italian Brenner motorway. Local and regional resistance against the growth of this traffic was similar to resistance in Austria and Switzerland. However, the Italian government was steady in its commitment to maintain the free flow of traffic across the Alps at relatively low cost, since this is its main link with the other countries of the European Community. If any particular region exercised strong influence on national policy, it was Lombardia – given its close integration with southern Germany – rather than South Tyrol–Trentino (Wicki, 1999, pp149–150). Nevertheless, the Italian system permitted surprising regional initiatives in favour of shifting road freight to rail.

The Italian National Railway Company (Ferrovie dello stato, or FS) is not a likely candidate for offering competitive freight transport services. Neglected after World War II, it is still plagued by heavy debts, old and insufficient equipment, long delays, overstaffing and frequent strikes. It will hardly be able to make the very substantial investments in rolling stock, terminals and safety necessary for expanding rail traffic. However, FS was transformed into a stock corporation in 1992, and liberalization began in 1998; this opened the way for competition by non-FS trains (Lüfter, 1998, pp179–182, pp235–244).

The Italian system of motorways, by contrast, was always flexible in its instruments and market orientation. Concessions to build and operate an '*autostrada*' are granted for a certain period (in most cases 30 years). The costs are to be amortized mostly by tolls. Motorways are operated almost exclusively by public bodies. The Italian *autostrada del Brennero* is owned primarily by provinces and regions of the area. The autonomous region of Trentino–South Tyrol owns 30.29 per cent; together with the provinces and cities of Bozen/Bolzano and Trentino, their chambers of commerce and their savings banks, the regional share amounts to nearly 54 per cent (Lüfter, 1998, p215). Since 1992, the *autostrada* presidency is held by Ferdinand Willeit, himself close to the Südtiroler Volkspartei (SVP), the main political party of South Tyrol.

In 1995, Willeit started a new approach to investing the substantial operating profits of the *autostrada*. The Motorway Corporation would, in future, compete with the Italian railroad – on rail, by participating in an international rail freight venture with the task to purchase multisystem locomotives and railroad cars and to invest in rail terminals for the North–South route of Munich–Verona. This material would be placed at the disposal of freighters at competitive prices. The *autostrada* would benefit by a reduced need for repairs and by improving its acceptance with the public (Lüfter, 1998, pp216–219); most importantly, the need to add a third lane in each direction might be avoided. The venture (Brenner Schienentransport AG) was set up in October 1997 and also involved several Italian provinces, the Austrian province of Tyrol and Bavaria. However, the *autostrada del Brennero* played a dominant role and furnished 85 per cent of the starting capital. Nor was Willeit content with this. He hoped to raise enough funds from tolls not only to finance this rail freight group and to carry out track improvements, but also to help fund the Brenner tunnel as the long-term solution to the transit problem (Lüfter, 1998, pp220–225). This did not really conform to the old Vignette Directive 93/89/EEC, according to which tolls may only charge for construction, operation and expansion of an existing motorway. However, there is no indication that the European Commission is questioning Willeit's approach.

Although South Tyrolean political leaders strongly supported this policy, the Brenner Schienentransport AG is still having trouble getting off the ground. But, in the meantime, the private sector has become active in the same direction. In early 2000, one of Italy's largest freighters, South Tyrolean Eduard Baumgartner, ordered several dozen locomotives and hundreds of railroad cars to expand the freight-carrying capacity of the railroad (*Standard*, 16 February 2000). Because of railroad liberalization, other actors are joining the game and freight trains across the Brenner are becoming more frequent.

SUMMARY AND CONCLUSION

What does this record tell us about the chances and possibilities of integrating environmental priorities within transport, particularly freight transport? Where are such initiatives likely to originate, and are there certain institutional arrangements that are more favourable to policy integration than others, particularly at the level of the EC? This section reviews the three cases.

Switzerland had traditionally followed a proactive policy of constraining road freight for environmental reasons. It also maintains what is probably the best-functioning railroad system in Europe (offering a viable alternative to long-distance trucking) and, in the 1980s, introduced the principle that traffic should pay for its full costs. While it could preserve its proactive approach in the first transit agreement of 1992, its government came under pressure to yield to the EC policy of facilitating road transport when it decided to apply for EEA membership. The government was prepared for major concessions but was, in turn, confronted with a popular movement that it could not control – the Alpen Initiative and its successful referendum banning all Alp-crossing transit trucks. The Swiss government now used this impulse to build a system that aims at transferring most long-distance truck traffic, including domestic Swiss traffic, to rail. Trucks going by road will have to pay steep fees that will chiefly go to financing railroad construction. The Swiss government's leeway was also increased by the fact that EEA membership had been rejected in another referendum, so there was no question of having to accept the *acquis* in the near future. In this situation, the EC first aimed at overturning the referendum but came to accept the new Swiss approach and concentrated its efforts on reducing LSVA fees. In this, it was fairly successful; as a result, LSVA will not cover the full cost of traffic (Wicki, 1999, pp39–53).

Austria has some features in common with Switzerland. It too has a strong railway system and the highest share of rail freight of any state within the EC. However, it has no long tradition of checking road freight. Partly for budgetary reasons, partly because of a strong popular movement against transit traffic, it attempted to develop a solution to this problem in the late 1980s that claimed to be more sustainable than EC practices. Confronted with determined EC insistence on the principles of free transport, Austria formulated its eco-points system (to stabilize the number of transiting trucks while reducing pollution), and an ambitious railroad scheme to step up combined traffic. It managed to secure EC acceptance (probably in exchange for a small 'miscalculation' at the expense of the people most directly affected). However, during the accession negotiations, much of these achievements was bargained away under EC pressure. The transit agreement of 1991 was hollowed out and road freight became more competitive. As a result, the expected shift to rail can by no means be taken for granted, especially if current Brenner toll rates have to be reduced (the numerical limitation of transit trucks will expire anyhow in 2003). On the other hand, Austria was never prepared to accept high tolls for all trucks on the Swiss model. It is true that the EC made some environmental concessions to Austria in the Brenner toll controversy and offered new possibilities for integrating environmental concerns through the 1999 Eurovignette Directive. These possibilities have not been taken up so far in Austria, partly due to domestic conflict over the issue, and partly because of organizational rivalry or inertia.

The case of South Tyrol demonstrates that even a region, in a country not much given to environmental concern over transport, can (under strong pressure from its constituent population) find ways to promote sustainable transportation despite EC law. The EC tolerated Willeit's creative practices of investing *autostrada* surpluses in the rail system and inserted a clause in the 1999 Eurovignette Directive that seems to sanction this practice.

What these cases show is that the EC took few, if any, initiatives of its own to integrate transport and environmental policies. It responded to innovations, which the Alpine countries (and sometimes regions) had themselves developed under very strong pressure from their own populations. Until the late 1990s, the EC's chief contribution was to press for easier, faster and unrestricted flow of road traffic. It also insisted on keeping tolls (and taxes) on road freight low (for example, by excluding external and, in particular, environmental costs from their calculation) and blocked cross-financing of rail by road. As a result, it made rail freight still less competitive.

The only major EC environmental initiative on transport was to reduce limits for truck emissions, an end-of-pipe strategy that could not contribute much to sustainability because its effects were immediately overcompensated by rising traffic volume (European Commission, 1999, figures 4.1 and 7.1). At best it was inclined to make temporary or ad hoc exceptions to its general approach to accommodate environmental concerns (limits on trucks crossing Austria until 2003; Brenner toll compromise; provision for special tolls for 'sensitive areas' such as alpine passes included in a draft of the new Eurovignette Directive, although dropped again later on).

The last few years seem to indicate a shift towards greater environmental policy integration in this area. This fits the recent policy of promoting rail freight (although its chief motivation is economic, and this policy may only partly compensate the shift to road achieved by the one-sided road liberalization policy of the 1980s). It is also reflected in the 1999 Eurovignette Directive, which provides that a certain percentage of toll revenues may be set aside for environmental protection or the balanced expansion of the transportation network concerned. This seems to imply the acceptance of some measure of cross-financing of rail by road traffic, as is practised already in South Tyrol. The chief problem here is that there is no indication of how much cross-financing of rail (and of environmental expenditures) is permissible under this provision.

This invites a more fundamental question. Much of the evidence supports the conclusion that the evolution of transport in the EC is unsustainable because transport is too cheap. It is too cheap because it does not pay for its full cost – including external costs – and this is accepted by the EC for another decade or more. According to economic theory, such a price level is bound to lead to excessive demand, which in turn will induce unprofitable infrastructure investments. Such conclusions regularly emerge from recent expert reports.[1] Underpriced traffic, furthermore, concentrates production in a small number of agglomerations (where it enhances congestion) and often leads to regional decline. Of course, the political problems of making traffic (primarily road freight) pay for its full cost must not be underestimated. But as long as this issue is not addressed, sustainable transport is likely to remain an evasive goal – or more precisely, one that so far was consistently pursued with insufficient instruments.[2]

Is there also a lesson to be drawn in institutional terms regarding environmental policy integration within the transport area or beyond? In the three cases reviewed, environmental concerns were taken into account in transport policy primarily due to public pressure by those directly affected by the negative impacts of trucking who organized strong grassroots movements. Due to the 'democratic deficit' of the EC, such voices are not often heard in Brussels, where economic interests are clearly privileged. It is likely, however, that they will be more easily heard in an elected assembly (and, indeed, the European Parliament argued in favour of a shift from road to rail quite early on in the game). It should be added, though, that the regulation of trucking is more likely to invite parliamentary treatment for sustainability than, say, private motoring.

National governments, in general, tend to downgrade environmental concerns; this is forcefully reflected in the dominant approach of the Transport Council as described at the outset of this chapter. Those at the helms of power – at the national as well as EC level – tend to view environmental concerns as something of a luxury in the context of the global economic struggle. The most promising way to modify this view is probably to bring the very real, long-term costs of environmental degradation out in the open. After all, external costs are eventually shouldered by people. To calculate those costs and make them transparent and widely accessible may yet be the best strategy to induce change. This is why the stakes of the current EC discussions on making all modes of transport pay their full costs are really quite high.

REFERENCES

1992 Agreement between the Republic of Austria and the European Economic Community on the Transit of Goods by Road and Rail, BGBl, 280/823, 4558–4568, 29 December

Arnold, A (1993) *Dokumentation*, Alpen Initiative, Brig

Bernhard, A (1995) *Österreich im Gemeinsamen (Straßengüterverkehrs-) Markt*, Verwaltungsakademie des Bundes, Arbeitspapier no 02/1995, Vienna

Bertsch, J (1991) 'Transitwiderstand in Tirol' in H Koch and H Lindenbaum (eds) *Überrolltes Österreich. Zukunft unter dem Transitverkehr*, Verlag für Gesellschaftskritik, Vienna

CIPRA Österreich (2000) *Die Alpenkonvention*, no 19, 1/2000, Vienna

1993 Directive of 25 October 1993 on the Application by the Member States of Taxes on Certain Vehicles Used for the Carriage of Goods by Road and Tolls and Charges for the Use of Certain Infrastructures (Vignette Directive 93/89/EEC)

1999 Directive of the European Parliament and of the Council of 17 June 1999 on the Charging of Heavy Goods Vehicles for the Use of Certain Infrastructures (Eurovignette Directive 1999/62/EC)

Eidgenössisches Verkehrs und Energiewirtschaftsdepartement (1996) *Wege durch die Alpen. Alpenquerender Güterverkehr auf Straße und Schiene*, Eidgenössische Drucksachen- und Materialzentrale, Bern

European Commission (1992a) *Green Paper on the Impact of Transport on the Environment: A Community Strategy for 'Sustainable Mobility'*, COM (92) 46, Brussels

European Commission (1992b) *The Future Development of the Common Transport Policy: A Global Approach to the Construction of a Community Framework for Sustainable Mobility*, COM (92) 494 final, Brussels

European Commission (1998) *Communication on Transport and CO_2: Developing a Community Approach*, COM (1998) 204 final, Brussels

European Commission (1999) *Transport in Figures*, http://europa.eu.int/en/comm/dg07/tif/contents.htm#Goods Transport

European Environmental Agency (EEA) (1999) *Environment in the European Union at the Turn of the Century*, EEA, Copenhagen

EEA (2000) *Term 2000: Transport and Environment Reporting Mechanism Report*, EEA, Copenhagen

Goodwin, F (2000) *Transport, Infrastructure and the Economy*. T&E report 00/6, Brussels

Hirter, H et al (1994) *Année Politique Suisse 1993*, Institut de Science Politique à l'Université de Berne, Bern

Hirter, H et al (1995) *Année Politique Suisse 1994*, Institut de Science Politique à l'Université de Berne, Bern

Hummer, W (1993a) *Alpenquerender Transitverkehr aus regionaler und überregionaler Sicht*, Böhlau, Vienna

Hummer, W (1993b) 'Verkehrspolitische Bedingtheiten des alpenquerenden Transitverkehrs' in W Hummer (ed) (1993a) *Alpenquerender Transitverkehr aus regionaler und überregionaler Sicht*, Böhlau, Vienna, pp3–12

Hummer, W (1993c) 'Der österreichische und der schweizerische Transitvertrag in vergleichender Sicht' in W Hummer (ed), (1993a) *Alpenquerender Transitverkehr aus regionaler und überregionaler Sicht*, Böhlau, Vienna, pp339–376

Kobach, K W (1997) 'Spurn Thy Neighbour: Direct Democracy and Swiss Isolationism', *West European Politics*, vol 20, no 3, pp185–211

Kramer, H (1996) 'Foreign Policy' in V Lauber (ed) *Contemporary Austrian Politics,* Westview, Boulder CO, pp151–200

Lauber, V (1997) 'Austria: a Latecomer which Became a Pioneer' in M Skou Andersen and D Liefferink (eds) *European Environmental Policy: The Pioneers,* Manchester University Press, Manchester and New York, pp81–118

Lüfter, U (1998) *Die Verkehrspolitik der Europäischen Union, Italiens und Südtirols im Hinblick auf den alpenquerenden Gütertransit insbesondere am Brenner,* MA thesis, University of Salzburg, Salzburg

Maibach, M, Ott, W and Schreyer, C (1999) *Faire und effiziente Preise im Verkehr,* Rüegger, Zürich

Organisation for Economic Co-operation and Development (OECD) (1999) *Environmentally Sustainable Transport,* Final Report on Phase II of the OECD EST Project, Paris

Ogrinz, T (1993) 'Entwicklung und gegenwärtiger Stand der Transitverhandlungen Österreichs mit der Europäischen Gemeinschaft' in W Hummer (1993a), *Alpenquerender Transitverkehr aus regionaler und überregionaler Sicht,* Böhlau, Vienna, pp143–152

Pösel, E (1991) 'EG-Beitritt' in H Koch and H Lindenbaum (eds) *Überrolltes Österreich: Zukunft unter dem Transitverkehr,* Verlag für Gesellschaftskritik, Vienna, pp179–202

Sickinger, H and Hussl, R (1993) *Transit-Saga: Bürgerwiderstand am Auspuff Europas,* Thaur, Innsbruck

Stampfli, K (1993) 'Schweizer Transitprobleme: Ein zielgerichteter Aufbruch – Das Projekt Alpentransit und der kombinierte Verkehr für das Europa von morgen' in W Hummer (ed) (1993a) *Alpenquerender Transitverkehr aus regionaler und überregionaler Sicht,* Böhlau, Vienna, pp187–198

Topmann, G (1993) 'Die Position des Europäischen Parlaments zum alpenquerenden Transitverkehr' in W Hummer (ed) (1993a), *Alpenquerender Transitverkehr aus regionaler und überregionaler Sicht,* Böhlau, Vienna, pp175–182

Trechsel, A H, and Sciarini, P (1998) 'Direct Democracy in Switzerland: Do Elites Matter?', *European Journal of Political Research,* vol 33, no 1, pp99–124

Urstöger, C (1997) *Die Verkehrspolitik Österreichs, der Schweiz und der Europäischen Union und deren Auswirkung auf die Entwicklung des alpenquerenden Güterverkehrs seit 1985,* MA thesis, University of Salzburg, Salzburg

Wicki, C (1999) *Nachhaltige Alpenverkehrspolitik,* Rüegger, Zürich

Newsletters and Newspapers

Acid News, Gothenburg, Sweden

Commissione Internazionale per la Protezione delle Alpi (CIPRA) Info

Environment Watch Europe (EWE), formerly *Environment Watch Western Europe* (EWWE), Agra Europe, Brussels

Euro Echo, Vienna

Europa-Info, Vienna

European Voice, Brussels

Neue Zürcher Zeitung, Zurich

Salzburger Nachrichten, Salzburg

Standard, Vienna

Transport and Environment (T&E) Bulletin, Brussels

Verkehrsclub Österreich (VCÖ) Zeitung, Vienna

NOTES

1 See, for example, the British SACTRA report discussed in *T&E Bulletin*, vol 81 (39) August/September 1999, p1; see also the report by Oxford Economic Research Associates and the report by the US Federal Highway Administration in *T&E Bulletin*, vol 76 (36), May 1999, p4. These arguments are applied to EU circumstances in Goodwin (2000).

2 The issue is discussed in the Commission at least since the early 1990s (*T&E Bulletin*, vol 55, January 1997, p3), but always as a measure for a fairly distant future. In a 1998 White Paper the Commission proposed to deal with this problem during the first half of the coming decade (*Acid News*, 3 October 1998, p3). Commission initiatives in this direction were already modest, action by the council even less satisfactory. Recent progress is not very encouraging (see the sceptical TERM report by the European Environmental Agency (EEA, 2000) and its discussion in *EWE*, 12 May 2000, p5).

9

EU Energy Policy in a Changing Climate

Ute Collier[1]

INTRODUCTION

There can be little doubt that energy policy is a crucial area for environmental policy integration (EPI). Energy production and use is a major contributor to a number of environmental problems. Detrimental effects can result during all stages of the energy cycle, from exploration to the final use of energy and the disposal of waste products. Of particular concern is the contribution of emissions from fossil fuel combustion, which are implicated in both air pollution and climate change. In the European Union (EU), fossil fuel combustion accounts for 98 per cent of carbon dioxide (CO_2) emissions (the major culprit of climate change), as well as a large proportion of sulphur dioxide (SO_2), and is implicated in acid rain and local air pollution, and nitrogen oxide emissions (NO_x). Energy production and use accounts for more than 70 per cent of CO_2 emissions, the rest coming from the transport sector (DG for Energy, 1999).

In the case of SO_2 and NO_x, end-of-pipe technologies can, albeit at a relatively high economic cost, lead to substantial emission reductions. Indeed, EU power station emissions of these gases have been regulated since the early 1990s and considerable reductions have been achieved. However, in the 1990s, the emerging concern about global climate change has raised new questions about the sustainability of current energy systems.

Climate change has rapidly advanced from scientific theory to the top environmental threat. While there are still considerable scientific uncertainties, the evidence of human-induced changes has been mounting. Seven of the hottest years on record have occurred in the 1990s, 40 per cent of the Arctic sea ice has disappeared and during the last decade the cost of natural disasters added up to four times the bill of the 1980s.[2] The issue is now being taken seriously not only by politicians but also by businesses. Large multinational companies such as BP, Dow, IBM and Johnson & Johnson have recently made voluntary commitments to reduce their emissions.

With CO_2, the most important greenhouse gas, emission abatement is a much more complex process than with SO_2 and NO_x, requiring fuel switching, efficiency improvements and a greater role for renewable energies. Fundamental changes in energy policy are needed to achieve this. EPI has to become a reality for energy policy; otherwise, emission reduction targets will not be realized. Nuclear power, while low in CO_2 emissions, entails other environmental risks and produces large quantities of extremely hazardous waste for which no long-term disposal option has been found.

At the same time as causing substantial environmental damage, energy production and use pervade all economic activities. While its significance as an input factor in industrial production has declined as a result of the shift to a more service-based economy, energy production nevertheless remains important, especially in the form of electricity. Electricity has become an indispensable, if often unnoticed, element in our daily lives, reducing both the time needed to perform daily chores as well as allowing us access to the information highway. The challenge is for energy policy to cater for energy needs without compromising environmental quality.

Energy's pivotal role in the quest for sustainable development has been acknowledged almost universally, as statements from the EU, Member State governments, industry and environmental pressure groups demonstrate. The EU's fifth Environmental Action Programme (EAP), for example, states that (European Commission, 1992a, p6):

> *Energy policy is a key factor in the achievement of sustainable development...*
> *The challenge of the future will be to ensure that economic growth, efficient and secure energy supplies and a clean environment are compatible objectives.*

Yet, during most of the 1990s, there was little progress with the 'greening' of EU energy policy. Directives on renewable energy sources and energy efficiency had little impact, while decisions to liberalize the EU energy market were likely to fundamentally change the EU energy economy. No environmental impact assessment was carried out until long after the crucial directives were passed.

Meanwhile, the negotiations for the Kyoto Protocol under the United Nations Convention on Climate Change (UNCCC) focused attention on the need for changes in energy policy. The EU aimed to position itself as a leader in the negotiations but its past record on EPI raised doubts about the credibility of its position. The EU signed the Kyoto Protocol as a block and is required to reduce its greenhouse gas emissions by 8 per cent by the years 2008 to 2012 (compared to 1990 levels).

In the year 2000, as greenhouse gas emissions continue on an upward trend, both the EU and its Member States are struggling to draw up credible plans to implement the Kyoto commitments. EU energy policy finds itself at the cross-roads – either it continues with business as usual and ignores the legally binding obligations under the Kyoto Protocol, or it institutes some serious changes, both at EU and Member State level.

This chapter examines the history of EU energy policy and EPI, current emission trends and the implications of the Kyoto Protocol for energy policy both at the EU and Member States level. It then specifically looks at the development of renewable energy sources as a case study. Finally, conclusions are drawn about the future prospects for EPI in the energy policy area.

EU ENERGY POLICY AND EPI: PAST FAILURES

When discussing progress towards EPI in EU energy policy, it has to be recognized that the EU as a supra-national body has limited energy policy competencies. Member States have been very reluctant to cede sovereignty in this sensitive area of economic policy (Collier, 1994). The Treaty on European Union talks specifically of 'measures' rather than a 'policy' in the energy area. While around 100 directives, regulations and decisions are in existence relating to energy, these have been relatively inconsequential, with the real power remaining with the Member States. Nevertheless, there are a number of measures in the areas of energy efficiency and renewable energies, as well as a technology research and development programme, with a focus on environmentally beneficial technologies.

Furthermore, there have been various Commission communications and council resolutions on the theme of a common energy policy, including periodical resolutions setting common energy objectives, although Member States have seldom taken much notice of these common objectives. Environmental concerns were first mentioned in the 1973 'guidelines and priority actions for Community energy policy', while the 1986 common objectives (to be achieved by 1995) for the first time included the objective to achieve balanced solutions between energy and the environment (Collier, 1994).

The theme of integrating an environmental dimension within EU energy policy subsequently gathered speed, mainly as a result of the emerging climate change concern. A *Communication from the Commission to the Council on Energy and the Environment* in 1990 (European Commission, 1990) was followed in 1992 by Commission proposals for a climate change strategy (European Commission, 1992b). This promised some real progress towards greater sustainability, providing for a carbon/energy tax, an energy efficiency programme (SAVE) and a renewable energy programme (ALTENER). However, the realization of the proposals has proved difficult (Collier, 1996).

Firstly, the carbon/energy tax has had a troublesome time. Industrial opposition led to concessions for energy-intensive energies early in the negotiations, although the Member States have found no agreement. A number (Denmark, Finland, the Netherlands, Sweden, and to some extent Austria) have introduced their own carbon taxes and are still keen on pushing for a common tax. The proposal has now been downscaled to such an extent that it would have little effect, yet there is still no prospect of agreement. Even though what is on the table would effectively entail little more than a harmonization of existing energy taxes with plenty of flexibility, countries such as the UK are still opposed, in principle, to the involvement of the EU in taxation matters. A common approach to cost internalization is thus likely to remain elusive.

Secondly, ALTENER is a very weak programme. Renewable energies have featured in EU energy discussions since mid 1985, but it was not until 1993 that specific numeric targets were adopted in conjunction with ALTENER (Grubb, 1996). According to this, in order to reduce CO_2 emissions by 180 million tonnes by 2005, the following must be achieved (European Commission, 1993a):

- increase renewable energy sources' contribution in the coverage of total energy demand from 4 per cent in 1991 to 8 per cent in 2005;
- treble the production of electricity from renewable energy sources (excluding large hydro);
- secure for biofuels a market share of 5 per cent of total fuel consumption by motor vehicles.

In 2000, with five years to go, these targets appear unrealistic. This is not surprising, considering that only 40 million ECU of EU funding were allocated over the first five years, mainly to be used for various pilot studies. One analyst estimated that achieving the electricity sector target alone would require the allocation of over 20 billion ECU of investment from 1995 to 2005 (Grubb, 1996). Later sections in this chapter will look at the situation regarding renewable energies in more detail.

The situation is similar as far as the SAVE programme for energy efficiency is concerned. This initially consisted of financial assistance for various pilot projects (a total of 40 million ECU during the period of 1992–1996) and a so-called framework directive (European Commission, 1993b) which left Member States so much flexibility in its implementation that the Commission itself commented early on that the effects of SAVE were highly uncertain (European Commission, 1994). The Commission proposed a budget of 150 million ECU for the period of 1996–2000 (SAVE II), aiming at energy savings of 60–70 million tonnes of oil equivalent (toe) per year by the year 2000. However, the proposal failed, mainly because of German opposition to increased expenditure, and a budget of only 45 million ECU was approved. So far, SAVE II has not been any more effective than SAVE I. It has produced many studies but few tangible results.

Meanwhile, the most significant development for the energy sector during the 1990s was the decision to liberalize energy markets. At the end of the 1980s, EU energy markets were essentially heavily regulated and dominated by large monopoly companies, often state-owned. Market liberalization was on the EU agenda since the late 1980s, as discussion started to create an internal energy market (IEM). After a long deadlock, the council finally agreed on market liberalization in the electricity sector in 1996[3] and in the gas sector in 1998.[4] National energy markets are now gradually being opened up.[5]

The ultimate aim of the IEM was to achieve lower energy prices as a means of improving industrial competitiveness. However, low energy prices are not necessarily desirable environmentally since they provide a major disincentive to energy efficiency and also make it more difficult for renewable energies to compete, in particular while there is no internalization of external costs. Yet, these issues received little consideration during the negotiations for liberalization (Collier, 1994). Liberalization was driven by economics ministers and, at the time, few economics or trade ministries felt the need to give due consideration to environmental concerns.

The need to reconcile competitiveness and environmental protection objectives in energy policy was one of the themes of the 1995 Commission White Paper on energy policy. This stressed the need to meet environmental challenges but offered little in terms of actual measures (European Commission, 1995, p9):

> *Exploring the complementarities between energy and environment must be done in the framework of sustainable development; there is, in particular, scope for a closer interface between competitiveness, job creation and environment.*

The White Paper proposed a number of initiatives, including communications on energy efficiency, cogeneration and renewable energy sources. However, while these have since been published,[6] there has been little corresponding action on the ground. A 1999 *Communication on the Single Market and the Environment* (European Commission, 1999a) acknowledged that a liberalized market could put a brake on the development of renewable energies and a less carbon-intensive energy system. A recent report for Greenpeace has confirmed these findings (Froggatt, 2000).

Some Member States are now beginning to address these problems and are introducing environmental service obligations on energy companies, largely as a result of their climate change policies. However, there are a number of instances of 'too little, too late'– for example, with regard to energy efficiency obligations in the UK. At the time of privatization and liberalization, the UK government insisted that the market would deliver greater energy efficiency. In reality, this did not happen and there has been a considerable increase in energy consumption (for example, 17 per cent for electricity since 1990 in the domestic sector), linked to lower prices.

Today, the true environmental effects of liberalization are not clear since only a few Member States have a fully liberalized market. It appears that there are some benefits (for example, consumers in Germany and the UK can now choose 'green', 100 per cent renewable, electricity tariffs), as well as clear threats, for instance in terms of energy efficiency. The lesson from the UK is that liberalized energy markets need careful regulation and this should happen when primary legislation is drawn up, not as an afterthought a few years later. However, the UK is not alone in its reluctant attitude. In most EU Member States (with the exception of Austria, Germany, Denmark and the Netherlands) there was little environmental concern in the energy sector, pre-liberalization.

Overall, energy trends in the Member States have yet to show substantive progress towards more sustainable energy options and emission reductions. During the 1990s, emissions continued to grow in most Member States except Germany and the UK. And in these two cases, this was fortuitous. In Germany, unification meant the collapse of industry in the old German Democratic Republic (GDR) and, hence, much lower energy demand. In the UK, the liberalization of power generation led to a 'dash to gas' as many old coal-fired plants were replaced by combined-cycle gas turbines. Due to greater efficiencies and the lower carbon intensity of natural gas, emissions declined considerably. However, the move to gas-fired generation was not due to EPI and other environmental options were ignored (Collier, 1997).

Despite fine words in the EU's 1990 communication, progress with EPI has thus been slow. There are a number of explanatory factors for this. Firstly, energy policy-making is dominated by economics ministries which tend to fare much better than environmental ministries in the ministerial hierarchy. Economics ministries are also heavily lobbied by the energy industry, which has been somewhat slow to react to the environmental agenda. Secondly, while environmental issues raised their profile in some EU countries (such as Germany and Denmark), others remained much less interested. Thirdly, liberalization came to dominate the policy agenda and environmental issues were essentially seen as a distraction in the process (requiring yet more regulation). However, towards the late 1990s, a change in attitudes gradually emerged. Crucial to this change was the Kyoto climate summit in December 1997, which aimed to set legally binding targets for greenhouse gases. This implied that fundamental changes in the way we produce and consume energy would soon be needed.

THE EU AND KYOTO

In the run-up to the Kyoto summit, the EU, spurred on by a number of progressive Member States, tried to position itself as a global leader on climate change issues. The EU had the most ambitious negotiating target for Kyoto – namely, a 15 per cent cut in the three greenhouse gases: CO_2, CH_4 (methane) and N_2O (nitrous oxide). It also proposed a number of common policies and measures to be agreed as part of the Kyoto accord. The feasibility of this target was supported by research from leading analysts, and a Commission paper concluded that such emission cuts were readily available at low or no cost. A series of policies and measures were identified that could cut CO_2 emissions alone by 800 million tonnes, 17 per cent below the 1990 level by 2010 (European Commission, 1997). However, not surprisingly, other negotiators (in particular, the Japanese and the Americans) questioned the achievability of the EU's proposals, especially in light of its less than exemplary record as far as emissions or common policies and measures in the energy field were concerned (see Ott, 1998, for more detail).

In the end, the EU signed up to an 8 per cent reduction in six greenhouse gases by the period 2008 to 2012: CO_2, N_2O, CH_4, sulphur hexafluoride (SF_6), hydrofluorocarbons (HFCs), and perfluorocarbons (PFCs). This compares to a 6 per cent reduction for Japan and 7 per cent for the US. The target was then subsequently divided up between Member States. Luxembourg (28 per cent), Denmark (21 per cent) and Germany (21 per cent) have the largest reduction commitments, while some Member States are allowed substantial emission increases (Greece: 25 per cent, Portugal: 27 per cent).

In June 2000, there was still considerable uncertainty about the Kyoto Protocol. While 84 countries had signed it, only one EU Member State (France) had ratified it. Question marks remained over the ratification of the protocol by the world's largest emitter, the US. Considerable opposition by the US Senate means that ratification might be some years away. The EU supports ratification by 2002, the anniversary of the Earth Summit in Rio, at which the United Nations Framework Convention on Climate Change (UNFCCC) was signed. However, as the evidence of climate change continues to mount, opposition to the protocol will hopefully dispel. By April 2000, EU countries were busy drawing up Kyoto implementation plans and the Commission had produced several papers on the implementation of the protocol. Quite clearly, if the Kyoto targets are to be achieved, business-as-usual trends have to be broken and substantial changes are required, in particular in the energy and transport sectors.

So, what are the prospects for a more integrated energy policy, both at EU level and in the Member States? As the next section shows, not all developments are pulling in the same direction.

THE CHANGING CONTEXT OF ENERGY POLICY

The circumstances governing energy policy decisions have changed considerably since the EU first looked at the integration of energy and environment policies in 1990. The last decade has seen a definite move away from concerns about energy scarcity and energy security. Oil prices have fallen significantly in real terms, while natural gas, once considered a scarce premium fuel, is now considered plentiful. State involvement in energy markets is now primarily through regulation rather than ownership. Within this framework, environmental concerns, and in particular climate change, have become the major constraints on business-as-usual behaviour and otherwise unfettered energy markets. While there undoubtedly has been much rhetoric, some of this is slowly translating into action, as exemplified by measures such as the climate change levy on business energy use in the UK.

According to the Directorate-General for Energy (1999) (since January 2000, the Energy and Transport Directorate-General), several core imperatives can be identified as the ingredients in a new approach to ensure that the energy system plays its part more effectively in a more sustainable development of the EU:

- provision of diverse and secure supplies;
- provision of adequate, full-cost and low-price energy supplies;
- reduction in the wide range of environmental impacts and control of the speed of climate change at the global level;
- measures to stimulate more efficient energy use, especially at a time of lower real energy prices;
- industrial policy and plant procurement issues;

- social and health dimensions of energy use, given ageing populations and fuel poverty.

Some of these policy imperatives are part of 'traditional' energy policy; others form significant components of macro-economic, fiscal, environmental and social policy. Quite clearly, a sustainable energy policy needs to be more complex and inclusive, thus presenting a real challenge to policy integration.

To achieve this ideal, a combination of EU and national measures is needed. At least in theory, climate change as well as a number of other developments (continuing liberalization of the energy market and cross-border mergers of energy companies) will lead to a strengthening of EU-level policy measures. For example, it is likely that an EU-wide emissions trading system will be developed that will allow greater flexibility in meeting emission targets. However, there is still great resistance by some Member States to agree to greater EU involvement in some measures, such as energy taxes or certain energy measures. This may well cause further conflict in the future.

EU Energy and Environment Trends

Energy and environment trends in the EU reflect the tension between economic logic, on the one hand, and climate change pressures, on the other hand. At the end of 1998, only three Member States (Germany, Luxembourg and the UK) had seen any emission decreases, while EU emissions overall had increased by 0.5 per cent.[7] According to Commission projections, CO_2 emissions in the EU are expected to increase by 7 per cent from 3079 million tonnes in 1990 to 3298 million tonnes by 2010 in a business-as-usual scenario (DG for Energy, 1999). Primary energy demand, however, is expected to grow at more than double that rate – namely, 18 per cent – implying a relative decrease in the carbon intensity of energy demand. This is expected primarily due to a switch away from coal to gas, as well as an increase in the contribution of renewable energies. But, given the rising energy demand, this switch is not sufficient to reduce total emissions.

Transport emissions are expected to grow particularly fast, with an increase of 39 per cent between 1990 and 2010. However, growth in this sector is notoriously difficult to address (as is reflected in Chapters 7 and 8 in this book). There will thus be considerable pressure to obtain emission reductions from the energy sector. At the same time, the downward push on energy prices due to liberalization will decrease the incentives for a more efficient production and use of energy.

A variety of policies and measures will thus be needed to achieve the Kyoto targets. A recent modelling exercise from the DG for Energy suggested that nearly half of the required emission reductions in the energy sector could be achieved through improved efficiency, while the rest could come from less carbon-intensive fuels and renewables (DG for Energy, 1999). The costs of this would be small, amounting to 0.02 per cent of gross domestic product (GDP). Yet, some vested interests are likely to object to new policy measures, in particular if they involve taxation proposals.

Not everyone agrees that emission reductions are that easy to achieve. A study published in early 2000 by the consultancy firm ERM Energy for the Commission (ERM, 2000) suggested that the Kyoto targets could only be achieved by building 85 new nuclear power plants. However, such a scenario is highly unlikely in view of the huge public opposition to nuclear power in many Member States. Nuclear power is also an incredibly expensive generating option. In any case, while electricity generation from nuclear power does not entail CO_2 emissions, this energy source is not without its own environmental problems, particularly in relation to waste disposal. These scenarios illustrate that there are likely to be different paths to achieving emission reductions, all of them associated with considerable uncertainties.

The Post-Kyoto Context: Making EPI a Reality?

The EU has signed the Kyoto Protocol as a block. The legal responsibility for emission reductions is shared between the EU and the Member States, although how this arrangement would work in practice was still uncertain in June 2000. The Commission published a first post-Kyoto communication in May 1999 (European Commission, 1999b). In it, it notes that early action is critical in order to retain the EU's credibility on the international scene. The main responsibility for taking action is given to the Member States, but the Commission sees measures taken at EU level as a useful complement to national initiatives. Progress to date is denounced by the Commission as too slow, particularly in the areas of energy taxation. Despite the urgency of the Kyoto targets, disagreements about policy competencies thus continue.

In March 2000, in a further communication (European Commission, 2000a), the Commission proposed a programme of stakeholder consultations to cooperate in preparing common and coordinated policies and measures. This preparatory work is to include representatives from industry and environmental organizations. Furthermore, action plans on energy efficiency and renewable energy sources were also announced, as well as an imminent renewable energy directive. At the same time, the Commission once again laid blame on the council for not making any progress with key proposals such as the energy tax proposal and the weakening of the SAVE and ALTENER programmes. As a result, at a crucial time for implementing the Kyoto targets, the Commission still appears to be fighting a losing battle in the face of reluctance from the Member States to agree on common energy and environment policy measures.

Due to the lack of progress with regulatory measures, the Commission also investigated the alternative approach of voluntary agreements with industry. After agreeing a voluntary deal with the European car manufacturing industry to reduce average carbon dioxide emissions of new cars by one third by 2005, the Commission explored a similar approach with other industries, according to an energy efficiency action plan published in April 2000 (European Commission, 2000b). The plan threatens mandatory standards for industries that refuse to cooperate. However, it is debatable whether such standards could ever be agreed at EU level. The plan seeks to cut EU energy intensity by 12 per cent over the next decade and is supposed to meet two-fifths of the EU's Kyoto commitment.[8]

In the plan, the Commission states that it will play an increased 'supporting and coordinating role' in the process of concluding agreements for industries, and was to publish guidelines in 2000 to create an EU-wide 'level playing field'. The Commission expected the chemical industry to sign an EU-level energy efficiency agreement later that year. By 2002, the pulp and paper, steel, textile, cement and energy supply industries should sign similar deals. It does not say whether these will be at EU or national level. Steel firms have already refused to contemplate an EU-wide initiative, saying it would be unworkable.

Other measures in the plan include new regional funding rules to encourage energy efficiency, while a household appliance energy-efficiency labelling scheme, already in operation, will be expanded and reinforced. Previous plans to introduce a directive on procurement of energy efficiency equipment have been changed in favour of a voluntary approach. It remains to be seen whether the voluntary approach is workable at EU level. Experience with voluntary approaches in the Member States has shown mixed results (cf Rehbinder, 1997). A compliance regime for EU-level agreements will be a particular challenge. However, in the absence of progress on issues such as energy taxation, voluntary agreements with companies may well be one of the few instruments available at EU level.

In addition to these new initiatives at EU level, several Member States were preparing their own Kyoto implementation plans. Do these plans present evidence of better EPI? Yes and no. On the one hand, the plans do contain new measures for energy efficiency, taxation and renewable energy. On the other hand, these measures only serve to repair some of the damage caused, for example, by recent energy policy decisions. For example, liberalization in the UK energy sector has meant fierce competition and considerable price falls in the industrial sector. The UK government is now introducing a levy on the business use of energy (the so-called climate change levy), which will increase prices, albeit not even to pre-liberalization levels. At the same time, energy efficiency obligations for domestic-sector energy suppliers will only target a limited number of households, while liberalization has meant decreased incentives for energy efficiency for all. In Germany, a new combined heat and power (CHP) law is being introduced after liberalization threatened to close down numerous small-scale, efficient CHP plants.

In general, joined-up thinking is still a rarity and tensions between environmental and other energy policy objectives continue to affect policy-making. However, Kyoto has ensured that, at least on paper, the environment has become a clear objective of energy policy, both at EU level and in the Member States.

PROSPECTS FOR RENEWABLE ENERGY IN THE EU

Energy efficiency and renewable energy sources form the cornerstone of a sustainable energy system. At the same time, they can play a major role in achieving other energy policy objectives, such as security of supply.

Developments in these areas thus provide a good test case of policy integration in practice. This section focuses on renewable energy, in particular, and discusses current trends and policies in three Member States which are generally regarded as particularly progressive on renewables.

Until recently, renewable energies were seen as niche sources with limited potential. However, in Lauber's view (2000), it is now fairly realistic to expect that these technologies will become mainstream over the next 10 to 15 years. Indeed, wind energy is already competitive with certain fossil-fuel technologies (for example, new coal-fired plant with flue-gas desulphurization). Yet, the picture is not all positive. While renewables should, on the one hand, benefit from the liberalization of energy markets and trends away from large, monopolistic suppliers, they are, on the other hand, threatened by the downward pressure on prices that liberalization creates (European Commission, 1999c; Froggatt, 2000). In addition, the price of fossil or nuclear energy still fails to reflect the external costs this type of energy production entails. To create a level playing field, renewables thus require special support, either through the imposition of carbon taxes or through direct grants and subsidies.

The share of renewable energy in energy supply varies from country to country. For the EU as a whole, it stands at 5.8 per cent. Renewable sources are mainly used in Sweden, Austria, Finland and Portugal, with a national share of between 16 and 27 per cent. In Denmark, Italy, France, Spain and Greece, their share is between 5 and 8 per cent, while their use remains almost negligible in the other Member States (DG for Energy, 1999). Most of the high shares of renewables in countries such as Austria and Sweden are due to hydropower, much of which has been developed over the last 50 to 100 years. However, these figures do not necessarily reflect renewable energy potentials, especially as far as the 'new' renewables sources are concerned (wind, solar, biomass and wave power), but often reflect the variation of government support for these technologies between countries. Nevertheless, even countries such as the UK, where renewables account for less than 1 per cent of energy supply, have seen a substantial increase in capacity over recent years.

Apart from the small sums available through ALTENER and other EU funds, renewable energy support remains a national domain. In May 2000, the Commission adopted a proposal for a renewable energy directive that sets indicative renewable energy targets for the EU (European Commission, 2000c). Cutting CO_2 emissions is a main objective of the directive. While the proposal allows much flexibility for Member States to set their own targets and to choose their support mechanism, the Commission has hinted that mandatory national targets might be needed if Member States do not come up with new proposals.[9] It has been suggested that the directive will put at least six countries under pressure to launch new, more ambitious policies – namely, Finland, France, Greece, Luxembourg, the Netherlands and Portugal. Although EU Energy Commissioner Loyola de Palacio announced that the targets were to be non-binding, she stressed that, under her plan, the Commission would monitor countries' progress and 'present proposals' should any fall behind. Even without this threat, Loyola suggested that it would be politically difficult for countries to fail to meet approved targets.[10]

Table 9.1 *Proposed EU Renewable Electricity Targets (Per Cent of Electricity Generated)*

	1997 actual	2010 targets	Per cent increase
Austria	72.7	78.1	7
Sweden	49.1	60.0	22
Portugal	38.5	45.6	18
Finland	24.7	35.0	42
Spain	19.9	29.4	48
Italy	16.0	25.0	56
France	15.0	21.0	40
Denmark	8.7	29.0	233
Greece	8.6	20.1	134
Germany	4.5	12.5	178
Ireland	3.6	13.2	267
Netherlands	3.5	12.0	243
Luxembourg	2.1	5.7	171
UK	1.7	10.0	488
Belgium	1.1	6.0	445
Overall EU	13.9	22.1	58

Source: European Commission (2000a)

Table 9.1 shows how the Commission thinks the 'burden' should be shared in terms of increasing the overall EU share of renewable electricity from (currently) 13.9 per cent to 22.1 per cent in 2010. The energy directorate has calculated that this would fulfil the Commission's 1997 goal of doubling the share of renewables in overall energy production from 6 per cent to 12 per cent by the same date. For seven countries, the directive effectively endorses current government policies to increase the share of renewable electricity by reflecting the targets already adopted.

Members of the European Parliament welcomed the new draft directive on renewables promotion,[11] but called on governments to agree on a clearer treaty commitment to promote renewable energy and expressed concern over EU guidelines on state aids for environmental protection. These were under review in June 2000 but to date have made no allowances for environmental criteria and have severely limited the opportunities for governments to offer environmental subsidies.

It remains to be seen whether this new initiative will be any more successful than previous attempts by the Commission to influence the development of energy policy. However, market forces may result in a greater EU harmonization of renewable energy developments due to the introduction of 'green certificates'. Such certificates would allow renewable energy produced in one country to be sold to customers in another, thus enabling companies to achieve their national obligations (where they exist) through purchasing certificates elsewhere. However, there is still much uncertainty about the green energy market and renewable energy developments remain driven by national developments. The following sections provide case studies of three Member States and examine their developments in more detail.

Germany: Rapid Growth During the 1990s

Germany has seen a huge increase in renewable energy capacity over the past decade, particularly in the field of wind power. At the end of March 2000, Germany had a wind capacity of 4635 megawatts (MW) (cf Bundesverband WindEnergie eV, 2000), more than ten times that of the UK despite much more favourable wind conditions in Britain. The spur for this development has been the introduction of the so-called feed-in law, which was introduced in 1991 and offered guaranteed rates of reimbursement for the supply of electricity from renewables. It made investment in renewable energy very attractive and gave a particular boost to wind energy in northern Germany. The law was not very popular with energy supply companies which had to pay for the reimbursements and even challenged the law in the constitutional court. It was eventually revised in early 2000 and new rates were introduced, supplemented by new government support programmes for solar and other renewables, including financial incentives for 100,000 solar photovoltaic (PV) roof installations. The solar PV programme was oversubscribed immediately and the overall favourable regime is leading to a boom in renewable energies in Germany (WWF-Germany, personal communication). Climate change has become a major driver for renewable policy; the German government has set an ambitious domestic target of a 25 per cent reduction in CO_2 emissions by 2005. Renewables are an important component of the policy for achieving this target. However, at the same time, the German government continues to subsidize the coal industry to the tune of billions of Deutschmarks (DM), a major policy inconsistency (WWF-Germany, personal communication).

Denmark: A New Export Market

The Danish government has supported the development of wind power for over a decade and during this period, Denmark has become the world leader in wind turbine technology. The Danish example is frequently quoted in discussions about the economic and employment benefits of renewable energies. The Danish government has a target of 1500 MW of onshore wind power by 2005 and 4000 MW of offshore wind power by 2030. This would result in wind accounting for 50 per cent of the electricity generated in 2030 (currently 9 per cent), quite clearly an ambitious target. Wind power does not attract capital investment subsidy, but does benefit from an electricity production subsidy, funded under a system of CO_2 and SO_2 taxes.

The government's targets for renewable energy are laid out in its energy plan, Energy 21. In this document, the government confirms a 20 per cent CO_2 reduction by 2005 and the aim to halve CO_2 emissions by 2030. Renewables are to contribute 29 per cent of total electricity production by 2010 and 68 per cent by 2030 (currently 8 per cent). It is expected that post-liberalization, compulsory renewable energy quotas will be introduced with financial penalties for non-compliance (similar to the proposed UK scheme). Furthermore, it is likely that a green certificate market will run alongside the quota system, with the possibility of granting extra green certificates to the less developed technologies.

For instance, biomass could be granted 150 kilowatt hours (kWh) of certificates for every 100 kWh delivered (WWF-Denmark, personal communication).

The UK: Great Potential, Slow Progress

The UK has one of the best potentials for renewable energy in Europe because its island situation means high wind speeds, as well as a long coastline and large estuaries ideal for wave and tidal power. However, since the UK is also rich in fossil fuels, it is not surprising that successive governments have neglected renewable energy. Nevertheless, the last decade has seen a shift in direction and privatization was accompanied by a support system for renewable energies through the so-called non-fossil fuel obligation (NFFO), initially set up to protect nuclear power.

The climate change issue has given a new impetus to the development of renewable energy policy in the UK. NFFO has been abolished and, in June 2000, the government was working out the details of a new renewable energy obligation to be imposed on all energy supply companies. The aim is to achieve a 10 per cent share of renewables in electricity generation by 2010. However, there are some concerns, both from the renewable energy industry and non-governmental organizations (NGOs), that this obligation may mean that suppliers will try to meet the obligation from the cheapest available option. Longer-term, less economically viable options are unlikely to progress under such a system. Furthermore, doubts have to be raised about the feasibility of the 10 per cent target from a planning perspective (CREA, personal communication). In recent years, a large number of projects approved under NFFO have failed to get planning permission, largely due to local opposition – particularly in the case of wind farms and waste incinerators. The government has promised to address these planning issues but the extra capacity required to achieve the 10 per cent target will undoubtedly provide a real challenge to local planners.

Summary: Renewables in the Member States

As the above case studies show, the last few years have seen a rapid growth in renewable energy capacity. In Denmark, Germany and the UK, renewable energy programmes have been driven largely by environmental concerns, initially as a result of a general greening of government but more recently heavily influenced by the Kyoto targets. As efforts to implement national climate change programmes continue, support policies for renewables are likely to strengthen all over the EU. However, at the same time, renewables continue as a small proportion of overall energy production in most countries. In terms of cost-effectiveness and technology, progress is still needed.

CONCLUSIONS

As this chapter has shown, EPI has been fraught with difficulties as far as EU energy policy is concerned. A number of explanatory factors for this slow progress can be identified, including:

- powerful vested (economic) interests;
- real or perceived economic costs of action;
- differing priorities;
- reluctance to cede competencies to the EU.

Energy policy (and other areas linked to it, such as tax policy) has traditionally been influenced by vested interests which have been reluctant to change. The energy industry adhered to a large-scale, supply-side philosophy; as a result, more environmentally sound options were unable to play a role. Options such as renewable energy and energy efficiency are also relatively unattractive at times of low energy prices – for example, during much of the late 1980s and the 1990s. While there has always been a number of win–win options (particularly in energy efficiency), inertia and vested interests militated against progress.

Energy policy priorities have not facilitated progress either. During the 1990s, there was a great political momentum (supported by business and industry) behind energy liberalization. The momentum was so strong that, for once, EU competency issues became less important and EU-level agreement on liberalization was reached. However, environmental concerns were largely seen as a distraction and another complicating factor; accordingly, they received little attention.

There has been some change since climate change became a new driver for the integration of EU energy and environment policies. However, at EU level to date, this integration consists mainly of paper statements rather than action on the ground. Energy policy continues to be primarily the responsibility of Member States and there is little political will to agree to EU-level measures. The Commission has tried its best, especially in the area of energy taxation; but differing views on energy policy competencies continue to impede progress with the EU's climate change strategy (see Chapter 7, which highlights a similar problem in the transport sector).

There has been consistent, if slow, progress in some Member States, in particular those that are generally more progressive on environmental issues. The EU has had little influence on these developments. Action has been motivated both by national concerns about climate change and the international obligations under the UN climate convention (UNCCC) and the Kyoto Protocol.

However, despite some progress, joined-up thinking and consistent policy development is still the exception rather than the rule. This is exemplified by developments in renewable energy. Most governments now have support programmes for renewable energy technologies, but they are still not a top priority and allocated funds are often dwarfed by support to unsustainable technologies, such as coal and nuclear.

Unless the situation improves, the EU is likely to miss its Kyoto targets. It is crucial that changes get under way now; Kyoto was only a first step towards the much larger emission reductions that are necessary to halt the threat of dangerous climate change. Policy integration in the energy field means allocating priority to energy efficiency and renewable energy. However, in most Member States, low prices, a lack of environmental cost internalization and a supply-side mentality jeopardize the small steps forward achieved through renewable and energy-efficiency support programmes. Fundamental changes in attitude are needed and the next decade will be a real testing ground for EPI in the energy policy field.

The EU could have a role to play in this, although much scepticism about greater EU involvement in the energy field remains. It thus seems likely that EU-level measures will continue to consist mainly of broad frameworks and 'soft instruments', such as voluntary agreements and monitoring. However, the implementation of framework measures may be taken more seriously in the future because there will be the additional pressure of complying with the Kyoto Protocol obligations. It is therefore significant that the EU and the Member States are jointly responsible for achieving the Kyoto targets. The EU also has a role in facilitating the exchange of policy experiences and ensuring a better dialogue with stakeholders. Overall, EPI now stands a better chance as far as energy policy is concerned than during the past. Much of the future success will depend upon ratification of the Kyoto Protocol and concern among voters in EU Member States about the climate change issue.

REFERENCES

Bundesverband WindEnergie eV (2000) *Windkraft bundesweit wieder auf Rekordkurs*, Pressemitteilung, 26 April, Osnabrück, www.wind-energie.de

Collier, U (1994) *Energy and Environment in the European Union: the Challenge of Integration*, Avebury, Aldershot

Collier, U (1996) 'The European Union's Climate Change Policy: Limiting Emissions or Limiting Powers?', *Journal of European Public Policy*, vol 3, no 1, pp123–139

Collier, U (1997) *Cases in Climate Change Policy: Political Reality in the European Union*, Earthscan, London

Directorate-General for Energy (1999) 'Economic Foundations for Energy Policy', *Energy in Europe*, Special Issue, December 1999

Eising, R (2000) *Liberalisierung und Europäisierung. Die regulative Reform der Elektrizitätsversorgung in Großbritannien, der Europäischen Gemeinschaft und der Bundesrepublik Deutschland*, Leske + Budrich, Opladen

ERM (2000) *The Dilemma Report*, http://europa.eu.int/en/comm/dg17/dilemma.pdf

European Commission (1990) *Communication from the Commission to the Council on Energy and the Environment*, COM (89) 369 final, Brussels

European Commission (1992a) *Towards Sustainability*, COM (92) 23 final, Brussels

European Commission (1992b) *A Community Strategy to Limit Carbon Dioxide Emissions and to Improve Energy Efficiency*, Communication from the Commission, COM (92), 246 final, Brussels

European Commission (1993a) 'Specific Actions for Greater Penetration for Renewable Energy Sources – ALTENER', *Official Journal of the EC,* L235, 18 September 1993

European Commission (1993b) 'Council Directive 93/76/EEC to Limit Carbon Dioxide Emissions by Improving Energy Efficiency (SAVE Programme*)', Official Journal of the EC,* vol 237, pp28–30

European Commission (1995) *White Paper – An Energy Policy for the European Union,* COM (95) 682, Brussels

European Commission (1997) *Climate Change – the EU Approach for Kyoto,* COM (97) 481, Brussels

European Commission (1999a) *Communication on the Single Market and the Environment,* Brussels, http://europa.eu.int//comm/internal_market/en/update/general/263en.pdf

European Commission (1999b) *Preparing for Implementation of the Kyoto Protocol,* Communication to the Council and the Parliament, COM (99) 230, Brussels

European Commission (1999c) *Electricity from Renewable Energy Sources and the Internal Electricity Market,* Working Paper, 13 April 1999, Brussels, www.europa.eu.int/en/comm/dg17/reselecen.pdf

European Commission (2000a) *Communication from the Commission on EU Policies and Measures to Reduce Greenhouse Gas Emissions: Towards a European Climate Change Programme (ECCP),* COM (2000) 88, Brussels

European Commission (2000b) *Communication from the Commission: Action Plan to Improve Energy Efficiency in the EC,* COM(2000) 247 final, Brussels

European Commission (2000c) *Proposal for a Directive of the European Parliament and of the Council on the Promotion of Electricity from Renewable Energy Sources in the Internal Electricity Market,* COM(2000) 279 final, Brussels

Froggatt, A (2000) *The Liberalisation of Europe's Electricity Markets – is the Environment Paying the Price for Cheap Power?,* Report commissioned by Greenpeace, Greenpeace International, Amsterdam

Grubb, M (1996) *Renewable Energy Strategies for Europe, Volume 1: Foundations and Context,* Earthscan, London

Lauber, V (2000) 'Politik und die Zukunft erneuerbarer Energien', *Wissenschaft und Umwelt interdisziplinär,* vol 2, pp51–58

Ott, H (1998) *The Kyoto Protocol to the UNFCCC – Finished and Unfinished Business,* Wuppertal Institut, www.wupperinst.org

Rehbinder, E (1997) *Environmental Agreements: A New Instrument of Environmental Policy,* Jean Monnet Chair Paper – Environment, No 97/45, Robert Schuman Center for Advanced Studies, Florence

Schmidt, S (1996) 'Sterile Debates and Dubious Generalisations: European Integration Tested by Telecommunication and Electricity', *Journal of Public Policy,* vol 16, no 3, pp233–271

NOTES

1. This chapter was written by the author in a personal capacity and does not necessarily reflect the views and policies of the WWF.
2. 'Millions pay a heavy price for a warmer world', *The Guardian,* 28 April 2000
3. Directive 96/92/EC
4. Directive 98/30/EC

5   Initially (as of 1999), 23 per cent of markets were to be opened up, increasing to 33 per cent after six years. For detailed studies of the EU liberalization process in the energy and electricity markets, see Eising (2000) and Schmidt (1996).

6   COM (97) 599 (renewables), COM (97) 514 (CHP), COM (98) 246 (energy efficiency)

7   These figures are for three greenhouse gases: CO_2, CH_4, N_2O (European Commission, 2000).

8   *ENDS Daily*, 27 April 2000

9   *Wall Street Journal*, 10 May 2000

10   *ENDS Daily*, 10 April 2000

11   *ENDS Daily*, 17 May 2000

Dynamics in a Multilevel Polity: Greening the EU Regional and Cohesion Funds

Andrea Lenschow

INTRODUCTION

'Wetlands destroyed', 'biodiversity threatened', 'nature reserves disturbed': all of this with the 'help' of European Union (EU) funding. These were news headlines in the early 1990s, preceding a series of reforms to the Community's regional and cohesion funds. Arguably, these funds were the first EU policies that went – and continue to go – through a conscious greening process. This chapter will investigate this progress more closely and attempt to uncover the conditions for, and the obstacles to, integrating environmental considerations in non-environmental policies. This task is helped by a comparative design in the first part of the analysis, comparing the experience of the EU's regional development policy with the cohesion policy.[1]

However, even though the greening of the structural funds – consisting of the European Regional Development Fund (ERDF), the European Social Fund (ESF), the European Agricultural Guidance and Control Fund (EAGGF) and the Financial Instrument for Fisheries Guidance (FIFG) – and, with some delay, the Cohesion Fund, are often portrayed as success stories, the success is a partial one. The third section of this chapter provides evidence that despite a 'greened' legal and operational framework on the EU level, the conflict between regional development programmes and environmental protection remains often unresolved on the ground. The funds demonstrate the multilevel nature of the environmental policy integration (EPI) project (Jordan/Lenschow 2000), where Member States and local actors do not necessarily follow policy shifts on the EU level. The structural and cohesion funds indicate that the adoption of the EPI principle may encounter many bottlenecks that may stop the whole process. At the same time, however, the funds offer a unique opportunity for enforcing EPI in the Member States, through the linkage of funding to environmental conditions; this may prove more effective than the threat of legal action. As a result, there may be a shift in the Commission's strategy from a defensive to a more active approach towards EPI.[2] The question remains whether such a strategy is also conducive to developing EPI mindsets outside the EU policy-making elite.

THE EVOLUTIONS OF THE REGIONAL DEVELOPMENT FUND AND THE COHESION FUND

Comparing the 'greening' of the European Regional Development Fund, as the largest of the structural funds, and the Cohesion Fund is most instructive for understanding the complex dynamics behind introducing integrative policy-making in the EU. The 'most similar cases' design of the comparison facilitates the identification of crucial variables. Before analysing the *politics* of change, however, this chapter reviews the results of the environmental evolution in the two cases under investigation. It is the observed variance that needs to be explained in the proceeding section.

The European Regional Development Fund (ERDF)

The goal of the ERDF, when it was first created in 1975 (Regulation EEC 724/75 of the Council of 18 March 1975), was to correct regional imbalances within the Community resulting, in particular, from agricultural preponderance, industrial change and structural unemployment. This basic goal did not significantly change until today, except that the emphasis has shifted to the latter two problems. However, both the management of the fund and the attention given to environmental protection have altered quite dramatically.

Initially, the environmental impact of industrial or infrastructure projects financed through the ERDF was not considered problematic; hence, environmental protection did not feature as a limiting criterion in the regional planning process. The management of the fund reflected an 'intergovernmental' philosophy in which the distribution of the resources was negotiated among the Member States, while the Commission's administrative role consisted of facilitating the 'hand-outs' with little influence on the way these were spent. This pattern began to change with the 1979 and 1984 reforms of the fund; indirectly, these reforms also laid the foundation for a greening process that would start in the late 1980s.

The first reforms of the ERDF in 1979 and 1984 led to an increase in regional policy spending and a refocus on support for southern European regions. Importantly, they provided the Commission with enhanced opportunities to influence and select national project proposals, as well as to engage in trans-regional and trans-national Community projects. With these changes, the Commission's role slowly evolved from that of a bookkeeper to that of a development agency with increased control over the allocation of the resources (Marks, 1992; Hooghe and Keating, 1994). This shift in policy responsibilities proved crucial for the EPI process later on.

In 1988, a more far-reaching reform of all structural funds took place and doubled the overall financial commitment for the fund, increasing spending for environmental activities.[3] This reform took place before the background of the adoption of the Single European Act (which had established environmental policy as a Community responsibility) and in an internationally favourable climate for environmental protection measures (cf the Bundtland Report). Increased spending for the environment does not constitute integrated policy-making, however, as long as the environmental impact of other projects remains in the dark. But even in this regard, further changes in the management of the funds appeared promising. The reforms led to the adoption of a programmatic approach, facilitating trans-regional and long-term planning and the coordination of different funding sources. Theoretically, at least, the programmatic perspective allowed for the recognition of, and reaction to, the environmental impact outside the immediate territorial limits of any given funded activity. Furthermore, the Commission gained some control over the planning and evaluation processes, which had previously been the sole responsibility of national authorities. This enhanced – again theoretically – its ability to bring ERDF funding in line with Community environmental rules.

While the 1988 reform began to establish a framework for environmentally conscious regional policy, several obstacles stood in the way of EPI. This section focuses on the legal and operational side, turning to the political bottlenecks in the next section. Firstly, the 1988 regulations limited environment-related programmes and projects to 'productive investment and investment in infrastructure aimed at environmental protection *where such investment is linked to regional development*' (Council Regulation (EEC) no 4254/88, Article 1f, emphasis added). Consequently it treated environmental protection as a secondary objective. Secondly, despite the declaration to engage in environmental policy integration (cf Council Regulation (EEC) 2052/88 of 24 June 1988, Article 7.1), no operational steps to link environmental and regional policy-making were developed. In fact, the council rejected operational measures proposed by the Commission, such as a set of mandatory environmental instructions to be followed in the planning phase of regional programmes.

In July 1993, the structural funds went through a new round of administrative reforms that resulted in an improved framework for environmental policy integration. The reforms targeted poor planning and monitoring performance, the limited eligibility criteria for environmental programmes or projects, and the tendency to support so-called end-of-pipe projects. The revised regulations reinforced the EPI by requiring that:

> ... *development plans ... must in the future include an appraisal of the environmental situation of the region concerned and an evaluation of the environmental impact of the strategy and operations planned, in accordance with the principles of sustainable development and in agreement with the provision of Community law in force. The plans must also mention the arrangements made by the Member States to associate their competent environmental authorities in the various stages of programming.* (CEC, 1993, p29, referring to the new Framework Regulation, Article 7)

Apart from providing a more operational framework for sustainable planning (the kind that had been rejected in 1988), this clause had important implications for the constellation of actors involved in EU-funding regional policy. It not only confirmed the monitoring responsibility of the Commission, as the watchdog of the EU treaties. It also began to turn environmental authorities into an 'in-group' in the preparation phase of regional programmes.

The legal evolution was paralleled by procedural changes leading towards fuller integration. The Commission developed an aide memoire (known as the environmental profile) for the Member States to clarify what information was to be supplied under the revised regulations. Although this profile had no legal standing, it served to assist public authorities to fulfil their legal obligations. It also facilitated the harmonization of the national information submitted to the Commission. While the profile was targeted at the regional plans, a questionnaire was drawn up for the same purpose and directed at large operational projects. A list of indicators and a handbook were prepared with the intention of assessing the environmental impact of the regional programmes and its associated costs (Lenschow, 1997, 1999). Hence, between 1988 and 1993, the policy evolved from a 'reminder' to comply with EC environmental law to an obligatory procedure to protect the environment.

At the turn of the 20th century, the EU structural policies came up for another round of reforms in the context of devising the 'Agenda 2000' that would facilitate the further narrowing of the disparities in income between, and within, the Member States. These reforms would include the future enlargement of the Community to east and central Europe. Not surprisingly, most of the political battles preceding the reforms focused on the distribution of the resources among the Member States rather than on the quality of the spending.[4] Nevertheless, the Commission had set the stage to ensure that the environment and sustainable development would be considered as a horizontal principle governing spending decisions (CEC, 1998). The final council regulation laying out the general provisions on the structural funds (EC no 1260/1999 of 21 June 1999) includes a number of provisions furthering the integration of environmental consideration within the operations of the funds:

- The EPI principle, especially the need to ensure compliance with EU environmental policy, is mentioned unambiguously and early in the regulation (Article 1; Article 2(5); cf also Article 12).
- Environmental needs are added as a criterion, justifying funding under objective 2 of the funds (Article 4(7)).
- Member States are encouraged to include environmental representatives in the planning and management of the funded programmes and projects. 'According to national rules and practice', they shall 'take account of the need to promote sustainable development through the integration of environmental protection and improvement requirements' (Article 8(1)).
- The new regulation explicitly allows for differentiated contributions to the fund in the light of the priorities from the Community viewpoint, where appropriate, for the 'protection and improvement of the environment,

principally through the application of the precautionary principle, of the principle of preventive action, and the polluter pays principle' (Article 29).

- The indicators used for monitoring the spending 'shall relate to the specific character of the assistance concerned, its objectives and the socio-economic, structural and environmental situation of the Member States concerned and its region' (Article 36(1)).

- The ex-ante evaluations of the regional development programmes will take into account the situation of the environment. It will include an ex-ante evaluation of the 'environmental situation of the region concerned, in particular of those environmental sectors which will presumably be considerably affected by the assistance; the arrangements to integrate the environmental dimension into the assistance and how far they fit in with existing short- and long-term national, regional and local objectives (eg environmental management plans); the arrangements for ensuring compliance with the Community rules on the environment'. The ex-ante evaluation will use quantified data, as far as possible, to describe the existing environmental situation and estimate the expected impact of the strategy and assistance on the environmental situation (Article 41(2)).

- On the basis of these provisions, it will be possible to suspend or withdraw regional funding if EU environmental law is discovered to be violated (Article 39).

Obviously, the success of these legal clauses to integrate the environment depends upon the organization of the programming and monitoring processes on the ground. This, in turn, depends upon the participation of environmentally conscious actors. The new regulation broadens partnership and (more explicitly than the previous regulation) encourages the participation of authorities and societal actors who push for the EPI principle (Article 8(1)). Nevertheless, the participation of environmental authorities or non-governmental organizations (NGOs) remains subordinate to national rules and practices. Hence, the involvement of NGOs, which had been exceptional in the past (cf Kelleher et al, 1999) may be strengthened in the current programmatic period. On the other hand, the Commission itself plans to take a more decentralized, or hands-off, approach. National and regional 'managers' of the fund will be informed of the principles and guidelines set out in the legislation and 'various working papers will be produced on sensitive or difficult issues ... to operators so as to facilitate their tasks: subjects will cover the application of the environmental Directives' (CEC, 2000). The Commission therefore adopts an indirect, facilitating role, relying on a positive take-up in the Member States and regions. Among the responsible 'partners' on the ground, the environmental authorities and environmental NGOs are likely to remain the least powerful ones.

The possible dangers implied in the Commission's pursuit of a more hands-off approach will become visible when looking at the dynamics of the earlier reform processes in the proceeding section.

The Cohesion Fund

The decision to establish the Cohesion Fund was taken during the negotiations leading to the Treaty on European Union (TEU), in part overlapping with the process of reforming the ERDF. The fund is dedicated to assisting the four poorest members of the EU (Greece, Ireland, Portugal and Spain) through projects in the fields of the environment and transport infrastructure. Both the parallel ERDF reforms and the specific objectives of the fund suggested successful environmental policy integration in this policy case. In practice, the Cohesion Fund was initially disappointing with regard to the environment.

Even though the original cohesion instrument was decided prior to the ratification of the Maastricht Treaty, it was linked to the treaty's Article 130r-s, which elaborated the 'environmental rationale' of the fund. Pointing to regional diversity and the need to take account of 'the economic and social development of the Community as a whole and the balanced developments of its regions', it stated that:

> ... [w]ithout prejudice to the principle that the polluter should pay, if a measure based on the provisions of paragraph 1 involves costs deemed disproportionate for the public authorities of a Member State, the Council shall, in the act adopting that measure, lay down appropriate provisions in the form of:
> * temporary derogations; and/or
> * financial support from the Cohesion Fund ... pursuant to Article 130d.

Rephrasing this somewhat cynically, depending upon the budgetary situation of the Member State and its capacity to meet the convergence criteria for joining the Economic and Monetary Union (EMU), the polluter pays principle may be suspended and the Cohesion Fund may be used to meet environmental obligations. Such a rationale indicates that the fund was never primarily thought off as an environmental instrument, but rather as a financial transfer mechanism with macro-economic objectives. The Cohesion Fund implied that there were no efforts to ensure that the four countries in question took consideration of environmental impacts in their attempts to join the EMU; hence, it was not integrative as the EPI principle demands.

Related to the fund's primarily economic objective, its institutional and procedural framework was also problematic from an environmental point of view, although advances were made after the Cohesion Fund passed from its pre-TEU 'interim stage' to a final status. Firstly, even though the 1993 reforms of the structural funds attempted to increase coordination among individual funds, this did not include the Cohesion Fund, which was spent on a disjointed project-by-project basis. This arrangement encouraged domestic pork-barrel politics and militated against a coordinated and integrated approach to cohesion. With regard to the environmental dimension, no special efforts were made to embed environmental projects in a larger regional development plan and to ensure that non-environment projects take account of environmental impacts.

Table 10.1 *Distribution of Funds under the 1993 Interim Cohesion Instrument*

Recipient	Per cent of total	Per cent for environment	Per cent for transport
Spain	54.8	29	71
Portugal	18.2	43	57
Greece	17.9	62	38
Ireland	9.1	39	61

Source: adapted from Agence Europe (no 6142, 6 January 1994)

Secondly, the procedural rules of the fund provided only limited tools for (systemic) environmental impact assessment and monitoring (on the European or national level). Furthermore, they offered only limited societal control due to their bilateral (central government/Commission) nature. Contrary to the structural funds, no management committee was established to control the expenditures. Equally, the Commission's powers of control were limited because the funding for each beneficiary was politically set[5] and left little discretionary powers to the Commission to chose among proposed projects and link those decisions to environmental criteria.

Thirdly, the interim instrument's environmental spending was biased towards large infrastructure projects. In order to lower the public borrowing needs of the government, it was decided that any individual project had to amount to at least 10 million ECU. This effectively prevented spending on small, less capital-intensive, but often more innovative, projects. Equally unfortunate was the initial distribution of expenditure between the two sectoral targets: transport and the environment. National discretion resulted in a severe bias towards transport projects in all countries except Greece (see Table 10.1).

The regulation establishing the fund in 1994 (Council Regulation (EC) 1164/94 of 16 May 1994) showed some progress from an environmental perspective. It made reference in its recitals to the fifth Environmental Action Programme (EAP) (CEC, 1992a), the Commission's *Green Paper on the Impact of Transport on the Environment* (CEC, 1992b) and the need to account for environmental costs. On the operational level, both spending and monitoring modalities were adapted, partly in response to environmental critics. Cohesion funding became available to 'groups of projects' and to technical support measures, facilitating a more strategic approach. On the level of monitoring and controls, the Commission was given the right for 'on-the-spot' checks and could request from Member States the reimbursement of any 'sums unduly paid'. The appraisal and monitoring process was formally strengthened by calling for environmental impact assessments supported by physical and financial indicators.[6] The final regulation also called for particular attention to transparency of management and the possible involvement of regional and local actors in the monitoring committees. Finally, it called for a 'suitable balance' between environment projects and those targeted at transport infrastructure.

Table 10.2 *Distribution of the Cohesion Fund During 1993–1995 in All Four Countries*

Year	Environment (ECU)	Transport (ECU)
1993	606,016,992	958,253,511
1994	923,430,183	929,157,266
1995	1,036,709,677	1,113,119,907
1993–1995	2,566,156,852	3,000,530,684

Source: Annual Report of the Cohesion Fund 1995, reprinted in Kouvelis et al (1997, p35)

Nevertheless, the appeals for environmental impact assessment, monitoring and the participation of environmental authorities, regional authorities and social and economic partners were mainly declaratory and lacked the support of operational measures similar to those developed for the Regional Fund. Criteria for environmental projects were poorly specified; transparency and access to information were lacking.

Some real progress toward EPI was made under the Santer Commission, when the portfolio of the fund was moved from the Secretariat General and budget directorate to the Regional Policy Directorate-General (DG XVI) under the leadership of (new) Commissioner Monika Wulf-Mathies. In November 1995, the Commission presented a communication entitled *Cohesion Policy and the Environment* that had been jointly prepared by the services for the environment and regional development. It declared that (CEC, 1995, p9):

> ... *for the future a 50/50 distribution between transport and environment should be an allocation target which must be aimed at... [T]he Commission will analyse further the possibilities for better co-ordination between the Cohesion Fund and the Structural Funds with regard to environmental monitoring and assessment.*

In fact, the distribution of the resources had already approached a 50/50 ratio by the end of 1995 (see Table 10.2).

The latest reforms of the Cohesion Fund (also as part of Agenda 2000)[7] imply further greening attempts, including efforts to improve operational aspects. However, in contrast to the structural funds, the old regulations are only amended rather than replaced. Hence, the overall macro-economic frame was maintained. The amended regulations insist on a fuller assessment of environmental impacts and project alternatives, which may enable the Commission to intervene in the project decisions on behalf of the environment:

> *The beneficiary Member States shall provide all necessary information, as set out in Article 10(4), including the results of feasibility studies and ex-ante appraisals. In order to make this appraisal as effective as possible, Member States shall also provide the results of the* **environmental impact assessment in conformity with the Community legislation,** *and their consistency with a general environmental or transport strategy at administrative unit or sector level, and, where appropriate:*

- ***an indication of the possible alternatives that were not chosen;*** and
- *the links between projects of common interest located along the same transport corridor* (Article B(2), second sentence, emphasis added).

While the amendment establishes a clear link to the Community's environmental impact assessment (EIA) directive, which had been missing before (see endnote 6), the sectoral separation between environmental and transport projects is maintained and the obligation to consider alternative choices remains ambiguous.

The amended regulation also seeks to correct the fact that the fund, in the past, gave disincentives to Member States for implementing the polluter pays principle (CEC 1999a). Article 7 provides for the adjustment of the rates of assistance in order to take account of 'the estimated revenue generated by projects and of any application of the polluter pays principle'. Article F establishes that 'an indication of the environmental protection measures taken, and their cost, including compliance with the polluter pays principle' shall be given in the national cohesion reports.

Looking at the history of EPI in the Cohesion Fund, we are faced with two questions. Why did the original fund of 1993 violate against the principle in such a dramatic way despite the good example of the similar regional policy area? And what explains the reform process during the last few years? The following section answers these questions from a comparative perspective, juxtaposing the 'politics' of the ERDF and Cohesion Fund reforms.

THE POLITICS BEHIND ACHIEVING EPI

This chapter suggests that the acceptance of EPI as a policy principle for structural policy is multidimensional, involving ideational, institutional and societal factors. The following analysis of the process towards EPI in the Regional and the Cohesion Fund shows that EPI implies the acceptance of new points of reference (frames) that guide the policy-making process. These may compete with 'old frames' such as the developmental paradigm guiding the old ERDF and a macro-economic stability frame of the Cohesion Fund. The comparative analysis shows variance in the frame adaptation process, and this section argues that this is related to institutional factors. However, actual adaptation also necessitates actors mobilizing and pushing for change – within this more or less hospitable institutional context.

ERDF

Framing the policy

The implementation of EPI has a lot to do with the 'policy mission' as identified by the policy-makers and its compatibility with environmental concerns. By examining the 'discourse' behind the EU's regional policy, it is possible to observe a shift from benign neglect of the environment, to sectoral thinking (treating the environment as external), to an increasingly integrated understanding.

The following illustrates this point. When establishing the ERDF, EU policy-makers anticipated that regional development would reduce:

> ... *the mounting environmental poverty of the areas of concentration. The pressure on housing, the miseries of commuting on overloaded roads or overcrowded trains, the pollution of the air and the water – all these developments mean that the environmental case for closing the geographical gaps is as powerful a one for those who live in the so-called prosperous areas of the Community as it is for those in the poorer regions.* (CEC, 1973, p10)

As a result, the EU's regional policy started from the notion that it would be compatible with environmental concerns. Indeed, it was thought to create a win–win situation in which the donors to the policy would be rewarded with environmental benefits. This image gradually changed and gave way to a very sectoral understanding. For instance, when DG XVI was approached in the late 1980s by a delegation of the WWF, who were concerned about the lack of mechanisms to assess the environmental impact of projects funded by the ERDF, a DG XVI official allegedly replied: 'We are a development institution; what do we have to talk about?' (interview, WWF, 4 August 1994). Despite the publication of the Brundtland Report only a few years earlier, which had linked the issues of development and environmental protection, regional policy in the EU was perceived as an isolated, sectoral matter, and the environment was perceived to be the domain of other policy-makers – for example, the Environment Directorate-General in the Commission.

As described above, this sectoral understanding began to change in the early 1990s and the notion of 'sustainable development' achieved the status of a horizontal principle guiding the policy. In a working paper tabled by Commissioner Wulf-Mathies (responsible until 1999 for regional policy), the Commission confirms this horizontal approach (CEC, 1999b, p2). Furthermore, the new general provisions governing all structural funds (Council Regulation (EC) No 1260/1999 of 21 June 1999) confirm: 'by promoting cohesion, the Union is encouraging harmonious, balanced and sustainable economic development of employment and human resources, environmental protection and upgrading' (Article 1). In addition, the new Council Regulation on the ERDF (No 1783/1999 of 12 June 1999) establishes sustainable development as one of its indicative guidelines and will especially support innovative actions in the field of promoting sustainable development.

Mobilizing for EPI and removing institutional bottlenecks

The reinterpretation of policy missions or 'frame shifts' is rarely an unconscious process. More typically, it involves political actors who mobilize to alter the policy discourse. The following account of the campaign to 'green' the EU regional policy shows the crucial role of the institutional context for such politics of change.[8]

The greatest mobilizing effort to 'green' the ERDF was performed by environmental NGOs in the late 1980s. As 'out-groups' in EU regional policy-making, the success of the NGO campaign ultimately depended upon gaining allies 'inside' and on weakening the story line of traditionally thinking actors at the institutional 'core' of the EU. The initial strategy was one of disseminating information in order to prove the environmental impact of the regional fund. The environmental NGOs, most notably the WWF, supplied DG XI, the Environmental Committee in the European Parliament (EP) and the European Court of Auditors (ECA), as well as several national governments, with such evidence. In particular, a report of the ECA (1992), which used some of the NGO evidence, seriously undermined the legitimacy of the fund's operation (and of DG XVI); it also gave additional credibility to actors demanding a 'greening' of the fund.

The institutional structure of running the fund is crucial to understand the delegitimization process. In short, the administrative reforms during 1984 and 1987 provided an institutional context that allowed for the successful environmental campaign. As a result of these reforms, DG XVI became vulnerable to external critics. By gaining powers in the selection of project or programme proposals, and in monitoring their implementation, the Commission accepted an increased level of responsibility for the outcome of spending. Hence, once environmental interest groups discovered violations of several EU-funded projects with EU environmental law, they could blame the Commission for ignoring its own commitments. Interested in maintaining its institutional legitimacy, the Commission joined the alliance for EPI, and DG XVI adjusted its mission in order to protect its institutional standing.

A second strategy of the green alliance assisted this rather speedy shift. It implied the threat of real sanctions[9] and the presentation of a package of policy alternatives (cf WWF/IEEP, 1989 and 1990; WWF, 1993 and 'no date'). Nevertheless, in order to change the overall framework of the Regional Fund, it was not sufficient to 'shake up' the Commission; it was necessary to also target the responsible Council of Ministers. Here, the environmental alliance benefited from a coincidence of interests with the Danish government, which shared the NGOs' environmental concerns, and the British government, which was concerned to secure 'value for money' in the context of the structural funds. The Danish government held the Council of Ministers presidency during most of the negotiation period for the proposed structural fund reforms in 1993, and the council followed most of the proposals formulated by the environmental campaigners (Corrie, 1993; WWF, 1993).

According to NGO observers, the 1993 reforms did not merely represent the results of a policy crisis, forcing the environment on to the agenda; they were also part of a real learning process and subsequent frame shift among EU policy-makers. Officials in DG XVI, who used to have a strong pro-development identity which often brought them into conflict with DG XI, in particular changed attitudes. Shaken by the skilfully presented evidence, DG XVI became more open-minded toward policy advice offered by colleagues from DG XI. DG XI actors, in turn, adopted a less adversarial approach and improved their understanding of the operational regional policy. These institutional adaptations provided for a more open, communicative climate; they also strengthened and helped to maintain a frame shift that was pushed by an NGO-led environmental campaign. Later cooperation between Commissioners Wulf-Mathies and Bjerregaard, as well as today between Commissioners Wallström and Barnier, must be seen in this context.

Yet, the NGO campaign did not rest. Approaching the 1999 reforms, several environmental NGOs conducted studies evaluating the performance of the structural funds and the Cohesion Fund and formulated a new 'wish list' (cf Bina et al, 1997; Kouvelis et al, 1997; WWF, 1997, 1998). As far as the clear declaration of the integration principle and the provision of differentiated funding according to environmental criteria are concerned, their campaign was successful. Also, there has been some movement with regard to requiring environmental indicators and facilitating the participation of environmental authorities and NGOs, though not quite as far reaching as demanded by the environmental campaigners.

To sum up, what are the elements that contributed to the 'greening' of the Regional Fund? To facilitate the frame shift in the Commission and the Council of Ministers, as the two crucial institutional actors in EU policy-making, it seemed important to delegitimate old non-integrative practices. Evidence of the 'scandalous' environmental effects of EU-funded projects served as a focal point in the mobilization effort for the reform (cf Long, 1995). The effectiveness of this 'good story' depended upon the institutional access and support given to the campaigners. In order to further 'lock in' EPI as a policy principle, institutional practices need to adapt. In this context, the 'stories' that motivated the initial change may serve as a constant reminder. At the same time, however, 'new stories' must be voiced to keep the reform process alive.

Cohesion Fund

Framing the policy

The Cohesion Fund policy went from blocking to accepting primarily procedural changes toward environmental integration. At first sight, the objectives of the Cohesion Fund seemed to correspond with the EPI principle. The fact that the fund was dedicated to support environmental and transport projects suggested, at least in part, an environmental frame guiding the policy-making. In practice, however, the EPI principle was ignored during the first operating period of the fund; environmental projects were instrumentalized in order to serve primarily macro-economic objectives without accepting environmental rationales. The fund came into existence as a side-payment to poorer Member States in return for their agreement to the Maastricht Treaty's EMU convergence criteria (Marks, 1992; Pollack, 1995). Due to intense pressure from Spain, in particular, which gained relatively little from the region-based ERDF, the Cohesion Fund was devised as a cash flow to national governments. The donor countries, in turn, insisted on the fund's link to macro-economic performance. Faced with Euro-sceptic sentiments among many Member States, the Commission developed a framework for economic cohesion and monetary union to which other policy objectives became subordinate (Ross, 1995).[10] In short, 'the Cohesion Fund was never intended to be primarily an instrument of the Community's environmental policy'. Despite its emphasis on environmental projects, the 'principal function of the Fund [was] to provide a financial transfer mechanism from the richer to the poorer of the EU's Member States' (Wilkinson, 1994).

This non-environmental frame of reference changed somewhat in the context of institutional reforms. Under the Santer Commission, the Cohesion Fund was moved from the Budget Directorate-General (DG XIX), where it had been placed by the Delors Commission, to DG XVI, which in the context of the ERDF was becoming increasingly receptive to the need for EPI. Since then, the Cohesion Fund has been perceived as more closely linked to the ERDF and some coordination is attempted. DG XVI states in its work programme for 2000 (CEC, 2000, p4):

> *Although the Cohesion Fund finances individual projects, this does not prevent the Commission and the Member States concerned from embedding them with strategic guidelines... Internal organisations with the Directorate General to bring together those responsible for managing the Structural Funds and for managing the Cohesion Fund should greatly contribute to this approach. To still further the quality of such funding, Commission officials will be drafting some working papers and procedural manuals.*

The strategic guidelines have been defined already in a previous communication, which highlights the two horizontal principles of sustainable development and equal opportunity. Making reference to the commitments under the Amsterdam Treaty and the agreements of the European Council at Vienna (CEC, 1999b, p2, emphasis added):

> *... environmental considerations, and in particular compliance with Community environmental and nature protection legislation, must be incorporated into the definition and implementation of measures supported by the Structural Funds and the Cohesion Fund.*

Nevertheless, the initial association with the EMU and macro-economic growth and stability has not been cut, as is evident in the amended regulations. Considering the high priority of EMU in the overall mission of the EU, the challenge of EPI remains substantial. However, the shift is remarkable and the process behind it deserves closer analysis in the next section.

Mobilizing for EPI and removing institutional bottlenecks

As already inferred, the negligence of the EPI principle in the early period of the Cohesion Fund and the subsequent environmental reforms are closely linked to the institutional framework in which the Cohesion Fund operated. At the time of its adoption, the fund was housed in DG XIX (and the Secretariat General adopted an additional supervisory role). The institutional hacking order in the Commission made the Cohesion Fund less penetrable than the Regional Fund, and hence immune to input from DG XI or environmental NGOs.

Furthermore, the operational structure of the Cohesion Fund made the Commission, as a whole, hardly vulnerable to environmental critics. The Secretariat General and DG XIX were responsible for the macro-level financial management of the fund, whereas the project planning and management was completely devolved to the Member States. These were not obliged to follow specific procedures to ensure environmental integration or even to integrate environmental authorities. Hence, the opportunity structure for environmental advocates to adopt a 'delegitimization' strategy as in the context of reforming the ERDF was much less favourable.

With regard to the actor side of the story, there were additional obstacles. Environmental activists failed to uncover any particularly scandalous cases of poor implementation with which to push the environmental principle prior to adopting the final regulation in 1994. Furthermore, the political stakes for some potential 'insider' allies were especially high. The Commission and the EP reacted more timidly than during the ERDF campaign because they feared that the Council of the European Union would withdraw funds from the cohesion instrument altogether (EP, 1993). Consequently, no effective policy network emerged against the final regulation establishing the fund. It should be noted, however, that the NGO campaign – led by the WWF and the European Federation for Transport & Environment (T&E) – quite successfully criticized the skewed balance between transport and environment projects (WWF and T&E, 1994), contributing to the adjustment in the distribution described above.

The institutional and, hence, strategic situation changed when, under the Santer Commission, the responsibility for the Cohesion Fund was moved to Regional Policy Commissioner Wulf-Mathies and DG XVI. The greater institutional vulnerability, the adaptations already under way in the context of the ERDF and the personal beliefs of key actors provided a context more supportive of EPI. In addition, the fast response in the form of the communication on *Cohesion Policy and the Environment* (CEC, 1995) was due to active integration pressure, particularly from the European Parliament. Already in the approval hearings for the Commission, the EP had pushed an environmental agenda. Benefiting from the move of Laurens Brinkhorst, formerly director-general of DG XI, to the EP's budget committee, the EP intensified its efforts to influence EU spending practices and insisted on better environmental controls in negotiations of the 1996 and 1997 budgets (Wilkinson, 1997, pp165–166).

In sum, the Cohesion Fund shows the close link between the construction of policy problems and objectives and the institutional opportunity structures. In the initial phase, an institutional home that was insulated from environmental movements impeded a 'greening' of the Cohesion Fund. Institutional reform, going hand in hand with the creation of a new policy context and a change of personalities, altered the situation on the cognitive and structural dimension and created opportunities for EPI.

EPI AS A MULTILEVEL PROBLEM

The previous analysis has shown that there is considerable progress in adapting the legislative and operational framework to the principle of EPI. However, practical experience shows that the implementation of the principle is not yet wholly successful. Only some of the remaining problems, which are identified in this section, seem reparable on the EU level and much responsibility for the actual integration of environmental concerns lies with the Member States and sub-national actors – indicating the multilevel nature of EPI. This is particularly true, as the latest reforms have shifted responsibility from the EU to the Member-State level.

What are the prevailing problems in applying the EPI principle in the EU's regional and cohesion policy? On the basis of the past reform efforts and the ongoing critical assessment, especially on the part of environmental NGOs, it is possible to identify five main (and highly interdependent) problem areas:

1 funding of environmental protection projects and programmes;
2 application of strategic environmental impact assessments (SEIAs) for regional development programmes, as well as EIAs for individual measures;
3 lack of environmental indicators for performance monitoring;
4 integration with EU environmental directives such as the Habitats Directive and the Birds Directive;
5 participation and information of environmental actors.

Funding

Environmental NGOs have criticized that too few resources are available to support environmental protection measures. From the perspective of EPI, it is more worrying that some so-called environmental projects prove harmful to this objective. The majority of environmental programmes funded by the Structural Funds are aimed at the establishment and operation of infrastructure, whether for water treatment and supply or waste managements. Similarly, the Cohesion Fund focuses its environmental spending on water treatment and supply. While wastewater treatment projects, in particular, tend to have a positive effect on the environment, many projects aimed at water supply and distribution do not guarantee the sustainable management of water resources. The WWF identifies a Structural Funds project to transfer water from the Rivers Tajo and Seguro to the Guadiana River basin in Castilla-La Mancha as a typical example of an unsustainable 'environmental' project (Kouvelis et al, 1997, pp37–38). While the project may be capable of solving the problem of domestic water supply in the La Mancha plain, it also supports unsustainable farming practices in the region and undermines a local agri-environment scheme. This scheme is supported by the EAGGF of the EU and was introduced to stop irrigation and encourage dry cultivation.

This example – where so-called environmental projects prove harmful to the environment or where EU funding policies are poorly coordinated – is no isolated case.[11] In part, the situation is due to the obligatory link of environmental projects to regional development and economic cohesion. But even within this narrow frame, Member States have the choice to stretch the definition and to propose environmentally sustainable programmes and projects. The main responsibility for programming and planning lies with Member States and the regions; therefore, it is important that the EPI principle will gain acceptance below the EU level.

Environmental Indicators

The country case studies in Part II show that the ongoing EU initiatives to push EPI make a difference in the domestic politics of Member States, strengthening environmental policy objectives and policy actors. Yet, there are also capacity problems, especially on the regional and local level. In this context, clear guidelines would facilitate a shift in the planning, as well as in the monitoring process of regional development activities. The development of environmental indicators could serve as tools to connect (and embed) the regional or national development plans with a national sustainable development strategy, facilitating cross-sectoral cohesion in a wider context.

The wording in the new Structural Funds Regulation makes explicit that the indicators used in the monitoring of the funds will relate also to the environmental situation of the Member State. Yet, the actual tools still need to be developed. Several organizations – ranging from the Organisation for Economic Co-operation and Development (OECD), the European Environment Agency (EEA) and the European Commission to environmental authorities in several Member States – are currently working on elaborating sustainability indicators. So far, few environmental indicators are used to evaluate the impact of the funds.

Impact Assessments

Moving from the macro- to the funding-specific context, there are two points in the planning process for ERDF- or Cohesion Fund-financed programmes and projects (environmental and others) during which the environmental impact should be assessed:

1   formulation of the regional (or national) development plan;
2   formulation of individual projects.

The relevant regulations appear increasingly explicit in calling for such assessment; even the amended Cohesion Fund Regulation includes a clearer statement in this regard. Nevertheless, evidence shows that most Member States interpret the legal obligations in a rather minimalist manner (cf Kouvelis et al, 1997, pp10–18). Formal impact assessments are avoided where possible. EIAs are conducted for individual projects or even project fragments without considering the impacts on (or of) other activities in the region. EIAs are conducted late after the planning has been completed, making the consideration of alternative arrangements very difficult, in practice.

The Commission may further strengthen the legal obligations to conduct (strategic) environmental impact assessments. However, given its limited capacities to intervene in all planning stages, it heavily depends upon the support of national actors. In the absence of a general political acceptance of (S)EIAs, in turn, such support depends upon the mobilization of environmental authorities and activists in the political process. Considering that environmental authorities are often poorly equipped to monitor the application of the EIAs for all projects being executed in the region, environmental activists (and the support of the national legal system) are particularly important. In Greece and Spain, for example, environmental federations protested against the insufficient or late application of EIAs with respect to major infrastructural development (the Acheloos River diversion project and a dock development in Tenerife) and won subsequent high court cases. In these instances, the Commission received necessary 'bottom-up' backing for suspending the funding for the activities.

Nevertheless, the participation of NGOs in the planning and monitoring process often remains precarious. Even on the EU level, NGOs continue to have considerable difficulty in gaining access to the European Court of Justice. In several cases, the court denied the NGOs the *locus standi*, and hence the right to represent the environmental interests, on the basis that the claimants were not 'directly affected' by the project in question. A recent example is Greenpeace versus the European Commission, Case No C-321/95P of 2 April 1998. Such rulings prevent effective bottom-up pressure on which EPI depends in regional and cohesion policy.

Implementation of EU Environmental Legislation

Compliance with EU environmental policies in the context of regional and cohesion policy depends upon the formal transposition of the relevant EU directives into national law and their practical implementation. Even though the failure to implement EU law does not remove the obligation for compliance, regional policy actors may not be aware of the environmental violations implied in their action. Environmental authorities, in turn, will lack the 'legal stick' to insist on revisions in regional policy plans.

Poor compliance with the EU's Birds and Habitats Directives,[12] for instance, have contributed to the negligence of nature conservation issues in many development plans and projects (cf Valaoras et al, 2000; Kouvelis et al, 1997, pp29–31). The *Financial Times* of 13 March 2000 reported: 'Germany, Ireland and Portugal … have yet to submit a full list of reserves. Together with France, the UK, Belgium, Sweden and Finland, they have all been subject of legal proceedings for failing to submit adequate proposals on the [Habitats] directive' (Smith, 2000). Such poor implementation often has to do with serious political conflicts between environmental and economic authorities, the latter fearing constraints for developmental and growth strategies. The Commission, in the past, felt trapped in the same choice dilemma – for instance, with regard to the A20 motorway in Germany, which passes through several special protection areas under the Birds Directive.[13]

More recently, however, the Commission seems to be steering a harder course in enforcing the EPI principle. Environment Commissioner Wallström warned that if governments breached EU environmental laws, 'they risked delays in receiving billions of euro in regional aid from Brussels' (Harding, 1999). She received backing from Commissioner Barnier, responsible for the regional policy portfolio, and the rest of the Commission (Smith, 2000). Indeed, the Structural and Cohesion Funds offer a special opportunity for enforcing EU environmental law and, consequently, the EPI principle. Financial sanctions may have a more immediate policing effect than long-term legal proceedings. To the extent that the Community's funding instruments are used to enforce the implementation of environmental legislation, it will be difficult to ignore this legislation in the operational practice of the funds. This may be true, although the Commission has given up some of its direct involvement in the management and control of the funds. As a result, we may witness the beginning of a rather virtuous circle.

Nevertheless, the link to dishonoured EU directives may not always be easy to establish. Violations of the sustainability concept underlying the EPI principle are more ambiguous, especially in the absence of clear indicators, and the Commission will have more difficulty in imposing sanctions in those cases. In the end, compliance with the EPI principle in the planning and monitoring stages depends upon environmental 'watchdogs' on the ground.

Participation and Information

As indicated, EU powers and capacities will never be strong enough to fully ensure the integration of environmental consideration within regional policy planning and operation. This depends at least as much upon the systematic involvement of environmental authorities as well as on societal control. The relevant EU regulations have gone a long way in facilitating broad 'partnerships' and public access (see preceding section). Nevertheless, the national experiences still tend to be on the restrictive side.

Despite the regulatory reforms, the participation of environmental authorities in the planning, and to a lesser extent in the monitoring, stage has been inadequate prior to the last reform of the Structural Funds. They are considered marginal players and their concerns are perceived as interventions delaying the cash flows from Brussels (Kouvelis et al, 1997, p22). Furthermore, their resources are frequently insufficient to play a stronger role. At the monitoring stage, environmental authorities tend to be involved only in the evaluation of specific environmental activities rather than in the overall environmental performance of the programmes (Kouvelis et al, 1997, p23).

'On the issue of participation', a recent WWF publication observes, 'although there has been an increased effort on behalf of most authorities to open up the discussion to social and economic partners (following the new Regulation), environmental NGOs have in general been excluded (except for the nature conservation parts of some Plans)' (WWF, 1999, p7). In particular, locally based environmental groups would be able to inform the programmers of the local environmental parameters and dangers and, hence, would complement the less detailed knowledge of the environmental authorities involved.

The informal participation of civil society and environmental NGOs through public campaigning or protesting remains limited due to a generally restrictive information policy, even though the regulations call for information and publicity on the Structural Funds. In this context, the generally resistant attitude on the part of national and regional authorities in implementing the EU Directive on the Access to Environmental Information forms an additional obstacle (cf Kimber, 2000).

CONCLUSIONS AND SOLUTIONS?

To conclude, open participation and information practices constitute the 'missing links' (Kouvelis et al, 1997, p45) for ensuring EPI in the multilevel governance structure of the Community's regional and cohesion policies. The reform processes of the ERDF and Cohesion Fund, described and analysed in the first sections of this chapter, revealed the crucial role that was played by environmental NGOs. The evidence presented by these groups with their close links to the local level contributed to a learning process on the part of EU administrators. To ensure that regulatory change is translated into operational practices in the Member States and regions, such a learning process needs to be repeated here. Hence, environmental authorities supported by civil society groups must be given systematic access to the entire regional and cohesion policy process.

A further lesson that can be learned from the EU-level reforms relates to the crucial role of institutional structures as facilitators or obstacles in the shift of policy frames. In this respect, EPI in regional policy remains an open-ended story. On the one hand, the EU legal framework may contribute to loosening institutional rigidities on the ground; on the other hand, sectorally autonomous policy-making structures are prevailing in most Member States (see Chapters 3–5 in Part II).

Considering these bottlenecks in the Member States, what is the appropriate role of the Commission as 'guardian of the treaties' and 'co-administrator' of the funds? A recent statement by Environment Commissioner Wallström is revealing in this regard: 'In the long run I would prefer to be more of a consultant or advisor to Member States, but until then I will have to be more of a policewoman' (Harding, 1999). In the last decade, the Commission has made great progress in building a facilitating framework for environmentally sustainable regional policy. Until the 'message' trickles down to the regional and national level, the Commission may need to reinforce the process through more active pressure, such as the recent threat to withhold funding in cases of non-compliance with EU environmental policies.

REFERENCES

Agence Europe (1994) *General News*, 6142, 6 January, Agence Internationale D'Information Pour la Presse, Luxembourg, Brussels

Bina, O, Cuff, J and Lake, R (1997) *EU Cohesion and the Environment: a Vision for 2000 and Beyond*, Report for the BirdLife International Regional Policy Task Force

Commission of the European Communities (CEC) (1973) 'Report on the Regional Problems in the Enlarged Community', *Bulletin of the European Communities*, Supplement 8/73, Office for Official Publications of the European Communities, Brussels

CEC (1991) *Improve Your Environment – Using Financial Instruments of the European Community*, CEC, Brussels

CEC (1992a) *Towards Sustainability: A European Community Programme of Policy and Action in Relation to the Environment and Sustainable Development*, COM(92) 23 final, vol II, 27 March, Brussels

CEC (1992b) *Green Paper on the Impact of Transport on the Environment: A Community Strategy for 'Sustainable Mobility'*, COM (92) 46 final, Brussels

CEC (1993) *Community Structural Funds: 1994–1999. Revised Regulations and Comments*, CEC, Brussels

CEC (1995) *Communication from the Commission to the Council, the European Parliament, the Economic and Social Committee and the Committee on the Regions: Cohesion Policy and the Environment*, COM (95) 509 final, 22 November, Brussels

CEC (1998a) *Proposal for a Council Regulation (EC) Laying Down General Provisions on the Structural Funds*, 98/0090 (AVC), Brussels

CEC (1999a) *The New Programming Period 2000– 2006: Technical Papers by Theme. Technical Paper 1: Application of the Polluter Pays Principle. Differentiating the Rates of Community Assistance for Structural Funds, Cohesion Fund and ISPA Infrastructure Operations*, 6 December, CEC, Brussels

CEC (1999b) *The Structural Funds and Their Coordination with the Cohesion Fund*, Draft Guidance for Programmes during the Period 2000–2006, tabled by Mrs Wulf-Mathies in agreement with Mr Flynn, Mr Fischler and Ms Bonino, Working Paper of the Commission, 3 February, CEC, Brussels

CEC and the Directorate-General for Regional Policy (2000) *Directorate-General for Regional Policy Working Programme for 2000*, CEC, Brussels

Corrie H (1993) *Campaigning to Green the EC Structural Funds*, mimeograph

Coss, S (1999) 'Report Points to Winners and Losers in Battle for Regional Aid', *European Voice*, News, 21–27 October, p8

European Court of Auditors (1992) 'Special Report 3/92 Concerning the Environment Together with the Commission's Replies', *Official Journal of the European Communities*, no C245, 23 September

European Parliament (EP) (1993) 'Debates', *Official Journal of the European Communities*, no 3–429, Annex, 10 March

Hajer, M (1993) 'Discourse Coalitions and the Institutionalization of Practice: The Case of Acid Rain in Britain' in F Fischer and J Forester (eds) *The Argumentative Turn in Policy Analysis and Planning*, Duke University Press, Durham, pp43–75

Harding, G (1999) 'Wallström Vows to "Name and Shame" Environmental Laggards', *European Voice*, News, 10–17 November, p2

Hey, C (1996) *The Incorporation of the Environmental Dimension into the Transport Policies in the EU: Short Version of the EU Study*, EURES Institute, Freiburg

Hooghe L and Keating, M (1994) 'The Politics of EU Regional Policy', *Journal of European Public Policy*, vol 1, no 3, pp367–393

Jones, T (1999) 'Reform Plans Focus on UK Rebate', *European Voice*, News, 10 March, p2

Jordan, A and Lenschow, A (2000) 'Greening the European Union: What Can Be Learned from the "Leaders" of EU European Environmental Policy?', *European Environment*, vol 10, no 3, pp109–120

Kelleher, J, Batterbury, S and Stern, E (1999) *The Thematic Evaluation of the Partnership Principle*, First Synthesis Report, prepared by the Tavistock Institute Evaluation Development and Review Unit with the assistance of ECOTEC Research and Consulting Ltd and experts in each of the Member States, February

Kimber, C (2000) 'Implementing European Environmental Policy and the Directive on Access to Environmental Information', in C Knill and A Lenschow (eds) *Implementing EU Environmental Policy: New Directions and Old Problems*, Manchester University Press, Manchester, pp168-196

Kouvelis, S, Corrie, H, Meldon, J and Schubert, D (1997) *Tools for Economic and Social Cohesion in the European Union: An Environmental Mid-Term Review*, WWF International, Brussels

Lenschow, A (1997) 'Variation in European Environmental Policy Integration: Agency Push within Complex Institutional Structures', *Journal of European Public Policy*, vol 4, no 1, pp109–127

Lenschow, A (1999) 'The Greening of the EU: the Common Agricultural Policy and the Structural Funds', *Environmental and Planning C: Government and Policy*, vol 17, pp91–108

Long, T (1995) 'Shaping Public Policy in the European Union: a Case Study of the Structural Funds', *Journal of European Public Policy*, vol 2, no 4, pp672–679

Marks, G (1992) 'Structural Policy in the European Community' in A Sbragia (ed) *Euro-Politics: Institutions and Policymaking in the 'New' European Community*, Brookings Institutions, Washington DC, pp191–224

Neligan, M (1998) 'To Stay a "Winner", the Objective Is to Be Judged "Poor"', *European Voice*, Features, 3–9 December, p17

Nollkaemper, A (1998) *The Integration Principle and the Search for Normative Closure in European and International Environmental Law*, Paper Presented at the Environmental Summer Workshop Environmental Policy Integration: The 'Greening' of Sectoral Policies, European University Institute, Florence

Pollack, M (1995) 'Regional Actors in an Intergovernmental Play: the Making and Implementation of EC Structural Policy' in C Rhodes and S Mazey (eds) *The State of the European Union. Vol 3: Building a European Polity?*, Lynne Rienner/Longman, Boulder CO, pp361–390

Ross, G (1995) *Jacques Delors and European Integration*, Polity Press, Oxford and New York

Smith, M (2000) 'EU States' Aid at Risk over Environment', *Financial Times*, 17 March

Valaoras, G, Rovisco, I, Grasso, M, Navarro, C and Sánchez, A (2000) *Assessing the Implementation of NATURA 2000 in Southern Europe*, Paper Presented at the Environmental Programme Workshop on Coming to Terms with the Mediterranean Syndrome, 19–20 May, European University Institute, Florence

Wilkinson, D (1994) 'Using the European Union's Structural and Cohesion Funds for the Protection of the Environment', *European Environmental Law Review*, no 2, pp2–3

Wilkinson, D (1997) 'Towards Sustainability in the European Union? Steps within the European Commission towards Integrating the Environment into other European Union Policy Sectors', *Environmental Politics,* vol 6, no 1, pp153–173

World Wide Fund For Nature (WWF) (1993) *Briefing for the Danish Presidency,* WWF, Brussels

WWF (1997) *A New European Community Policy – Sustainable Regional Development,* Umweltstiftung WWF-Deutschland, Frankfurt

WWF (1998) *12 Steps towards a Sustainable European Union Cohesion Policy. WWF's Proposals for the Reform of the Structural Fund Regulations 2000–2006,* Umweltstiftung WWF-Deutschland, Frankfurt

WWF (1999) *Preliminary Report on the Ex Ante Evaluation of the Regional Development Plans of five EU Member States,* WWF European Policy Office, Brussels

WWF (no date) *Towards the Greening of the EC Institutions. Integration of Environmental Objectives into EC Policy Making: Recommendations for Action,* WWF discussion paper, WWF, Brussels

WWF and Institute for European Environmental Policy (IEEP) (1989) *Reform of the Structural Funds – An Environmental Briefing,* IEEP, Surrey and London

WWF and IEEP (1990) *The EC Structural Funds – Environmental Briefing, 2,* WWF/IEEP, Brussels and London

WWF and Transport & Environment (T&E) (1994) *Briefing Paper – The Cohesion Fund: Proposal for a Council Regulation,* COM (93) 699 final, Brussels

NOTES

1   This and the next section rely heavily on previous work (Lenschow, 1997 and 1999).

2   For the distinction of defensive and active strategies, compare Hey (1996) and see proceeding section.

3   Environmental spending under the ERDF rose from 135 million ECU in the four years prior to 1988 to more than 2.5 billion ECU (or almost 20 per cent of the budget available under the structural funds) in the five-year period after the reforms (CEC, 1991).

4   A series of articles in the *European Voice* are very revealing in this respect (Neligan, 1998; Jones, 1999; Coss, 1999).

5   See Council Regulation No 1164/94 (Annex 1).

6   However, no formal reference to the Community's directive on environmental impact assessments (EIAs) (EC No 85/337/EEC) was made, making this obligation rather informal and subject to a minimalist interpretation on the part of the beneficiary countries (cf Kouvelis et al, 1997, p25).

7   Council Regulation (EC) No 1264/1999 of 21 June 1999, amending Regulation (EC) No 1164/94, and Council Regulation (EC) No 1265/1999 of 21 June 1999, amending Annex II to Regulation (EC) No 1164/64

8   See Hajer (1993) on the formation of 'discourse coalitions' and the role of 'discourse institutionalization' in the environmental field.

9   For instance, the European Parliament threatened to make use of its budgetary powers.

10   In the early 1990s, the EU's environmental policy had come under intense scrutiny due to its heavy intervention in national affairs without showing clear progress in improving the state of the environment in Europe.

11   Compare Bini et al (1997, section 2.2) for more examples.

12   Birds Directive No 79/409/CEC of 1979; Habitats Directive No 92/43/CEE.
     Both directives call for the designation of special zones, forming an ecological
     network. The final objective of the Habitats Directive is the creation of a
     European network – the so-called Natura 2000 network – guaranteeing the
     protection of habitats and species listed in the directive.

13   The Commission has decided in favour of the motorway on the basis of the
     special development needs of Mecklenburg-Vorpommern (objective 1 region) and
     the fact that the motorway would be part of the Trans-European Networks (cf
     Nollkaemper, 1998).

Part IV

CONCLUSION

11

Conclusion: What are the Bottlenecks and Where are the Opportunities for Greening the EU?

Andrea Lenschow

Most sectors of economic activity interact with the natural environment and carry the potential for its massive degradation. Energy and transport are the main culprits for air pollution and climatic changes. Modern agriculture is responsible for the pollution of soil and water and, especially in southern Europe, has contributed to major land erosion. Regional development policies that focus primarily on infrastructural measures often neglect their immediate impact on existing ecosystems, as well as the longer-term environmental consequences of new economic activities in the region.

The preceding chapters in this book do not only confirm the interconnected nature of economic activities and the state of the environment, they also indicate the need for a fresh look at public policy-making in the European Union (EU). In the past, EU and national policy-makers have treated environmental policy as just another 'sector' that could be managed in isolation of other policy domains. Environmental policy regulated economic activities, imposing certain limits but not directly intervening in sectoral programming and planning. Not surprisingly, most resources spent on the environment supported reactive or end-of-pipe measures, correcting environmental impact at the end – or even after – the production and consumption processes.

Remarkably, these patterns prevailed against the better knowledge of most policy-makers. The non-integration of environmental considerations within the sectoral planning and decision-making processes imposes considerable economic and environmental costs. Chapter 1 traced the evolution of the environmental policy integration (EPI) principle through EU policy-making, showing that it was acknowledged already in the mid 1970s and became a legal obligation with the signing of the Single European Act in 1987. And the EU was only following other examples. The influence of the Brundtland Report

(WCED, 1987) on European environmental policy discourse is widely known; in addition, several Member States had already moved ahead. Müller shows in Chapter 4 that Germany, for instance, was a programmatic front-runner in establishing the EPI principle in the early 1970s.

Yet, the actual application of the EPI principle in sectoral policy-making looks much less promising. The state of the environment in Europe is deteriorating and progress towards environmental integration is far from satisfactory (EEA, 1999a, b). Reacting to these deficiencies, the EU heads of state or government took the initiative in late 1997 and relaunched the EPI process. In the context of the so-called Cardiff process, most sectoral councils as well as the Member States are instructed to assess their environmental performance and develop better strategies for integrating the environment. In the course of such rethinking, policy priorities, as well as policy-making procedures and institutional arrangements, need to be reconsidered.

It was the objective of this book to analyse past attempts to implement the EPI principle in EU and national policy-making, as well as to identify the bottlenecks that have hampered change. This concluding chapter draws together the results of the nine case studies collected in this volume – three country studies and six EU policy studies – and suggests some lessons for the ongoing reform process.

GREENING ON MULTIPLE LEVELS

EPI in the EU involves not only cross-sectoral (horizontal) coordination; it equally depends upon vertical cooperation. Most EU policies need to be formally transposed and then implemented on the national and regional level, usually leaving discretionary space to account for national practices and traditions. With regard to novel normative principles such as EPI, a visible learning process on the EU level does not automatically ensure a similar rethinking on lower levels of governance. This is especially true because the legal status of the EPI principle remains somewhat ambiguous (see Chapter 2). The dissemination of new policy principles depends upon a cooperative climate conducive to joint learning processes. Obviously, this process is not limited to the implementation process but works in the interactions shaping the policy formulation and decision-making stages.

In this context, the subsidiarity debate has resulted in unhelpful divisions. Most political rhetoric about the subsidiarity principle in the past emphasized themes of national and, to some extent, regional autonomy and the protection against interventionism from 'Brussels'. In the environmental field, the subsidiarity concept fed into the post-Maastricht deregulatory paradigm of the EU (cf Collier et al, 1996, Collier, 1998). Often neglected in these debates was the mutually interdependent and potentially mutually supportive character of multilevel politics (Marks et al, 1996; Jachtenfuchs and Kohler-Koch, 1996). The main conclusion of the Cardiff Summit in June 1998 pointed to the no longer obvious by emphasizing that EPI depends upon a working *partnership for integration*, involving the Community institutions as well as the national governments (CEC, 1999a).

In the absence of this working partnership, the greening process may be interrupted or hindered on each of the multiple levels of governance in the EU. But the multilevel context may also allow for learning and reform processes that would not have emerged otherwise. The case studies in this book point to four possible scenarios, showing these joint responsibilities for EPI:

1   The EPI principle is disregarded in the EU policy formulation phase.
2   The EPI principle fails to gain acceptance in EU decision-making.
3   The sector-specific framework for EPI is set on the EU level but is disregarded in the national policy process.
4   The EPI discourse and policy development on the EU level triggers a 'greening' in national policy-making.

The EPI Principle in the EU Policy Formulation Phase

The fact that the EPI principle is outright disregarded in the policy formulation phase is becoming increasingly a pattern of the past. Agricultural, transport and regional cohesion policy used to be routed in policy paradigms that took little account of environmental impacts (see Chapters 6–10 in Part III). Either the natural environment was considered well served – by keeping rural areas from decline or by supporting the modernization of old (and dirty) industrial complexes – or the economic trade-off of protecting the environment 'at the expense' of 'developmental' activities was perceived too high.

In recent years, there has been notable evidence of a rethinking in several Commission services, often following a change in leadership. In Chapter 7, Hey shows the 'infiltration' of green ideas in the Energy and Transport Directorate-General (DG), responsible for transport policy, resulting in the publication of Green and White papers that acknowledged the problematic role played, in particular, by road traffic and that proposed some novel policy approaches. In Chapter 10, Lenschow describes a similar learning process within the Regional Policy DG resulting in now close cooperation with the Environment DG. The relative openness of many Commission services to ideas presented by expert and interest groups, as well as national policy-makers, constituted an important contributing factor, especially if these new ideas succeed in 'delegitimizing' old policy approaches.

Yet, the 'greening' of Commission services has been varied and is far from complete. In Chapter 8, Lauber's analysis of the Commission's handling of the alpine transit issue suggests a paradigmatic divide through the Energy and Transport DG. The provision of transport infrastructure, particularly if it serves market transactions, continues to receive clear priority over environmental concerns. Furthermore, the initial phase of the EU Cohesion Fund was shaped by a rather singular interest of the Commission in macro-economic performance (see Chapter 10). The Agriculture DG approached the greening process by proposing to *add* new environmental activities rather than suggesting fundamental reforms of environmentally unsustainable market support schemes (see Chapter 6). In the latter case, environmental activism, supported by international criticism of the economic support structure for European farmers as well as evidence of high environmental and economic cost, did not suffice to bring about a more substantial reform (see also Lenschow, 1998).

Marginal, partial or 'additive' greening proposals may well indicate anticipatory behaviour on the part of the Commission rather than internal resistance or unresponsiveness. Getting innovative proposals through the decision-making stage in the various Councils of Ministers may prove a real – and sometime insurmountable – challenge.

The EPI Principle Ignored in EU Decision-Making

The importance of agenda-setting and initiatives in policy-making and the impact on 'framing' subsequent discussions and decisions have occupied many scholars in public policy (cf Kingdon, 1984; Schön and Rein, 1994), including individuals investigating EU policy-making (see, for example, Pollack, 1997). Yet, policy initiatives may still be stopped in the decision-making phase, hence in the responsible Council of Ministers and, considering its increasing competencies, the European Parliament. Several case studies confirm the recent 'global assessment' of the Commission that 'the commitment by other sectors and by Member States to the Programme is partial' (CEC, 1999b, p3).[1] The decision-making processes in several councils show little evidence that the EPI principle served as a 'rule of reference' or was even accepted as an 'autonomous normative principle' (see Chapter 2 for an elaboration of these concepts).

Chapter 7 on environmental taxation for heavy goods vehicles offers the clearest example of how EPI initiatives were stopped or significantly watered down in the Transport Council. Following the consideration of various policy options to 'green' transport policy and to deal, in particular, with the environmental impact of heavy freight transport in the Commission (resulting in the preparation of various discussion papers that elaborated on the option of environmental taxation), the inputs were ignored in the first decision-making round. 'What is most apparent is that the parallel discussion on the environmental consequences of transport and on the Green Paper on Transport and the Environment had no visible effect on the council negotiations' (Chapter 7, p142). Ministerial positions held in the Transport Council were, of course, representative of the domestic acceptance of the EPI principle. Hey observes in Chapter 7: 'Environmental considerations had little influence in national transport politics. They slightly softened the Dutch and Danish positions; but in total national environmental ministries were marginalized as players in the sectoral decision-making process' (p144). In later council meetings, the issue of heavy freight taxation became coupled with the issue of transit traffic across the Alps, with Switzerland 'blackmailing' the EU from the outside to adopt a somewhat 'greener' position. Nevertheless, the final decision confirms the generally restrictive position of the Transport Council on the issue of 'greening' transport policy (see Chapters 7 and 8).[2]

The implications for the internal market, concerns over the competitiveness of national hauliers and insistence on national taxing autonomy were the main reasons why transport ministers were unwilling to prioritize environmental concerns in their decisions. In Chapter 9, Collier points to another issue that turns the Councils of Ministers into rather conservative actors – the spending of EU resources. The Commission's proposals to promote energy efficiency and renewable energies through the SAVE and ALTENER programmes were dramatically cut down in the Energy Council, preventing them from showing much effect. While it must be acknowledged that the overall EU budget is rather small and incapable of serving many funding needs, the fact that the bulk of the budget is allocated for a problematic agricultural market support scheme (with a very small environmental component) suggests that environmental concerns have not yet become a main determinant of EU funding decisions. Not even the Cohesion Fund, which distributes about half of its resources to environmental projects, was conceived of as a truly environmental instrument (see Chapter 10).

Until now, the technical Council of Ministers proved often to be a rather high hurdle in the EPI process. However, individual Member States have sometimes played an instrumental role in pushing the EPI principle. Denmark (with the assistance of the UK) joined the environmental alliance to 'green' the structural funds in the early 1990s (see Chapter 10). The UK hoped to restart the debate on 'greening' the transport sector in organizing a joint council with the environment ministers during its last presidency (see Chapter 3). In the case of alpine transit, it is possible to see how non-Member States, such as Switzerland, are sometimes able to push the EPI agenda onto the council level (see Chapter 8). Furthermore, the European Council, gathering the EU heads of state and government, has been the most important forum for relaunching the EPI process in recent years. Sweden had placed the EPI issue on the agenda of the Luxembourg Summit; the UK provided institutional structure in establishing the so-called Cardiff process; Austria, Finland and Germany used their EU presidencies to continue and widen EPI activities (see Chapter 1). Overall, we see that progress towards EPI in the European multilevel polity depends crucially upon the political will and initiative of the political leadership in the Member States.

Poor Responsiveness in National Policy Processes

The actual 'greening' of public policy does not necessarily follow from such general support of the EPI principle as declared in most Member States. There is a thorny path between the declarations of a policy commitment to compliance with it. Two of Part II's country studies serve as good illustrations.

As hinted above, Germany has been a 'programmatic front-runner' of the EPI principle. Germany's first environmental programme of 1971 contained the objective to integrate environmental concerns in all public and private decision-making processes and elaborated three further principles – polluter pays, precaution and cooperation – to guide the integration approach (see Chapter 4). Yet, the actual performance in EPI must be considered relatively poor. In most political and administrative activities in 'non-environmental' policy areas, the environmental ministry, authorities or interest groups play a subordinate role. EPI has been generally linked to the economic interest of relevant actors; it did not become institutionalized as an autonomous policy principle.

The British example goes in the same direction. Though never known as a pioneer in environmental policy-making, the UK has become one of the strongest advocates of the EPI principle. Furthermore, according to Jordan's analysis in Chapter 3, 'the UK possesses the necessary "hardware" (the organization and procedures of governance) needed to coordinate policy across the various strands of government activity, and the intellectual "software" (the knowledge about how to implement EPI) to make the government machine run in a more environmental direction' (p36). But Jordan points also to continuing centripetal forces at lower levels of the departmental structure of government, where 'departmental views' compete, leading to fragmented policy-making. Jordan's case evidence from the transport and energy policy domains illustrates how the EPI principle fails to permeate the core of sectoral activities. Despite all declarations to the contrary, the UK's transport policy continues to serve car drivers first. Its progress in cutting pollution from the energy sector has been mostly coincidental to the collapse of its coal industry.

The above examples indicate that the insertion of the EPI principle within the EU treaty texts are not sufficient to redirect national practices in sectoral policy domains. Several EU policies, however, have begun to provide more than a framework of principles and are developing an operational structure to guide EPI on the ground. The evolution of the European Regional Development Fund (ERDF), in particular, points in this direction. But even in this case, sectoral policy-makers in the Member States and regions were often incapable or unwilling to apply the principle (see Chapter 10). Environmental groups continue to uncover cases where regional development projects have harmful consequences for the environment and where the planners ignore environmental impact assessments. Environmental authorities and societal actors still play only a marginal role in the planning and monitoring processes. Even some activities that are conceived as environmental projects produce more harm than good. While there is still room for improving the EU operational framework, the main culprits for this implementation gap are the Member States (or regions).

Also in the farming sector, the EU Member States have much discretion within the 'accompanying' agri-environmental measures, however marginal. Buller's analysis in Chapter 6 shows varied national responses. While some Member States integrate more than 80 per cent of their utilized agricultural area in agri-environmental schemes, others, such as Belgium and the Netherlands, have a take-up rate of less than 2 per cent (see Table 6.4). Generally, Buller observes that these take-up rates correspond with the traditional agricultural production structure in the Member States and that there is little evidence that the agri-environment scheme contributes to substantive structural reforms in the sector.

In short, EU policy initiatives and reforms to integrate environmental concerns in sectoral policies depend for their success on the Member States joining the effort. Both the country studies and several policy studies presented in Parts II and III show notable differences in the capability and willingness of national and regional actors to 'green' public policy. Furthermore, there are differences within countries across policy sectors. In Chapter 9, Collier notes, for instance, interesting initiatives in several Member States to push the renewable energy sector (a case where national Kyoto commitments are the main impetus, not EU policies). Overall, however, there is more evidence of compliance problems than successes.

EU Reforms as Triggers for National 'Greening' Processes

EU reforms as triggers for national 'greening' processes imply that the previous scenarios could be successfully avoided. EU decisions complying with the EPI principle need to be received favourably on the national and often also the regional political and administrative level. In this regard, the implementation perspective – in which the EU establishes a concrete expectation for Member States' adaptations – is too narrow. A general normative principle such as EPI, while legally binding, is supposed to have a *multiplying* effect and serve as facilitator for reforms on the lower levels of governance that were not pre-structured on the EU policy arena. While much EU policy requires implementation in the Member States – in accordance with all treaty obligations, including EPI – the EU *acquis* also constitutes a general framework for domestic initiative from the 'bottom up'.

Despite the sceptical view presented in the previous section, the country studies in Part II also suggest a few examples where EU environmental policy, in general, and the discussions on the EPI principle, in particular, have triggered national responses that go beyond concrete implementation activities. There has been some evidence of learning.

In Chapter 4, Müller states: 'The history of German environmental policy, particularly its struggles with the EPI principle, has provided some evidence that the EU level has served on several occasions to break domestic political bottlenecks' (p73). Environmental instruments that facilitate EPI, such as information rights, environmental audits and environmental impact assessments (EIA), would not have developed in the German political context. Some, such as the EIA, had previously failed to be adopted and were introduced only due to EU environmental policy. While there exist some doubts about the implementation performance of these measures in Germany (cf Knill and Lenschow, 1998, 2001), Müller observes a loosening of political and institutional rigidities due to 'Europe'.

The multiplying effect seems even more significant in Italy. Helped by the political 'revolution' ending the Italian First Republic, Lewanski argues, the government responded favourably after 1996 to the EPI stimuli represented by international commitments (Kyoto) and EU policies (see Chapter 5). EPI has entered into the 'market of political ideas', shaping the present political discourse in Italy as well as concrete policy-making. Significantly, several recent initiatives are not merely implementation acts to comply with EU policies, but rather represent 'original' activities that 'green' regional development in southern Italy, urban transport and industrial policy.

To sum up, this section illustrates the multilevel nature of the EPI problem. EU activities depend upon the support of the Member States, not only during the decision-making phase but also in subsequent processes 'on the ground'. In many cases, this partnership for integration has not yet developed, even though there have also been several instances of a 'greening' of public policy. The evidence presented above leaves us with a question, however. What are the conditions that explain such varied experiences across countries and across policy sectors? The proceeding section will elaborate on the explanatory framework that was introduced in Chapter 1.

BOTTLENECKS AND OPPORTUNITIES

Framing the Issue

The environmental policy integration principle was formulated in the 1970s; in the EU context, it was subsequently 'forgotten' for approximately two decades before it was 'unearthed' again in the mid 1990s. This fluctuation of the principle does not correlate with the fluctuating environmental impacts of economic activities. Rather, it is due to the nature of the political discourse, in which the saliency of issues is constructed. As was elaborated in Chapter 1, 'EPI represents a first-order operational principle to implement and institutionalize the idea of sustainable development' (p6) that was formulated in the 1970s and spread widely after the publication of the Brundtland Report in 1987. Ideas, such as 'sustainable development', give structure and content to the definition of interests – they act as 'causal stories' or interpretative frameworks, giving new information their place in the story and structuring expectations. Political conflict is fought with the weapon of competing causal stories, which substantiate the interests of political actors. The country studies in Part II illustrate how environmental interests were empowered by the 'story' of sustainable development. Environmental ministries were established, environmental non-governmental organizations (NGOs) spread and the volume of environmental legislation increased.

Nevertheless, environmental policy tended to develop in policy niches rather than as an integrated component of sectoral policies. To the extent that we see a general paradigm shift, this is often restricted to programmatic declarations; operational changes are scattered rather than systematic. The case studies in this book point to two weaknesses in the 'framing' of the EPI principle: the causal story remains a skeleton and the story loses persuasiveness on lower operational levels.

The skeleton story
The persuasive character of the sustainable development concept is rooted in the argument that EPI produces positive-sum results. The natural environment will be protected from degradation and the economic basis of human existence will be sustained.[3] In the long term, the resource pool will be secured for future generations. But also in the short term, by avoiding a circle of environmental damage and subsequent repair – which is achieved by accounting for, and

internalizing, environmental costs in production and consumption behaviour – a higher rate of economic efficiency can be achieved. This is the general logic of the story!

In economic practice, we observe that the costs of unsustainable practice often remain elusive. Sectoral policy-makers are overtaxed in assessing the environmental impacts of their programmes and projects and in evaluating sustainable practice. Hence, 'greening' attempts tend to be piecemeal rather than strategic. The liberalization of the energy sector (see Chapter 9) and many regional development plans (see Chapter 10) illustrate this widespread incapacity (and often related unwillingness). Sectoral policy-makers need sustainability indicators and targets in order to comprehend what EPI 'means' and targets.

In the past, such instruments that facilitate an operational interpretation of the sustainability concept and, hence, EPI were missing, with the result that sectoral policy-makers neglected the very abstract – and therefore vague – EPI obligation. The development of indicators is one of the new priorities of the EU and may help to add flesh to the skeleton. Indicators allow for a regular review of progress towards achieving policy target and setting sectoral benchmarks. The publication of such indicators contributes to holding sectoral policy-makers accountable to the EPI principle. The Commission is currently developing environmental and sectoral integration indicators, which together inform on improvements in the state of the environment, on environmental progress made in key sector policies, as well as on the feasibility of achieving sustainable development targets (CEC, 1999c; see also EEB, 1999, for an example of benchmarking indicators).

Gaps in the logic

Even if more substance and therefore guidance is given to the concepts, a fundamental problem remains. The emphasis of the sustainability concept and EPI on 'win–win' scenarios, with regard to the environment and the economy, is persuasive from an aggregate and long-term perspective. There is little doubt that environmental degradation today will impose restrictions on the economic opportunities of future generations; this is most obvious with respect to the extraction of natural, non-renewable resources or soil erosion. But this win–win logic often breaks down on less aggregate levels. The sustainable development paradigm implies a restructuring of the economy with redistributive effects, where not every producer, farmer or consumer will gain.[4]

In political terms, this means that the EPI principle is more likely to gain acceptance on the top level or among conceptually working persons – for example, among heads of state or government or Commission officials – but will face resistance where immediate trade-offs are felt. In other words, the 'weapon' of the sustainability story often loses power on the ground. The case studies in this book show that concerns with the immediate costs of reforms prevail over responsibilities for a common good; variation in the acceptance of the EPI concept is closely related to the perception of short-term economic consequence.

This does not mean that EPI always breaks down on the ground. The story of mutual gains has inspired creative minds in political and economic planning, and more sustainable solutions were found for many economic activities. The development of new, less resource-intensive materials, recycling techniques, ecological housing projects or eco-tourism are only a few examples of 'green' niches in economic activities. Nevertheless, the two case studies on transport-related issues in Chapters 7 and 8 illustrate that such niches are not always easy to find. In Chapter 8, Lauber shows that the Austrian progressive stand towards restricting road traffic across the Alps, especially for heavy lorries, diminished once it became clear that local (Tyrolian) traffic could not be easily exempted from the costs; such discriminatory policy would violate against internal market principles. Hey provides a similar example in Chapter 7, tracing the 1993 Eurovignette Directive, among other things, to a significant fall in oil prices, allowing the introduction of an eco-tax without imposing new costs on the transport sector. While the latter case points to an economic window of opportunity for institutionalizing an environmental policy instrument, both examples show the economic limits on 'greening' sectoral policies.

If the political will to comply with the EPI principle and to produce environmentally sustainable policy outcomes is strong, it may be possible to solve these conflicts of interests by constructing a win–win solution. In other words, individual losers of 'greening' measures may be compensated, typically by subsidizing their adaptation processes. Subsidies, although controversial in the current political discourse, have the advantage that they allow for a steering of the restructuring processes, establishing clear incentives and disincentives. The agri-environmental measures of the EU agricultural policy move in this direction. The ongoing attempts to liberalize the energy and transport markets show the difficulty of 'internalizing' environmental cost, on the one hand, and of subsidizing providers of environment-friendly energy or modes of transport, on the other hand. In this context, political will is necessary in order to find sustainable solutions.

The Institutional Context

The sustainable development concept developed in the Brundtland Report established an explicit link to institutional structures, arguing that the establishment of cooperative structures between policy sectors and, vertically, between levels of governance is a necessary condition for achieving sustainable policy outcomes. More specifically, sustainable development implies that:

> 'central economic and sectoral ministries [be given] the responsibility for the quality of those parts of the human environment affected by their decisions, and [that] environmental agencies [receive] more power to cope with the effects of unsustainable development.' (WCED, 1987, p10)

Institutional fragmentation and insulation, therefore, constitute constraints to effective environmental policy integration and, hence, sustainable policy-making.

These conclusions of the Brundtland Report are easily confirmed with respect to the EU – both on the Community and the national level. The reforms in the EU regional policy, leading towards a significant 'greening' on the Community level, were shown to be clearly correlated with the development of good working relations between the Environment DG and the Regional Policy DG (see Chapter 10). This cooperation goes beyond the publication of joint working papers; it also appears to work on the more operational level where the environment service assists in evaluating regional development plans. Generally, however, the cooperation between the Commission's services has been assessed less favourably. Internal procedural reforms to force each DG to take responsibility for the environmental impact of its decisions and to facilitate cooperation with the environmental unit are faced with much resistance and perceived as unnecessary bureaucratic exercises (see Chapter 1; see also Favoino et al, 2000).

These problems tend to be even more severe on the national level. Reporting from Germany, Müller, in Chapter 4, identifies several institutional factors that hindered effective policy integration:

- The environment ministry and (however less so) its predecessor, the interior ministry, did not possess the institutional standing in the government and the procedural tools to intervene in the work of other ministries.
- The federal structure allows most sectors to build vertical alliances in the preparation of sectoral policies but environmental interests gain access only at late stages in the policy process (environmental policy-makers, on the other hand, are required to 'coordinate' from the bottom up).
- Day-to-day administrative procedures do not facilitate interministerial coordination and especially disfavour the environment. As Lewanski points out with reference to the Italian case in Chapter 5, administrative structures and procedures may equally hamper the execution of EPI in the implementation phase – for instance, by fragmenting the authorization procedures for new projects.

Institutional analysis in political science emphasizes how difficult it is to engage in institutional reforms. In this context, it is hardly surprising that there has been only slow movement in the Commission and in Germany. In Italy, the big political crisis in the mid 1990s facilitated a general reorientation with respect to environmental policy-making, including significant administrative adaptations. The crisis 'punctuated' the previous equilibrium (Krasner, 1984) and created an opportunity for change. In the regional policy case, mentioned above, the reform was equally triggered by a deep crisis – in this case, a crisis of the Commission's and the DG's legitimacy. Environmental NGOs could prove that the Commission's regional funding practices regularly violated EU law, mobilizing general critics of the Brussels bureaucracy, as well as environmental advocates. The already planned reforms of the structural funds provided the political window of opportunity to 'green' the funds.

In sum, there is wide agreement that horizontally and vertically integrated institutional structures are necessary ingredients for EPI. At the same time, institutional structures are difficult to reform unless there is a serious crisis. The concepts of sustainable development and environmental policy integration may be able to provide the vocabulary to 'green' an existing crisis scenario (as in the Italian case), or even to construct a new crisis (as in the regional policy case). In any event, people need to be mobilized in order to exploit the crisis scenario for change.

Mobilizing Actor Support for EPI

For people to mobilize in the name of EPI they need to be enabled. This tends to be one of the main demands of environmental NGOs, which have been driving forces in many greening initiatives on the EU and the national level. The regional policy case has already been summarized briefly. Lauber's case study on freight transport across the Alps (Chapter 8) comes to similar conclusions. In all three regions involved (Switzerland, Tyrol and Trentino-Alto Adige), 'environmental concerns were taken into account in transport policy primarily due to public pressure by those directly affected by the negative impacts of trucking' (p171). These impacts extend to individual persons, landscapes, natural and urbanized surroundings and sometimes even people's economic standing. In a political context, in which the environmental implications of economic activities continue to elude the sectoral policy-makers – not least due to underdeveloped methodologies for assessing such implications – the input of locally affected people will close a gap in policy planning. The Commission acknowledged this role in its fifth Environmental Action Programme (EAP) in 1992; it emphasized that the multilevel polity does not 'end' at the local governmental level but on the level of the general public (CEC, 1992, p26):

> *The concept of shared responsibility requires a much more broadly based and active involvement of all economic players, including public authorities, public and private enterprise in all its forms and, above all, the general public, both as citizens and consumers.*

Yet, the provision of environmental information to the general public and more open channels for participation in the public policy process remain issues to be placed on a 'wish list' for most of EU and national policy-making. Considering the EU's formal commitment to 'shared responsibility', it seems strange that the European Court of Justice has, in the past, denied environmental NGOs *locus standi* to represent local environmental interests against the Commission (funding regional development programmes) (see Chapters 1 and 2). Local people who feel the environmental impact of economic activities, especially in the context of large construction projects, are rarely capable of entering into expensive and time-consuming legal battles. If the wish for 'broadly based and active involvement' is to be taken seriously, access to the courts needs to be widened.

In the meantime, the Commission seems convinced that 'pressure from below' needs to be complemented by 'pressure from above'. In its *Partnership for Integration* Cardiff strategy paper, it argues: 'such an approach, across the sectors, can only come about by Heads of State and Government assuming responsibility' (CEC, 1999a, p3). In particular, Jordan's and Lewanski's country studies on the UK and Italy support this perspective (see Chapters 3 and 5). In Italy, progress towards EPI is largely due to the willingness of the Prodi and D'Alema governments to use the opportunities of the Second Republic for environmental reforms. The UK case contrasts with the Italian example. In the UK, many conditions for successful policy integration are already present; the idea resonates well with British emphasis on efficient government, and the institutional 'hardware' is assembled quite favourably. The informal cabinet principle of collective responsibility particularly contributes to internal coordination. Nevertheless, interdepartmental competition often produces failures of communication and requires strong executive leadership 'to pull departments into line' – provided that the core executive is willing to do so. Jordan shows that even the new Labour government, which in its political rhetoric leaves no doubt concerning its commitment to the EPI principle, failed to exercise the necessary political will.

SUMMARY AND FUTURE STRATEGIES FOR THE EU

In summary, compliance with the EPI principle depends upon conceptual, institutional and actor-specific factors. These factors operate in a complex dynamic, none succeeding without the other. Furthermore, they are operative on all levels of governance, of which 'Brussels' represents only one. Hence, there are limits for EU policy-makers to solve all persisting problems. Nevertheless, the previous chapters in this book and the comparative analysis of this conclusion suggest that additional initiatives could and should be taken on the Community level:

- EPI on the ground frequently fails due to insufficient capacities and a lack of substantive guidance. Environmental indicators and targets, as well as guidelines to conduct (strategic) environmental impact assessments, need to be developed and disseminated from Brussels. Such tools will improve the operation practice of EPI; they will also push the imagination of the sectoral policy-makers to develop sustainable policy solutions.
- Nevertheless, as elaborated above, there are limits to finding positive-sum solutions. The win–win story of the sustainable development concept risks losing persuasiveness on lower levels of abstraction where the economic costs of changing production and consumption patterns may be far higher than immediate gains. Hence, EPI on the ground often fails due to a 'good story or argument' for the self-interested addressee. From the long-term perspective implicit in sustainable development, sectoral policy-makers, and especially the short- and medium-term 'losers' on the ground, need to be compensated or enabled in order to restructure their activities. Resources need to be freed – on the EU and the national level – to alter the incentive structure and to create more bottom-up support for EPI.
- The Commission, in particular, has put much effort into providing information and channels for participation; there has been more resistance on the national and regional levels. In order to compensate further for national deficiencies, the legal opportunities for societal actors and their representatives must be extended. Access to the European Court of Justice remains far too restricted.

These measures have been mostly of a facilitating nature. They underpin the strategy that was adopted by the Commission in the past. In addition to moving the principle ever more prominently within Commission documents and the Community legislative framework, channels for communication and cooperation were built and reporting mechanisms were established. The less than satisfactory results of this strategy suggest that it needs to be complemented by a more active approach. A recent remark by Commissioner Wallström hints that the Commission is considering such strategy shift (see also Chapter 10): 'In the long run I would prefer to be more of a consultant or advisor to Member States, but until then I will have to be more of a policewoman' (quoted in *European Voice* of 10–17 November 1999, p2).

With regard to the European funding policies – the Common Agricultural Policy, the Structural Funds and the Cohesion Fund – the EU has a unique tool to enforce EPI by making funding conditional upon environmental criteria[5] and by adopting an active role. The warning to impose financial sanctions is also likely to be more effective than the longer-term threat of legal action.

These last remarks are not intended to suggest that there is, after all, an easy solution to achieving EPI in the EU and the Member States. EPI remains a complex problem and only a *mix of strategies*, tackling the conceptual, institutional and actor-specific bottlenecks, will succeed in triggering a learning process and in achieving wider compliance with the principle in the future.

REFERENCES

Commission of the European Communities (CEC) (1992) *Towards Sustainability: A European Community Programme of Policy and Action in Relation to the Environment and Sustainable Development*, COM(92) 23 final, CEC, Brussels, 27 March

CEC (1999a) *Partnership for Integration: A Strategy for Integrating Environment into EU Policies*, Communication from the Commission to the European Council, CEC, Cardiff, June 1998

CEC (1999b) *Europe's Environment: What Directions for the Future? The Global Assessment of the European Community Programme of Policy and Action in Relation to the Environment and Sustainable Development, 'Towards Sustainability'*, Communication from the Commission, COM(1999) 543 final, CEC, Brussels, 24 November

CEC (1999c) *Report on Environment and Integration Indicators to Helsinki Summit*, Commission Working Document, SEC(1999) 1942 final, CEC, Brussels, 24 November

Collier, U (1998) *Deregulation in the European Union: Environmental Perspectives*, Routledge, London and New York

Collier, U, Golub, J and Kreher, A (eds) (1996) *Subsidiarity and Shared Responsibility: New Challenges for EU Environmental Policy*, Nomos Verlag, Baden-Baden

European Environment Agency (EEA) (1999a) *Environment in the European Union at the Turn of the Century*, Environmental Assessment Report No 2, 1 December, Copenhagen

EEA (1999b) *Monitoring Progress Towards Integration: A Contribution to the 'Global Assessment' of the Fifth Environmental Action Programme of the EU, 1992–1999*, EEA, Copenhagen

European Environment Bureau (EEB) (1999) *Ten Benchmarks for Environmental Policy Integration,* EEB Position Paper on Targets, Indicators and Timetables, tabled for the Helsinki Summit, 29 September, EEB, Brussels

Favoino, M, Knill, C and Lenschow, A (2000) 'New Structures for Environmental Governance in the European Commission: The Institutional Limits of Governance Change' in C Knill and A Lenschow (eds) *Implementing EU Environmental Policy: New Directions and Old Problems,* Manchester University Press, Manchester, pp39-61

Jachtenfuchs, M and Kohler-Koch, B (1996) 'Einleitung: Regieren im dynamischen Mehrebenensystem' in M Jachtenfuchs and B Kohler-Koch (eds) *Europäische Integration,* Leske + Budrich, Opladen, pp15–44

Kingdon, J W (1984) *Agendas, Alternatives, and Public Policies,* Scott, Foresman and Company, Glenview IL, and London

Knill, C and Lenschow, A (1998) 'Coping with Europe: the Impact of British and German Administration on the Implementation of EU Environmental Policy', *Journal of European Public Policy,* vol 5, no 4, pp595–614

Knill, C and Lenschow, A (2001) 'Adjusting to EU Environmental Policy: Change and Persistence in Domestic Administrations' in J A Caporaso, M Green Cowles and T Risse (eds) *Transforming Europe,* Cornell University Press, Ithaca NY, pp116-136

Krasner, S (1984) 'Approaches to the State: Alternative Conceptions and Historical Dynamics', *Comparative Politics,* vol 16, pp223–246

Lenschow, A (1998) 'The World Trade Dimension of "Greening" the EU's Common Agricultural Policy' in J Golub (ed), *Global Competition and EU External Environmental Policy,* Routledge, London, pp161–188

Marks, G, Hooghe, L and Blank, K (1996) 'European Integration from the 1980s: State-Centric v. Multi-Level Governance', *Journal of Common Market Studies,* vol 34, no 3, pp341–378

Pollack, M A (1997) 'Delegation, Agency and Agenda Setting in the European Community', *International Organization,* vol 51, no 1, pp99–135

Schön, D A and Rein, M (1994) *Frame Reflection: Towards the Resolution of Intractable Policy Controversies,* BasicBooks, New York

World Commission on Environment and Development (WCED) (1987) *Our Common Future,* Oxford University Press, Oxford and New York

NOTES

1 Reference is made to the fifth Environmental Action Programme (CEC, 1992), which provide a first framework for EPI in the Community.

2 The fact that the greening proposals focused on the instrument of taxation, which implied unanimous voting rule in the Council, made the decision-making process even more difficult.

3 In addition, the sustainable development concept includes a third dimension of social equity.

4 This argument is made most clearly by Edda Müller in her case study on Germany (see Chapter 4).

5 The recent reforms of the CAP include a clause that gives the Member States discretion to implement such conditionality (see Chapter 6). This signifies a trend towards renationalization and a passive rather than active strategy of the Community in this policy field.

Index